CIRCLE OF DREAMS

A MEMOIR

*To friends
at TidePointe
Candi Ray*

MARGUERITE McEACHERN RAY

1stBooks – rev. 6/1/01

CONTENTS

The joys of life are caught like transient gems of dew in the tangled web of our experiences.

MMR

I

EARLY YEARS

Those of us who are born and grow up tucked snugly into a loving family have a support group that surpasses any other play of fortune. My good luck—the second of six children—cherished, but encouraged to grow and think as I wished, gave me a wondrous sense of freedom.

During the twenties and thirties of the last century, life seemed close to nature and full of mystery. My selfhood was formed by a spiral of dreams and realities as I wandered through the deep woods and explored the river by my home in northern Florida. Following these dreams, my voyage through the years has been one of wonderful diversity—a kaleidoscope of experiences, leading me to many parts of the world.

When we are young, looking at the world with imagination and energy, we dream and invent ourselves as we change. We gradually emerge from this self-made cocoon to fly free as thinking adults.

During our waning years, we often seek to examine the direction our dreams have taken us, hoping to understand our place and purpose in the world, and perhaps to help us face the future with serenity and hope.

My parents moved their growing family to our place on the St. John's river near Jacksonville, Florida when I was somewhere between three and four years old. The five-acre property on the river bluff was undeveloped—a virgin hammock of large oak trees hanging with Spanish moss. It must have presented a tremendous challenge to my young parents, as there was no water or electricity on the land. They later added three more acres to make a sizable estate, and worked hard to make their dreams come true.

In addition to the practical needs to be met, they did such imaginative things as entwining the branches of young trees to form a leafy arch at the property entrance where they hung MIRIAMARDON, a sign designed from the names of their three children. Early on my father drilled a fresh water well and later installed complicated electric motors. Keeping it all running properly seemed to take a lot of his spare time. Even so, I remember special things my parents did for us three young children. There were camping trips, a playhouse painted the

same color as the main house, a large goldfish pond with plants and rocks all around, special swings, a sliding board and various "acting" bars, where I later developed some daring feats, one resulting in a cracked head. I believe my dad tore down the bar after that.

When I began my formal education at Arlington Elementary School I started in the second grade, already having learned to read aided by books provided by a Miss Quinn, someone's live-in relative. Storybooks and poetry attracted me the most, but working out the puzzles of arithmetic was fun.

Music was an early interest, especially as my mother played the piano. I began violin lessons at the age of nine and continued throughout my formative years. During these years, I thought of my violin as a personal friend having a life of its own, and I often turned to it to express the developing, intense emotions of adolescence—the whole gambit from longing, frustration and sadness, to the almost overwhelming feelings of joy and hope for the future before me. Throughout my life my love of music has stimulated my imagination and expanded this joy of living.

Looking ahead as I approached my teens, I felt I could do anything or be anything I wanted to—an arrogance not unusual at that age. This confidence pushed me to try new physical things, sometimes with reckless disregard for the danger involved. Parachuting from our high bluff overlooking the river by using an umbrella taught me certain facts, as did swinging out over the bluff on a thin rope. Climbing trees and walking alone for hours through the woods where one seldom saw anyone else developed my independence and a closeness to nature. In the sixth grade I remember I felt that Nature was my own special secret—not really to be shared with anyone. Our eight acres on the river had deep woods and Indian mounds, that stimulated imaginative dreams.

Animals were always a part of family life. An old mutt named Buster was the first real dog friend I remember. He would follow wherever I roamed and during his long life accumulated a collection of scars from fights with aggressive dogs. Later there were others, a beautiful Irish setter named Jake who died when hit by a speeding car that didn't stop. I also remember miscellaneous cats and kittens and my pet tortoise, Nicodemus. A special surprise was a pony that appeared one Christmas morning with a big red bow tied around his neck. We learned to ride Brownie bareback since he was too round to hold a saddle firmly in place. Unfortunately, our pony died a few years later—a sad day, since we never discovered why, and poison was a possibility.

All of us learned to swim at an early age. I loved the water and would spend hours trying complicated dives from the diving board built by neighbors on their dock. We had a dock of our own that I enjoyed through the years, but we never had a diving board.

I had always wanted a boat, so in my early teens I began saving my nickels and dimes, earned by various projects such as selling Indian arrowheads and "relics" (broken pieces of pottery) or doing special chores. (Allowances were unknown during these depression years.) I finally saved all of ten dollars, a huge sum, which I used to buy an old wooden sailboat. It had a narrow deck and a centerboard which was useful on the river where winds and tides were sometimes strong. I usually used it as a rowboat and spent many hours exploring along the river and across to the nearby island. My boat brought me many years of fun, and sometimes I took my brother and younger sisters exploring with me. I remember the guilty thrill of climbing the long ladder arching out up the side of the beacon light near the island—illegal to do, of course. Many large ocean liners passed on the other side of the island headed to the docks in Jacksonville. Watching them from our high bluff through the years made me dream of travel to far off places.

We did not have a telephone during my early years. We had to go to a neighbor's house to phone. I called my grandmother in Jacksonville often, and somehow her number at that time (5-66-91W) is still etched in my memory. In those days we seemed to accept the reality of lacking such things as phones. Perhaps we didn't miss what we never had. Modern conveniences did gradually come into our lives, of course. I remember the shock I felt when I was about 11 or 12 years old and came home from school to find masses of lovely trees felled to make way for the city electricity line down our long driveway. I literally grieved for days, wandering among the fallen branches of the trees I loved. It did not seem worth it to me to have this happen, because, after all, we had more or less reliable electricity from the motors my dad had installed. I'm sure he appreciated this convenience more than I did.

In Junior High at Landon School, among other things I began the study of Latin that I enjoyed throughout high school. Miss Franklin was an upright, white-haired moral force and she also opened new doors for me to ancient history and far away places. One useful piece of advice she offered was never to let yourself be hypnotized or let your mind be taken over by others. My interest in mathematics continued and during the last years of high school I was the only girl in our large class of advanced algebra and trigonometry. The logic of these studies always interested me.

Since we lived some ten miles from Landon High School, I often rode in with my dad who left quite early for his job as an engineer at the Municipal Docks in Jacksonville. In those days I remember his singing as he drove—his same two or three favorites; and he often bought a cigar, which he enjoyed. When we were in elementary school he used to save time by crossing the river by ferry from Arlington. Later he changed his route to accommodate us children, or maybe the ferry stopped running about then. Sometimes I rode the school bus which took longer and meant we had to change buses at Arlington Elementary School. If I missed the bus, usually a neighbor driving to work would stop to offer a ride. My last year in high school I seemed to miss a lot of Mondays, one way or another! This meant I could take my boat out to explore wherever I wanted. My parents didn't seem too concerned with my choices at this time.

One Monday when I went to the island to pick blackberries, taking my youngest sister along with me, a strong storm came up. As I hurried toward home, an oar-lock broke and one oar fell overboard. Increasingly alarmed, I dived in and rescued it, but had to use the heavy oar to paddle all the way back across the river (about a mile if going straight). Although I was a good swimmer, I was frightened for my little sister, who was about five years old then. We were at the mercy of the wind that was blowing us off course, so I had to angle over, as one would in a sailboat, landing a long way from our place on the river and having to wade home along the shore pulling the boat. By the time I got there, I had blisters on both hands, feeling very guilty but having learned a lesson in safety and the vagaries of weather that I haven't forgotten. We did bring home a bucketful of blackberries!

Another dramatic event during those years was when my young sister, Cecil, came near to drowning by falling into our large goldfish pond. She was a mere toddler and was frantically brought back from unconsciousness by my mother after she had been alerted by Rosemary, the four year old. All of us older children were at school at the time so only learned of it later. Cecil seemed to be especially accident-prone as she was growing up. At one time her clothes were set alight from an open bonfire; she once swallowed gasoline and had other accidents. After these episodes Mother was firmly convinced that she was chosen by God to live a charmed and dedicated life. She has certainly followed that path with her selfless devotion to her family and doing good for others—an inspiration for many of us.

High school was a melánge of experiences. I played first violin in the school orchestra and entered other activities such as the Lionettes, a marching drill team that performed at the football games.

During these years of violin study I also played in the Jacksonville Symphony for several years. The conductor was my violin teacher, Mr. Orner, a real tyrant at times but an excellent teacher. Making music with other people, in an orchestra or other musical group, brings a special pleasure not experienced any other way. Perhaps the self confidence it brings or the discipline required in learning, seem especially important during adolescent years. The Jacksonville Symphony was an amateur organization at that time with lots of high school students taking part. I played in the second violin section and remember driving in to the evening rehearsals with good friends, our neighbors, the Pattishalls. Their son, Evan, played the French horn. These kind neighbors, both musicians, often invited me to accompany them and their children to concerts in Jacksonville. I owe them a debt of gratitude for providing these wonderful opportunities. I remember the joy of hearing Fritz Kreisler give a marvelous concert, and I was able to get his autograph afterward—with my leaky pen, as I remember! Rae Pattishall and her brother Evan were my closest friends.

Many other memories come back from those years on the St. John's River. My mother remains the central home influence. She was a free spirit in many ways, even though a bit hampered by the circumstances of rearing six children. But she always enjoyed children, and I remember when we were young she would think up imaginative games and "fairy surprises"—tasty treats of cookies or cupcakes hidden in the branches of trees or other places outside, which we had to search for when we came home from school. To me she always offered encouragement in all I wanted to do, plus enthusiastic applause for all of my modest accomplishments. I had started writing poetry while in elementary school and my love of poetry was certainly gotten from my mother—who had many verses published in the magazines of the day, plus a few anthologies. She also wrote articles on raising children, often using one or another of us as examples. I remember and admire all those efforts. Later she was to be honored as Mother of the Year from Florida, which she certainly deserved.

Mother was an energetic, artistic person who did a lot to bring beauty to our lives. Such things as hibiscus blossoms placed in a piece of driftwood on the dining room sideboard and other artistic touches remain in my memory. When I was in my early teens we had built a large new house on our property. It was an H-shaped log house set among the oak trees, and had a huge stone fireplace in the center room and many windows on all sides. Mother was the inspiration for the way the house took shape, in large part. She loved working outside to beautify the place. There were clusters of ferns and other plants placed among the trees. A real success was the table and seats made from a group of tree stumps that proved to be a perfect place to eat watermelon!

My relationships with my sisters and brother were close and followed a rather predictable pattern. I was probably closest to my oldest sister Jeanne, and I admired and emulated her, especially when I was young, although we developed different interests as we grew. She was particularly talented in drawing, and in some ways has always seemed more artistic than any of us. My own interest in art started early as well, and I remember trying sculpture at a young age, making models of feet and such things. A large black head carved from peat rescued from the bank of the river, rested on the floor of my bedroom for some time. My music came first during these years, however, and it was much later when I came back to trying my hand at various art forms.

My sister and I were both avid readers and we spent long hours in the public library, reading extensively while waiting to be picked up by our father after music lessons. At home I would often read my books perched in a tree or in an angle on the roof of the house above my room. One of my favorite places was in a large oak tree that was easy to climb because of a huge grapevine that encircled it.

We had lots of books and read practically all the books from our neighbor's, the Pattishall's, library. My maternal grandmother in Jacksonville provided an additional wide range of books, including a set of the Harvard Classics and many years' accumulation of National Geographic. The pictures of the naked natives were intriguing!

This eclectic collection of reading material must have had an influence on my developing taste. I read books ranging from fairytales and childhood adventure stories to "Pilgrims's Progress" and romantic Victorian novels. Thick books of poetry were filled with abstract concepts such as Life, Fate and Destiny, always capitalized, which seemed to give them some mysterious importance. Luckily, I seemed to prefer the poetry of Shelley and Byron (which I sometimes memorized).

My grandmother, who had been widowed when her children were very young, was an accomplished artist in earlier years. I remember some dramatic and impressive landscapes in oil and watercolor decorating her house. The daughter of a well-known doctor, she grew up in a large, culturally privileged family and was educated by a private tutor. In addition to her many books, she had a grand piano and an extensive collection of records, which we played on a wind-up Victrola with the famous picture of the listening dog as the logo. I remember an old Caruso record on a heavy disc used in those days. She also offered a selection of children's favorites of the time, many of which are heard today. My grandmother sometimes offered such well-worn advice as "Where there's a will, there's a way" and "If you wish in one hand and spit in the other, which will get full first?" Made good sense. Still does. As I remember, she described me at this age as "Standing with reluctant feet where the brook and river meet."—an image that appealed to me and was surely apt since I matured late and was not anxious to grow up. I remember vowing I would never get tired of climbing trees!

I loved exploring old cemeteries, and there was one near my grandmother's house where I spent long summer afternoons. In this mysterious, sun-dappled retreat, I would imagine all sorts of stories about the people who had been buried there. One summer I "adopted" an unmarked, unkempt grave. Mr. No Name's plot was looking pretty good after being weeded and decorated with various "extra" flowers from other graves nearby.

We drove in to Jacksonville almost every weekend to visit my grandmother. She had a garden filled with a variety of flowers and shrubs, which, in a way, seemed to reflect her personality. The "powder puff" tree (mimosa), kumquat tree and the "banana" shrub were some of my favorites. Two pools with goldfish and frogs were a delight for us children. My grandmother's death when I was thirteen years old left a real emptiness in my life.

My sister Jeanne and I often made music together. Our piano and violin endeavors sometimes became a battle as to whether we should keep perfect time (her idea), or play with "expression" (my choice). We were often called upon to play for visiting aunts and uncles who usually became bored and talkative after a piece or two, much to our amusement and intuitive understanding. My brother and other sisters all played musical instruments later, with varying degrees of success. The occasional "concerts" we produced were easily forgettable. The most valuable thing my brother accomplished on the trombone was taking turns with me in very early morning practice to help get rid of an aunt and uncle, who seemed to have extended a family visit into a permanent stay. Our plan worked and they left shortly afterward.

As my only brother, Don has a special place in my heart, and I felt especially close to him when we were young. I remember those years exploring the woods together, camping out with friends on the Indian mounds, riding bikes miles and

7

miles and swinging through the trees on grapevines, *a la* Tarzan. We spent many hours playing on the large sand pile next to our place on the river. Two hickory trees partially covered with the white sand that had been dredged from the river at some earlier time provided a great playground. I recall the wonder I felt when high tides produced lovely, delicate fairy castles shaped into the sand near the water. I seemed to spend more time with my brother than with my older sister at this age. One summer there was pole vaulting, and we always shared a love of boats and later an interest in flying. (I finally forgave him for sinking my little boat when I went away to college.)

There was a four-and-a-half year gap between the three older children and the younger girls, Rosemary, Cecil and Frankie (Austin, as she later called herself). They were a delight to me when I was growing up (except when they bothered my things!). I would always choose to tend to them rather than alternative chores offered. While my older sister preferred to help in the house, my main strategy was to get outside—with or without the children. I used to tell them imaginative stories and play special games with them. They later said that I manipulated them to do whatever I wanted. Partially true, but I prefer to think of it as developing psychology in dealing with people! I truly thought they were delightful as children and they seemed to love being with me, as well.

I remember my young father as inventive and adventurous, admired by all who knew him. He was always ready to help anyone in trouble, once temporarily adopting a six-foot five, red-headed giant named Frank, who had served a prison sentence for some misdemeanor or other. Frank was the strongest man I had ever seen and used to carry five gallon cans of water in each hand and another in his teeth sometimes! My memory of him is rather vague, but I remember he built himself a small house in the woods and did a lot of work to develop our property, helping with road making and other things. He once helped my father build a series of arbor supports over a sunny part of our driveway, which was planted with grapevines. It later produced a lovely shady retreat as well as lots of red, purple and green grapes. Frank adored my parents and was kind and helpful to us children.

My dad was good at mathematics and helped me with my homework from time to time. He could fix anything or build anything, it seemed, and was often called upon to help neighbors when they had problems. In any emergency, he was the first to respond. I loved him for that. He was always inventive and in the early days of radio I remember his putting together various sets and experimenting with all the new gadgets. As a young child, I sat entranced in the big leather chair nearby listening to the strange squawking and singing and wondered why no one let the poor lady out of the box! Later on, we were to listen to favorite old programs, such as The Shadow, Fibber Magee and Molly, Amos and Andy and Jack Benny. My parents always enjoyed music and we listened to the Firestone Hour, Saturday afternoon opera occasionally and other classical concerts. There was no TV at that time, of course.

Perhaps his adventurous spirit led my dad to experiment with many things he did not have a talent for. During my growing up years he was continually investing in one project or another, which he was sure would make him wealthy. Luckily, he kept his regular job during these depression years, as most of his projects did not work out, or were abandoned for various reasons. I remember when he was going to start a dairy and bought thirteen young calves, which we children loved and cared for until they were almost grown, but then he sold them for something else that was needed. My own calf, Star, was a special pet and I used to enjoy a comfortable seat leaning against her as she was resting under a large oak tree. My secret club at that age included both Star and several favorite trees, but no human other than myself. My diary from those days shows perfect attendance at our meetings! Star was later sold to pay for having my tonsils removed—bad for bad, I thought at the time.

Another project was investing in a farm in southern Florida near Ft. Myers. Dad arranged for two young relatives who needed work to move there and they planted many acres of tomatoes and other things. Unfortunately, that was a particularly hard winter and everything was lost. I remember a trip down there when we saw rotting tomatoes on the ground for as far as I could see.

Then there was the promising chicken farm and the building of a dozen or so chicken houses. This seemed to go well until there was an accidental fire in the brooder house, which he was never able to recover from financially. One of his successful projects was the planting of a wide variety of citrus trees—oranges, grapefruit, satsumas, lemons, kumquats as well as hybrids of all kinds. These thrived for many years and added a lot to our pleasure as well as our general health.

My Dad continued to invest in other projects. I remember the artesian well he drilled which was supposed to result in a swimming pool. Instead, sulfur in the water turned all the silverware black! I sometimes wonder how rich he would have become if he had just bought a few stocks with the money he spent on these things. Having the fun of trying new things probably made his life much more interesting, however, and besides, who knows how the children would have turned out if we had had more money? I have many fond memories of the daring young father I knew.

Looking back, it is rather ironic that even though my father was always trying new things, he would often say to me, "Jack of all trades, master of none." whenever I would become involved in some new activity. I'm sure I inherited some of those genes!

In addition to my immediate family, I was influenced by an array of aunts and uncles. My mother's only brother, Uncle Jim, was my favorite uncle, by far. He and my mother were very close and he took a delight in us three older children when we were young, often bringing us presents when he traveled, and telling us all about the stars, plants and flowers, (complete with Latin names), and other wonders of nature. He shared his love of all growing things with my parents throughout their lives. My sister and I still have the silver dessert spoons and forks engraved with our individual names given to us by Uncle Jim each birthday and Christmas. He seemed to love being the doting bachelor uncle until his rather late marriage (in his thirties) and having two children of his own, Nell and Jim. We children rather resented his wife—actually a fine woman, if rather cold—because she took his attention away from us. He continued an interest in us, however, and later helped me with a loan to finish my senior year in college. I remember him with love and appreciation.

My Dad had four older sisters, but no brother. These aunts were a rather interesting bunch. The oldest, Aunt Pearl, was a real business woman, a rarity in those days, and managed a series of luxury hotels in the Tampa area over the years. She was married a couple of times but had no children. She occasionally tried to interfere with my father's decisions, with little success and much to my mother's annoyance. Looking back, this is understandable since she had a lot to do with my father's growing up years, as he had lost his father at an early age and she was about twenty years older. His mother, quite old when my dad was born, lived with us the last few years of her life. I remember "Ba-Mama" as a kind, soft-spoken woman who used a cane and was bed-ridden a lot of the time. She loved us children and used to tie candy on her light cord for us. Seeing her in her coffin, peaceful and beautiful, holding a flower picked by my very young brother was my first encounter with death.

Aunt Hattie was what we would call "new age" now, into all kinds of food fads—whole kernels of wheat for cereal, olive oils and other healthy things. She also dabbled into such things as palmistry and astrology. She was married twice and had two children, Hal and Annetta, both much older than I was. Don was her favorite among us children.

It may have been Aunt Hattie who influenced my father to insist on healthy food for the family. Whatever the reason, when we were growing up we almost always had oatmeal for breakfast, lots of milk, fruit, chicken and fish, and liver about once a week (which I have never chosen to eat since!), plus eggs occasionally. The butter we had was made from cream skimmed from the top part of the milk, but mostly I remember having oleomargarine which in those early days came in a solid white block along with a small packet of coloring material. This was because of a law protecting the dairy farmers, since oleomargarine was much less expensive than butter. It was a chore to combine it into a spread that was appetizing looking. "Banner" whole wheat bread was always the bread we bought. I often wished I had sandwiches made from that soft white bread for my school lunches, as most of the other children had. Looking back, I realize how wise parents often are.

Aunt Bessie was energetic and interested in all of us children—especially Jeanne and me, perhaps because she had no children of her own. Her husband, at least the one I remember, was hugely overweight and not an attractive man, although he seemed fairly well-to-do and invested in stocks and other projects. He often talked about "waiting for his ship to come in", which to me seemed a puzzling thing to say. I remember his smelly black Cuban cigarettes, and he was certainly more interested in himself than others. Aunt Bessie seemed to have a lot of spare time and spent innumerable hours playing solitaire and other card games, but she was always kind to us children and made fancy doll clothes for Jeanne and me and occasionally took us on trips with them. She seemed to prefer Jeanne to me, which I sometimes resented, but I remember a vacation at a luxury hotel on Lake Okeechobee in southern Florida where I celebrated my fifth birthday. Photos of the event, with white-coated waiters formally serving a group of paper-hatted children, bring back that memory. A little boy named Warren Wood caught my fancy. I wonder what happened to him?

Aunt Rosa was perhaps the warmest and most loved aunt that I had. She had helped me be born—since the doctor was late in arriving at the private hospital in Jacksonville on that May seventh, and she seemed to favor me because of that. My mother opted to have all the following children at home—probably a wise decision. Aunt Rosa was married to a man with only one arm and she had two children, Elizabeth and Jack. I remember her as a caring, generous woman who adored cats and had many of them. She was probably the closest sister to my father, both because of age and because of living nearby.

Christmas was always a wondrous time for our family. First, there was the excitement of searching for just the right tree in the woods around. It had to be huge—to reach the ceiling—and cedar, not pine as some used. In addition to the tree, we had to find holly and large bunches of mistletoe, which always seemed to grow in the highest branches. We usually waited until right before Christmas to decorate the tree, and after lights and balls were all in place, I remember many "discussions" about not throwing the tinsel on in large globs. Our stockings, hung by the big fireplace, were filled by Mother and Dad when we were young— we older ones allowed to help later on. They were stuffed to the top with the usual fruits and nuts, plus packets of large raisins with seeds, dried figs and candies, and a small gift hidden in the toe. Mother was always the last to go to bed as she finished up some special project of sewing or some other surprise. I truly admire the way she always managed to make everything come out just right, with so many of us to think of.

We woke up at dawn but were not allowed to enter the living-room until a roaring fire was warming the room. Even then, I remember some chilly Christmas mornings, since of course there was no central heating in Florida in those days. These memories draw me closer in thought to my brother and sisters

11

during this magic holiday, and make me appreciate the value of carrying on family traditions through the years.

My parents were not regular churchgoers when I was growing up, attending only occasionally. We children went to the little wooden Methodist Episcopal church nearby more often. I can remember playing the violin at Christmas programs and other special events, accompanied by my sister, Jeanne. I was in my final years of high school when the family began going to the Southside Presbyterian Church in Jacksonville. I joined the church at this time, although my serious search for a spiritual life came later, with more mature and intellectual experiences in self-discovery through the years.

I must have been rather difficult to live with as a teenager. Perhaps typically, I often felt misunderstood and that my opinions were ignored. When anyone, especially my older sister, said I HAD to do something, my first reaction would be negative. (That character trait has stayed with me, I'm afraid.) Of course I did my share of arguing and teasing, ("I'm giving you only HALF a chubby for Christmas!") but by nature non-combative, I disliked the chaos that sometimes reigned in such a large, strong-willed family and would often retreat from angry confrontations. My older sister and brother seemed to enjoy a good fight, which was probably healthier than to become moody, as I often did.

My interest in boys, other than as good pals, developed rather late. Several young boy classmates would send me postcards from trips or write notes during school in my early teen years, and one used to bring me gorgeous double poppies from his garden, with their stems encased in wax. His mother, one of the mathematics teachers, had a hand in this, I believe, although he remained interested and I remember going to several school dances with him.

The first boyfriend I really found attractive, however, was when I was fourteen years old. Up until then I enjoyed boys as good friends and I preferred challenging them to a game of mumble peg or a swimming race rather than anything else. Bobby was something different, coming down to Florida for the summer from New York state where he lived with his father, to visit his mother who had remarried and lived in the neighborhood. He brought one of his friends with him, an equally attractive teenager named Jack.

We had lots of parties in those days—hayrides, scavenger hunts, dances and beach parties. This first sexual attraction, with no more than an innocent kiss or two, continued until almost Christmas. Bobby had decided to stay with his mother and she had given him an early Christmas present of a shotgun. Not a good decision. I'll never forget that fateful day when Bobby accidentally shot himself in the Pattishall's back yard, dying instantly. It was a terrible shock for everyone. All the men and boys used to hunt in those days, unfortunately. I never liked guns and after this horrible accident I disliked them even more.

During my last years of high school I remember several male friends— David, Tom, Charlie, and others. I have fond memories of dancing with them and going to parties, but nothing serious. Shortly after my seventeenth birthday I graduated from highschool and was eager to continue my education away from home, with only vague dreams of what lay ahead.

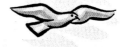

II

TAKING OFF

Leaving home to start my college education in North Carolina was a pivotal point in my life. I was not only excited, but felt a delicious sense of freedom, as I remember. My sister, Jeanne, had preceded me to Montreat Jr. College and had graduated and moved on before I arrived. For me, it was a new place, a new life on my own, with a variety of friends and a chance to explore the waiting world of ideas and philosophies.

Choosing subjects to study, within a prescribed framework built on the liberal arts, I studied Biology, French, higher Mathematics and other things new to me, as well as the usual History and English courses. Since Montreat was a church-oriented school, I also studied the Bible as history—Old Testament and New Testament in detail—all through the two years there. My teacher for this was Dr. Rachel Henderlite, a graduate of Yale Seminary, and she presented religion as a logical and interesting development of thought. We were all saturated with other religious influences as well—daily chapel, mid-week prayer meetings, plus the regular Sunday services. I took an active part in these activities  and for one brief period considered going into the missionary field. Looking at it honestly, however, I realized, even then, that it was mostly the travel and adventure that attracted me—hardly a firm basis to begin this kind of career.

While at Montreat, I often accompanied one of the teachers, a former missionary, to meetings of a small church for blacks nearby. Churches were segregated in those days, and I remember playing my violin as the congregation, mostly women, sang the hymns. I had grown up in this segregated, southern society, but from an early age had developed warm, friendly feelings for black people—Louise, Joe, Emma, Uncle William and others I had known.

Compassion and a growing understanding for the many problems they face have strengthened over the years.

These years at Montreat were busy ones; in addition to classes I was active in all sports offered, playing on the teams of soccer, softball and basketball. I also enjoyed the hiking club, which required walking 100 miles to join, with 10 miles a month required after that. It was no chore to get up for the early morning hikes that were scheduled, since the mountains of North Carolina are ideal for this. We often had breakfast hikes on the weekends. I had never seen mountains before, even though, at age 8, I had spent one summer with one of mother's cousins in Rocky Mount, North Carolina—a rather flat part of the state. The mountains were awe inspiring, and had an deep emotional impact on me, especially that first autumn. The unbelievably brilliant foliage, varying even within a single leaf, thrilled me and convinced me that mountains were for me! I still get that special lift of spirit when I am in the mountains, wherever they are.

At Montreat I had a fellowship to help with tuition and I worked in the library, choosing to be around books whenever I could. Miss Dickerson (Dickybird, as we called her privately) was the patient librarian, teaching me how to bind books as well as to take care of them. I read many novels, biographies and practically all the adventure books around. Those by the swash-buckling Richard Haliburton made a real impression. At this time I was also drawn to the writings of the transcendentalists, Emerson and Thoreau. Emerson's essays, especially his "Self Reliance" and "Nature", seemed to reflect my own philosophy. I still have his writings among my books, heavily underlined in many places and still inspiring to read.

I lived in the big, old, white wooden dormitory, the Alba (appropriately named), which hovered over small Lake Susan at the center of the ring of mountains surrounding Montreat. When working late at the library, I often missed getting back to the dormitory before the curfew, and resorted to climbing up the fire escape that had access to the hall near my shared room. My roommate, Rae, and suite-mates, Jean and Ruth, were always helpful by unlocking the window when needed.

Montreat was an extremely strict college even in those days. No smoking, of course, but also no dancing, playing cards or other such frivolous wasting of time. We had occasional trips to nearby Asheville for concerts and such, and were able to hike two miles into Black Mountain for a movie on our weekly Monday holiday. I seldom went to the movie, as I chose to work off most of my library hours on that day—for more freedom during the week.

One of the few times I got into "trouble" these years was when I wrote a satirical poem for a biology assignment. We had been asked to write sentences with all the words anyone had missed in a certain test. Boring, I thought, and since I knew the teacher well and liked her, I falsely assumed she would appreciate the wit of my clever poem. Alas, no. I was called before the straitlaced Dean, who made me feel so small I felt I could walk out of the door without opening it. I lacked the confidence to stand up for myself at that time, unfortunately. I was furious with Miss Smith, the biology teacher, and ignored her for ages. She finally apologized and we kept up a friendly correspondence for many years after I left.

The summer between the two years of classes at Montreat I stayed on to work in the Assembly Inn, waiting tables during the annual Presbyterian conferences held then. I spent a lot of time swimming with friends and got my Red Cross senior life-saving certificate with a young man named Bo. All of us thought he was a dream, probably because during the school year we seldom saw men, other than the postman or repairmen. Montreat College was known as Dr. Anderson's Angel Academy in those days! Looking back, it makes me rather wistful to think that we were only a few miles from Black Mountain College, the liberal, creative center of so much of the artistic development of the time. Oh well, lost opportunities!

During these years I must have been terribly earnest and overly judgmental. I know I did not "suffer fools gladly", and was scornful of hypocrisy. While I felt deep compassion for those handicapped by birth, such as the blacks, I had little patience with weakness. I'm sure I was very naïve then. In maturity I developed a much broader sense of compassion and acceptance of weakness, including my own.

But these were formative years and I now appreciate having had the chance to develop my independence of thought as well as a lasting love for learning. Genetically programmed to be a bit of a rebel, the years of being in an all-girls school in a protected environment paradoxically reinforced my independent nature. After graduating I was eager to move on to the wider world.

I entered George Peabody College in Nashville, Tennessee the following autumn and began a new phase in my education. I wanted to major in math and music, but was dissuaded since each would take so much time. I chose to work toward a B.S. in Instrumental Music Education with a major in violin. It was hard work, but enjoyable. I took several months of classes in various groups of instruments, and became relatively proficient in the bass clarinet, the flute (which I tutored for awhile) and the cello, which was easy for me. Advanced Harmony was especially enjoyable because of its mathematical basis, and I liked Conducting, although I don't remember being very good at it. I played first violin in the joint college orchestra (with Vanderbilt participating) and bass clarinet in the college symphonic band. Since the Peabody Music Department was just getting started at that time, we enjoyed a unique relationship with the professors. A small group of us were often invited to their homes to listen to records, sing Gilbert and Sullivan songs or take part in other social activities. Many good friends were made during those years. My roommate, Dot, played the piano and

we sometimes played together. I broadened my education with classes in psychology, art appreciation and other subjects, but my main focus was on music, working toward my senior violin recital.

During my junior year at Peabody I earned my Red Cross life-saving instructor's rating, and the following summer taught swimming, life-saving and canoeing at a Girl Scout camp near Nashville. That summer at camp, I had fun writing a water musical based on an Indian theme to entertain visiting parents. I remember the pride and pleasure of playing my violin, along with another counselor at the piano, to introduce the scenes, as we perched on the back of a truck near the dock of the lake.

At Peabody, I was increasingly attracted to a brilliant, young pianist, Jimmy, a fellow student. This developed into a more serious relationship some years later and we were engaged for a short period. Sadly, he was very unstable and later was diagnosed as a schizophrenic. He died in his forties or fifties, long after our relationship ended. But during those college years we had fun together and enjoyed life. When at home in Florida, I dated a good looking, young man who wrote me often and came up to visit while I was at Peabody. He was more serious than I was, and we drifted apart a year or so after college.

Gradually I became more aware of what was going on in the world beyond academia. At this time there was a strong movement to stay out of World War II, which had begun in Europe. I remember distinctly the day we heard of the Pearl Harbor bombing, Dec. 7, 1941. Many of the young men I knew realized they would soon be called upon to join the services. It was a sobering moment in our lives.

The spring term was full of various activities, however. I sang in the chorus and also in a small madrigal group at that time, along with my roommate, who had a much better voice than I. The group included several of the teachers in the music department. I think I was selected because I had a good ear and could read music and at least blend in, rather than for my singing voice. We took several trips, one up to Chicago and beyond, performing at various colleges. That was my first glimpse of a large metropolis and I loved wandering around in a spring snowstorm that March, visiting the Art Institute and other places. I rode an escalator for the first time there in the big department store, Marshall Field. I also remember a trip to Milwaukee where I played with a huge orchestra made up of various college groups, performing a special composition under the baton of Leopold Stokowski as guest conductor. It was a thrilling experience for a young violinist.

Mostly during the spring of 1942 I worked hard to finish my degree, practicing up to 8 hours a day. I gave my senior recital in May, playing a Handel sonata, a Mozart concerto and miscellaneous compositions by Ravel, Albeniz and others. There was a large attendance and my mother and various relatives were there. I was modestly pleased with the performance and remember the lovely dress I had and the white orchid that Jimmy gave me. While it was probably not the best recital given that year, it was certainly the most dramatic, since after playing the last selection, I fainted in leaving, falling down a short flight of stairs and breaking my violin into pieces. Anything to keep from playing an encore, I joked later. Luckily, I was unhurt and had my violin repaired the following summer—a long, tedious job done by an expert violin maker in Jacksonville. It was not that great a violin, but I was attached to it, and certainly could not afford a new one.

I graduated a short time after that and began thinking seriously about a career. During the summer I was offered several jobs teaching instrumental music in high school, which I had prepared for. While I was considering my choices, a development took place that was to change my career and my life. The Navy announced that a WAVES (Women's Auxiliary Volunteer Emergency Service) branch was to be started. I was immediately interested, since my father had been in the Navy during World War I, and flew in some of the early Navy planes, even parachuting to safety once. I went to be interviewed and was told they would get in touch with me. After a while, I decided I had better make some contingency plans in case I didn't get accepted. I therefore agreed to take a job as

instrumental music teacher in a high school in Humboldt, Tennessee, with the stipulation that if I were to be called into the Navy, I would leave.

I started teaching in September of that year, but a short time later I was called for further interviews for the WAVES. In all, I was in the teaching job for only one month, but enjoyed it, teaching the marching band new drills and generally entering into the life of the school. But then I was off to Charleston, South Carolina, for more interviews and a series of tests. At this time they were forming the first class of WAVE officers for training at Smith College in Northampton, Massachusetts. I remember arriving in Charleston after long hours on the train with no sleep. I arrived late, at noon rather than in the morning, which was not unusual considering train travel in those days. They said that the others had finished their physical exams and those who passed were now to take the mathematics and verbal parts of the tests, and that I could go ahead with them if I wanted to, taking the physical later. I did, and passed without trouble, I gather, since I was among a small group of women selected from the southeast region to enter training. It was an exciting time and I was anxious to be a part of the war effort. A new life was soon to begin.

III

SOLO FLIGHT

Along with about a dozen others, I left Jacksonville by train October 1942 for Northampton, Massachusetts. There, at Smith College, nine hundred women, almost all college graduates, began Midshipmen's training with a specialty in Classified Communications. This was the area most needed early in the war, and we were training to replace men in positions in the U.S. so they could be sent overseas. At that time, no WAVES were assigned outside of the U.S.—in contrast to the WACS, who were being sent overseas.

When we first arrived at Northampton we packed away our civilian clothes and were fitted for uniforms designed by Mainbocher, a leading designer of the day. They were navy blue, neat and smart, even if a bit long for the time, we thought. We had to have our hair cut above the collar line and wore little or no makeup. Luckily, they did not regulate underwear for the WAVES as they did for the WACS.

For the next three months we followed a rigorous schedule, full of classes and physical training such as marching, swimming and other prescribed athletics, on the Smith campus. Our instructors were men naval officers, and since we were the first class of women midshipmen, they were especially strict, determined not to be more lenient than usual just because we were women.

I lived in Hotel Northampton that had been taken over for the WAVES. (It is still a hotel there.) We had what seemed to be delicious and ample meals provided by the well-known Wiggins Tavern, a part of the hotel. There were ten of us in one of the largest rooms, in an annexed hall opposite the apartment of the owners of the hotel, Mr. and Mrs. Wiggins. Our group was made up of young women from all over the U.S. Three of us were from Florida, others from Ohio, Illinois, New York and elsewhere. It was a happy time getting to know these women from diverse backgrounds. I was the next to youngest in the group of ten, and later finished my training with the second highest rating (following "Tossie", a brilliant student, with a photographic memory who seldom bothered to take notes!). All of us made good friends with the Wiggins and used to "hide" our cider in their apartment when weekly inspection time came.

Sometimes during our rare leisure time, we would bicycle through the New England countryside, aflame with autumn foliage. This was where we got our cider! Bikes were lent to us by Smith College students. There were also trips to nearby Mt. Holyoke, Boston and once to New York City, my first visit there. What a fabulous weekend that was! One of my roommates had a brother who was training on the USS Prairie State, docked in the Hudson River. Between them, they arranged for five of us to go down as dates for five of the young men. We

girls stayed in midtown Manhattan in what was then the Sheraton-Plaza Hotel for Women, I believe. We shared rooms and enjoyed the luxury of continental breakfasts, slipped through a slot at the bottom of the door along with the morning edition of the New York Times. It was an exciting weekend—seeing Radio City Music Hall, Greenwich Village and other New York highlights for the first time. The young men, midshipmen as we were, paid all the checks except the hotel, although none of us had much money. We were all in uniform and in one restaurant (called No 1 Fifth Ave., I believe), a kind gentleman nearby saw all of us together and offered free drinks for all. I'll never forget wandering up and down the streets, arm in arm, singing and having fun. An ideal weekend for a 21 year old.

The only lonely time I had there in Northampton was at Christmas, my first away from home, when none of my gifts arrived on time. Tossie, who had not received hers either, and I shopped late Christmas Eve, I remember, and bought each other glamorous nightgowns. Mostly, however, it was a full, happy three months.

I graduated in early January 1943, one of five hundred out of the nine hundred who started—Ensign McEachern, a true ninety-day wonder, as we were called—and ready for action!

My first assignment was to report for duty at Commander Gulf Sea Frontier in Miami. My preference had been New York, a city I knew would be an exciting place to be. In true Navy fashion, I was sent to Miami instead, to a state already familiar to me. I managed to get transferred to New York two years later, but the intervening years proved extremely interesting. The Naval Communications office was open 24 hours a day and we were on scheduled 8 hour shifts, working different times every few days. There were between 20 and 30 officers on each shift, men and women, decoding messages as they came from the Radio room, routing information to appropriate offices, and then working with Naval operations personnel, sending out coded messages to all concerned ships and stations. There was a lot of enemy submarine action in the Gulf and southern Atlantic areas at that time, and we were in on the earliest reports coming in of ships in distress, among other things. All ships in the area that could offer help had to be contacted with the proper codes, giving the location of the distressed ship. Then the movements had to be followed continuously as the operations were carried out. Speed and accuracy were of prime importance, as was secrecy. I remember the horror of frequently hearing that a ship had been sunk or damaged, things not reported to the public until much later. We had all been cleared for highest security, of course, and felt we were playing a small but important part in the war effort, but we were well aware of the tragedies going on so near.

In the Navy we were all addressed by our last names while on duty. Since McEachern is so hard to fathom as McCann, as it is pronounced, I became Candi at that time among my friends and fellow workers. This nickname has stayed with me through the years.

In Miami we had no assigned officer quarters and found our own private accommodations. I first lived with three other women officers in an apartment right on Biscayne Bay. We often walked the mile or so to work in the center of town. Our apartment was brightened by a chirping, green parakeet and an old white piano with green keys that we bought. Cigarette burn marks here and there gave hints of a dark past—some smoky "Casablanca" bar of Miami long ago. Later, two of the girls moved out and Gretchen and I kept the apartment.

Our lives were active, often hectic, with people working different shifts. We managed to have busy social lives however, with frequent dates, mostly with other Naval officers. There were plenty of eager young men to choose from. Among others, I dated a tall, attractive Lieutenant from Long Island who was the Communications officer on DE 16 (one of the destroyer escorts serving as a training ship with weekly cruises out of Miami). I had met Marvin while on a visit to his ship, and from our positions in Communications, we managed to send each other obscure secret messages from time to time. He sometimes invited me on board for dinner in the officers' mess. Once a large cruiser arrived in port and docked just next to the DE 16. I was with a group of WAVES who had been invited on board for a tour of the ship. In the midst of this, a sailor came up with a message received by semaphore for Lieut. McEachern. (I had been promoted to Lieut. (j.g.) by then.) The message was from my friend on the DE 16 and said, "Don't let the big ship throw you!" Great fun!

This same friend had a small sailboat for awhile and he kept the "Fearless Flea" moored in front of our apartment. One afternoon we capsized in the middle of the bay, much to his chagrin. I thought it was a lark, especially when we were rescued by the Coast Guard. I have many fond memories of those days and the people I got to know.

While in Miami, I decided to learn to fly. It was something I had dreamed of ever since my first flight in a small sightseeing plane piloted by Wiley Post, when I was quite young. I enrolled in Emory Riddle Flying School, which specialized in seaplanes. In my off hours from work I took the ground courses— Meteorology, Aircraft and Engines, Radio and Navigation. (I knew that Geometry would come in handy!) Then began my flight training. My instructor was a patient, white-haired man, named Mr. Royce. Since my father had flown many years before and my brother, Don, was training as a Naval aviator, I was determined to get my private license, and I soloed after the minimum 10 hours instruction. I continued to receive more lessons and took a couple of "long distance" solo flights from Miami—one up to West Palm Beach and another down over the keys toward Key West.

All of flying was a thrilling experience for me. I loved the open cockpit, learning basic aerobatics, and the general feeling of freedom I felt. I was flying a Piper Cub seaplane, which was great to fly as there were plenty of places to land with all that water around. I took my solo test for a private license after the minimum number of required hours. I did the tailspin twice (to get it perfect), but passed without trouble, in spite of a rather strong cross wind. That was in the spring of 1944 when I was not quite 23 years old.

I still had a yen to go to New York, however, and early in 1945 I got my chance. A WAVE officer friend of my roommate, who worked in the personnel office in Washington, had a bit of a breakdown and needed a month or so away from the hectic office there. I was able to arrange a place for her to live in Miami to recuperate. She was grateful and said that if she could ever help me, to let her know. At this time, WAVES were beginning to be sent to Hawaii. Since this was too much like Miami, I asked instead for a transfer or trade with someone who wanted to leave New York. My friend in personnel managed to put my request on top of the pile and a three-way swap was made. It was hard saying goodbye to all the friends (male and female) I had made in Miami, but I wanted to move on. After a nostalgic farewell, I headed for the big city in March 1945.

When I arrived in New York, I was excited about the change of jobs and living in this large city. After staying with WAVE friends a few days, I moved into the old Henry Hudson Hotel, not far from Carnegie Hall. Shortly afterwards, I managed to find an apartment in a high rise on E. 79th Street with another WAVE. Beth, who worked in the Supply Corps, and I were on different schedules as well as different wave lengths—so didn't see too much of each other. This first apartment was in the Hungarian section of the city. There were a lot of good restaurants around—different from those I was used to. My "local" was just across the street, and before I made friends I ate quite a few meals there alone. The owners "adopted" me, in a way, so I always got special attention.

I was still in Classified Communications working in the Federal Office Building (USS Neversink!) at 90 Church Street—downtown near Wall Street. It is still there. There were five admirals stationed in the building with various Naval organizations. I worked in Comeastseafron with Admiral Kinkead, among others. This was exciting work, which we did not talk about outside the office. We still worked shifts and I remember so well being on duty when victory came to Europe, fighting actually ceasing on my birthday, May 7th. I phoned to wake up a WAVE friend with the news at 2 a.m. when the first reports came in to our Radio Center. (Don't think she appreciated the call!)

Another thrill was being in New York on August 6th when the atomic bomb brought an end to the war in the Pacific. The celebrations there at Times Square were something never to forget, even though I had, and have, mixed feelings about the U.S. dropping the bomb. I still feel it was a tragedy—even if a necessary one, as some argue.

The two years plus in New York were among the best years of my life. In addition to having a part in bringing the war to an end with rewarding work, I enjoyed many friendships and an active social life. For the first time I was able to indulge in as many concerts as I wanted, plus seeing many of the best stage productions of the day—enjoyed with a variety of interesting young men officers. Among the plays, I remember seeing Ingrid Bergman in "Joan of Lorraine", Judy Holliday in "Born Yesterday", Tallulah Bankhead in "Skin of our Teeth", "Streetcar Named Desire" with original cast, "Oklahoma", "Carousel" and "On the Town". I especially loved to go to hear the New York Philharmonic where Toscanini was conducting.

Shortly after V-J day, Anne, a WAVE friend from Miami moved in to live with Beth and me until her fiancé returned from service in England. Their greeting when he arrived was featured on the front page of the New York Times!

After that, I moved in with Alice, another WAVE, at 45 E. 72nd Street, where I stayed until leaving New York. Her cousin, Stokley, sang in the chorus of "Oklahoma", so we got free tickets!

The apartment was small, but much better located than the one I had moved from. It was between Madison avenue and Park avenue, only a short walk from Central Park. My friends and I enjoyed exploring the zoo, the skating rink and other parts of the park. It was quite safe in those days, which is not always true today, according to latest reports.

While in New York, I was able to buy my silvery-toned violin that was made in 1775 in Wein (Vienna) by a man named Matbius, according to the notation inside it. I found it at a violin place close to Carnegie Hall—upstairs. The elderly man who repaired and made instruments had a son in the Navy, so gave me a special price. On a recent trip to New York, I noticed the shop was still there! I wonder if he passed it on to his son or grandson?

By that time I had been made a Lieutenant. The Navy was busy putting most of our ships in "mothballs", stripped of armaments and moored at various stations up and down the coast. I had planned to leave the Navy early after the war, but I was offered a spot promotion to Lieutenant-Commander, along with two or three other officers, if I would stay on to help with this decommissioning of ships. Since I loved New York's attractions, it was not hard to decide to stay. Perhaps I was the youngest Lieutenant-Commander in the WAVES at that time.

When the war ended, the young men began returning from overseas, my pianist friend from Peabody days among them. Jimmy was a pilot with the Air Corps and had been stationed in South America and Italy. We had kept in touch with frequent correspondence, and in the autumn of 1945 he came to New York and proposed marriage. In the excitement of seeing him again, I accepted his ring. We had a wonderful few days exploring the sights together and going to nightclubs and jazz clubs to hear the leading players of the day. I remember my eyes streaming tears from the smoky rooms where I heard Art Tatum, Johnny Hodges and others. Jimmy was an excellent jazz musician and loved it.
Previously I had spent several afternoons in record shops off Broadway searching for early discs of Duke Ellington and others from lists Jimmy had sent me. The salesmen were impressed, assuming I knew a lot more about these musicians than I did!

Jimmy and I decided to get married as soon as he got settled and he returned to Nashville to decide on his future. It was not many months, however, before I realized that we had developed as different people. I sent his ring back in January 1946. He drove to New York in February to try to dissuade me from breaking the engagement, but I somehow knew we weren't right for each other. He never did get his life together, unfortunately, even though he was an extremely talented and intelligent young man.

The work was less exciting after V-J Day, but my social life was still great! I seemed to fall in and out of love every few months—all passing fancies. Pilot friends who were returning "war-weary" planes to bases in Florida would sometimes offer me a ride to visit my family. Once, I was even allowed to take the controls of a DC-3 for a couple of hours! It was not during landing or takeoff, of course, but I did log it officially in my flight book. Another pilot with the Coast Guard offered me a chance to ride (and try to fly) a helicopter. Lots of fun trying to hover, but it was a bit too complicated for me with so many variables—trying to control the angles of the rotor blades while doing everything else.

My brother was in flight training with the Navy at this time and I once visited him at the Naval Air Station in Jacksonville. He later transferred to the Marines and became a fighter pilot, flying in the Korean War.

My limited flying experience made me occasionally dream of starting a flying school in Florida after the war, and I remained fascinated with flying. But I began to realize that my education had not been as complete as I would like, and there were too many things that interested me that I didn't know much about. I had done a bit of painting in New York, caught up in the enthusiasm of the art revival of the 50's, but it was ideas I needed to explore more deeply. With the lure of the GI Bill, I decided to return to school. After the anonymity of New York (and the crowded subways), I decided to go back to Nashville and a more relaxed life, where I had friends and family.

I had a month's leave due me before officially leaving active duty in June 1947 (4 years 8 months and 9 days after I started!). I took a cross-country trip to California to visit friends, especially an ex-WAVE, Ellie, in Los Angeles and another N.Y. friend, Ben, who was working in Bakersville. This trip was taken courtesy of several Navy flights going my direction. In California I visited the huge Palomar telescope, then Hollywood and Pasadena, with the fabulous

Huntington Library. I even took a short tour up to San Francisco to see Fisherman's Wharf and the Art Museum there.

In Bakersfield, Ben and his friends took me camping in the High Sierras where there was still snow on the ground. A half-hour later we went swimming in the hot valley! Then, before heading back east I took a short bus trip down to Tijuana, Mexico, just to see a foreign country. A young Navy man I met on the bus who was also leaving the service spent the whole trip trying to get me to stay in California! I can't remember his name.

After taking a few courses at Peabody during the summer I felt I needed some time to truly relax before starting regular studies at Vanderbilt University. I invited Mother, who was visiting Jeanne, to go as my guest for a week in Gatlinburg, Tennessee. We stayed in a little cottage on the French Broad River, relaxing in the hammock on the porch with no pressure and no noise except the water rippling across the rocks in the shallow river. It was a delightful change. We did take a few easy hikes up the mountains, but mostly just enjoyed the solitude and each other. It was a week with my mother I will always cherish.

I was eager to begin my graduate studies at Vanderbilt. I had my B.S. in Music Education, but not enough credits in English to begin the master's program in English Literature that I wanted. That first year back, therefore, I concentrated on senior undergraduate courses in Literature and Philosophy, joining many other veterans, mostly men, working toward degrees. This was an exhilarating time after the war, and for me a time of creative intellectual development. Ideas seemed to fly in all directions—with unlimited scope. A strong feeling of camaraderie developed among the veteran students. I enjoyed a rather special status, being one of the few women veterans at Vanderbilt, and I was accepted as an equal among the men, which added to my enthusiasm. We were all a bit intellectually arrogant, sensing we had different experiences and more mature insights than the younger undergraduates. Competition was keen with all of us working hard and appreciating education much more than we had earlier. At this time most of my best friends were men, and I have a warm spot in my heart for Brockie, Dan, John and others who welcomed me as a pal and confidant.

After getting my B.A. in English I began working toward my M.A. the fall term of 1948. During this time, among others, I dated James Dickey, the poet, and author of the bestseller, "Deliverance". Other boyfriends I remember include Madison Jones who later wrote several novels, Carter, a long-time friend from music school days, Bud, who once hired a private plane to fly to see me in Florida and a nice guy named Bill McQueen, later a university professor.

The social scene for the students was stimulating. Some of the more interesting parties were given by an artist, Jack Kershaw, and his wealthy wife. They entertained lavishly, arranging imaginative events such as square dances (complete with authentic old-time fiddler and caller) and sleigh rides at their large estate. Many graduate students and young professors in the fields of music, art and literature were invited. I got involved through my old music buddies at Peabody. Jack was not a great artist by any means. He used an air brush for his paintings, which were too slick and commercial looking for my taste. In his studio, one wall was completely covered by a huge reclining nude (No one I recognized, thank goodness!). He would often "arrange" to take individuals alone to view this, just to see how they would react. A bit of a character, who loved to flirt with all the young girls, but few took him seriously. Still, I remember it all as being a lot of fun.

For me, it was an intellectually challenging time, intertwined with the social activities. I had courses and seminars in a broad range of literature, including Modern Poetry (with Jim Dickey alongside), the Lyric, and Classical Drama, as well as many philosophy courses (my minor). I especially enjoyed Logic and Ethics classes. I chose to do research on the author, Lafcadio Hearn, for my master's thesis, mostly because of his diverse ethnic background and his distinctive style. I became absorbed with this work during 1948-49, as well as finishing my formal classes then. Thinking ahead, I applied for a Fulbright Scholarship to do further study in England. I had passed the first round of applications and was moving ahead when I met someone who was to change my plans and my life.

Even though Bob and I had both been in Vanderbilt for a couple of years, we did not meet until one day in the university library where we both had graduate study carrels. I was deep in reading when a young man started talking to the girl in the next carrel. He mentioned his airplane! Ears perked up and I soon joined in the conversation. Bob had also been in the Navy during the war, graduating from flight school in Pensacola. He invited me for a ride in his small Taylorcraft, and we began spending more and more time together. I met and liked Bob's parents, but I thought of him as just another friend at first, and I was dating several others.

Gradually we found we had many things in common, in addition to an interest in flying and experience in the Navy. We had similar philosophies of life, and both wanted to do worthwhile work involving travel and adventure. During spring break we flew to Florida in his little Taylorcraft to visit my family. They liked Bob and the trip was great fun, even though we had a slight mishap during a stopover in Atlanta on the way back when a large plane tipped us to the side while it was taking off nearby. The wing was slightly damaged and we had to stay overnight to have it repaired.

Another incident that took place during this trip was when we were flying near Chattanooga and noticed that the fuel gauge was low. Bob switched to the alternate gas tank, but nothing happened! We were nowhere near an airport or any convenient landing place. Realizing something was probably blocking the fuel flow to the engine, he banked sharply left and right. Voila!, things were cleared and we flew on our way, although I was feeling slightly nauseous by that time! After landing we discovered that a dirt dauber had started to make a nest in the air hole to the fuel tank.

We were very much in love and it wasn't too long before we decided life would be much better together than apart. We became engaged in the spring of

1949 and spent the last quarter of graduate school madly finishing course work for our Master's degrees. Bob was getting his degree in Economics, and was not "into" literature or music, although he appreciated them. Some of my friends wondered why I was marrying someone so "different". Even though we were, and are, different, we have intersecting circles of talents and interests, and our goals and values are much alike, as has been proved through the years.

IV

FLYING TOGETHER

We were married on August 6, 1949 in the attractive Scales Chapel of the Methodist Church across from Vanderbilt. Rev. Anderson performed the ceremony and two of my friends, Bob and Almyra, from music school days, sang solos. My sister, Jeanne, was my matron of honor. Her five-year old daughter, Miriam, was an adorable flower girl. All the family members were there, plus other assorted relatives and friends—about one hundred in all. It was a small, but beautiful wedding—with a long white dress, made lovingly by Jeanne, and I carried a bouquet of small orchids and daisies. It was an event to remember with pleasure—even though the August temperature was breaking records. We went

to the cool mountains in Gatlinburg for our honeymoon. His parents had lent him a car and we explored Great Smoky National Park and over into North Carolina, even climbing up Mt. Lookout in Montreat, that I remembered fondly from earlier days.

Back in Nashville, Bob had a fellowship at Vanderbilt to work toward his doctorate. He began courses and teaching and I was finishing up my thesis, "Verbal Artistry in the American Writings of Lafcadio Hearn"—a Stylistic Study. I took a job as program director at the Nashville YWCA, to help with the finances. My work there kept me busy but was enjoyable. I arranged classes, dinners, twice-weekly dances and other things for various groups of young women.

We first lived in a tiny apartment (with shared bath!) near the University, then, thankfully, moved into an attractive little apartment on a quiet street. We borrowed some furniture from family and filled in with painted potato boxes as side tables. Even though we had barely enough to live on that year we were busy and happy. I worked in the library during free time to finish my thesis while Bob studied. It was completed and signed on Valentine's Day 1950, written under Donald Davidson and Richmond Beatty—well known members of the Vanderbilt faculty.

The summer of 1950 brought us an opportunity not to be missed. Bob was granted a fellowship in Latin American studies for six-weeks study at the University of North Carolina in Chapel Hill. I resigned my job at the YWCA without regret. We sub-let our apartment and headed for North Carolina in our little plane, which we had named "Skylark". I was eager to take some classes of my own at Chapel Hill, so I studied Modern Drama and Playwriting (one of the especially good courses offered there) while Bob followed his courses. We lived in one of the big men's dormitories, taken over for married couples. I remember having to wash out our coffeepot in the men's urinals!

As the term came to an end, Bob received an offer to interview in Washington for a research project in Puerto Rico. He had finished his course work for the doctorate, but was undecided about going straight on with his research. We decided to explore the offer, with the idea that the research there could possibly be used for his thesis. So, off we went to Washington in "Skylark", not knowing exactly what would happen.

Over Hopewell, Virginia we ran into a heavy rainstorm and flying became more and more difficult. Our maps showed a small airport down there somewhere, but we couldn't see a thing! After flying at tree-top level for awhile, we saw a bare space and just headed down. It was more like a lake than a landing strip—luckily, it was the airport. After getting a ride into town we stayed in a huge, old wooden hotel, almost deserted. Next day, on to Washington, which we knew had a choice of small airports. Bailey's Crossroads, Virginia was chosen (airport no longer there), and soon we were in DC looking for a place to stay. Innocently, both in casual flying gear, we went first into the famous Willard Hotel. It didn't take long to decide it wasn't our style and we found a modest hotel not too far away. Next day, we met Dan Darling at the Labor Department, who was to direct the study in Puerto Rico. Bob was offered, and accepted, the job to begin in September. That night we wanted to celebrate, but had little money. We found a neat little restaurant, the Olmstead, where we were able to afford nothing on the menu but Salisbury steak. It tasted delicious!

We flew back to Nashville through a beautiful sunset in the Shenandoah Valley, excited about plans for our first overseas adventure. There was much to do before we left. We thought briefly about taking "Skylark" with us—but soon realized how far we would have to fly over the water, and abandoned that idea. The Taylorcraft had a limited range, and only went about 100 miles an hour, tops. Sadly, we said good-bye to our little plane, and I was able to sell it to an old boyfriend—who didn't even know how to fly!

Our one-year stint in Puerto Rico provided a good introduction to foreign life. Even in 1950, of course, the island was not extremely foreign, and English was spoken in most of the shops and larger towns. We sought out chances to learn Spanish, but it was a long way from total immersion. Still, it was a different culture, as we soon found out. Stereotypical ideas of the "relaxed" idea of time, for example, are firmly based in experience. We were not met on our arrival as promised, and after phone calls, took a taxi to where we were to stay. This was some kind of guest house that had no guests except us—and no one to run the place at all. A young teenager let us in, then left. We were in a residential section with no transportation or shops, but managed to have a supper of avocados bought from a street cart, washed down with a bit of cognac, which we had. After climbing under our mosquito netting that night we finally got used to the constant chorus of kukis from the small pond outside. How can a little frog make so much noise? The next morning we were awakened by wild shouts and screams, later discovering that we were next door to the local home for the mentally deranged! The Director of the Social Science Research Center of the University of Puerto Rico soon arrived to show us around, however, and things went more smoothly after that. We found a small studio apartment—a fourth-floor walkup in a building within a few blocks of the University campus in Rio Piedras. Walking and climbing stairs kept us fit!

Bob did his research on anticipated labor needs of the island. This involved taking an extensive survey of all the manufacturing sector, so he was able to travel throughout the island (only 100 miles long). I went with him whenever I could, visiting Mayaguez, Ponce, and Arecibo. We went to the more exotic sites of El Yunque rain forest and Luquillo beach during our off hours, as soon as we were able to buy our first car. The "Green Queen" was a ten-year old bright green Plymouth coupe, which broke down periodically, but it did enable us to explore all the nooks and crannies of remote beaches and little mountain roads throughout the island.

Our family expanded a few months after we arrived when we bought a cocker spaniel puppy. Linda proved to be the best dog we ever had, perhaps because I had more time to train her. When she was small, sometimes we would put her into a bag and sneak her in to see a movie with us. Shortly after that we moved into a small house nearby, along with George, a fellow research student from Harvard. The new house was only basically furnished, and we couldn't even afford to have the hot water heater attached. The whole time we were there the men took bracing showers in the morning and I waited until noon for mine.

The *ménage a trois* worked out quite well, and at least we had a bit of a yard for Linda to run in. Our attempts to cut the grass with a machete didn't amount to much. I was the designated cook and concocted some filling, if unimaginative, dishes such as arroz con pollo. Meat was expensive and we mostly ate dishes with cod or other fish plus lots of fruits and vegetables. Every now and then on weekends we would go to the Navy Beach Club, where we could get delicious steaks rather inexpensively. George, ex-army, went along as our guest. It was a good place to socialize although we also made friends through the University. A lot of young people were doing research there at that time. Our evening get-togethers were intellectually exciting with earnest discussions about everything from politics and economics to art and metaphysics. Our choice of drinks was rum and Coca-Cola, with the rum, a major product of Puerto Rico, being much less expensive than the coke!

I hadn't been able to get any work at the University (rule against hiring wives) and spent my days keeping things running at home, plus writing numerous short stories. Naturally I sent them out only to the best magazines, such as The New Yorker and The Atlantic Monthly. When they were rejected I was too discouraged to waste any more postage. I read a lot, lugging arm loads of books home from the University library. In addition to my creaky little typewriter, we had brought all our books down to Puerto Rico with us, so the house was mostly furnished with them, plus a few plants.

In the Spring of 1951, we were hit with a double tax bill and were practically broke. Through the Navy, I was able to get temporary duty as the only WAVE attached to the Comgulfseafron headquarters in Puerto Rico. Since I was still in the Naval Reserve, going on temporary active duty saved our lives. I worked in the Communications office there for two weeks as Lieutenant Commander, and then was put on the payroll as a civilian for four more weeks, working until we left in the summer of 1951. Coincidentally, I discovered an old boyfriend from New York was also on duty there!

Bob and I had some wonderful memories to take home from this first year out of the U.S. On the way back to the States we went to Haiti for a few days. The dignity and carriage of the statuesque Haitian natives with huge loads on their heads impressed us and I was enchanted with their warm, French dialect. We stayed in a large, classic wooden hotel there and later hired a driver to take us to explore the mountains above Port au Prince. I'll never forget having tea and eating strawberries in front of a mahogany wood fire at a small inn high above the city. What a delight after our meager meals in the humid climate of Puerto Rico. It made me sad, however, to see all that mahogany go up in flames.

Bob had to return to Puerto Rico for a week or so, but I went on to the U.S. to wait for him. Around that time I was beginning to suspect I was pregnant, and after a stopover in Jacksonville, I headed for Nashville where this was confirmed. Bob's parents, Ruth and Joe, had invited us for a vacation in the Thousand Island area of New York, and Bob flew up to meet us there. His brother, Dan, also went along for an active week in a small cabin, with frequent boat trips with Bob's Uncle Lawrence, who lived nearby. Unfortunately, I had morning sickness much of the time.

After our vacation, we headed for Washington, since we had decided that was where we wanted to live and Bob was confident he could find work there. Dan Darling, the director of the project in Puerto Rico, had become a good friend, and through his contacts, Bob was hired by the Department of Labor.

We moved into an empty one-bedroom apartment on North Ode St. in Arlington, Virginia, just across the Potomac River from Washington. We bought basic necessities little by little, sleeping on a day-bed for some months and using a card table and chairs borrowed from the Darlings. Linda had been shipped to us from Puerto Rico, and we were happy together, making do with what we had and looking forward to the birth of our first child.

Carol Jeanne was born at 5 p.m., February 5, 1952 at Doctor's Hospital in Washington with Dr. Jay Bay Jacobs attending. The birth was not too easy as she was reversed in the womb, but after ten days in the hospital we took home our 7 lb. 14 oz. squirming, pink bundle with both optimism and trepidation. The next months  were busy ones—with a new baby and a dog. We did manage to rent a larger, two-bedroom apartment across the hall and even bought an old piano (with a high bid of $50.50!). With a few hundred dollars from my Dad (which I had lent him during my Navy days), we bought a second-hand gray Chevrolet. Believe it or not, I had not learned to drive before that, even though I could fly a plane!

Bob gave me a few lessons and I soon got my license. The day afterward, with Carol and Linda, I confidently drove in heavy traffic to 3rd and Independence in Washington to pick up Bob at work. That was an exciting experience. I think I stalled at every red light!

When Carol was three months old we took an extensive trip, driving down to Jacksonville to see my parents, then up to Nashville and Ohio and back. Carol slept a lot in her car bed, and Linda was a diverting companion—always well behaved. A month later, we went to Ohio again for the wedding of Bob's brother, Dan, and Joanne; then at Christmas, drove to Miami where my parents had retired. So, Carol began her life with lots of travel!

Shortly after that, I was thrilled and not too surprised when Bob called from work one day to say he had been offered a job in Peru to help set up an Employment Service. Knowing I would agree, he had already accepted! We began our plans and somehow managed to buy the things necessary for the move.

We flew to Miami for a brief visit with Mother and Dad since that was our taking off point for Lima. Carol, who was now 13 months old, loved playing on the beach, as did Linda. Much confusion saying goodbye and getting ourselves

aboard with all Carol's bottles, diapers and jars of baby food, as well as briefcases, coats and my violin. This was before the days of jet travel, so we had berths that were made up before we boarded. Carol took awhile to go to sleep and kept peeking at us as we ate dinner. She and I slept in the lower berth, with Bob in the upper. We landed at Panama City and Guayaquil, Ecuador, but Carol slept peacefully all night. Quite an exciting experience to sleep thousands of feet above the earth. We knew right then that Carol would be a good traveler.

V

OVER THE ANDES

Flying high over Peru, we awoke to a rosy dawn out of the window. Below us we caught glimpses of barren desert and mountains jutting through the clouds in the distance. We became increasingly excited as we approached landing and were thrilled to see the beautiful city of Lima spread out before us with many parks and wide boulevards. The city was completely different from anything we had seen or expected. We were fascinated with everything, eager to establish ourselves after our long plane trip. First we checked into the Hotel Bolivar on the Plaza San Martin—a dignified and impressive old place with unusual architecture. Its "snake pit" was a famous meeting place. In a few days we made arrangements to move to Pension Beech (a boarding house in the area of San Isidro). When Bob went to pay the bill at the Bolivar he found he did not have quite enough money. What to do? "Do you have a calling card?" the management asked. Of course he did. Then, "No hay problema", we could pay later.

At "Ma" Beech's pension—run by an expatriate Englishwoman—we were able to get a suite of rooms with a small garden, opposite the main house. We had our meals in the main dining room, but there was a basic kitchen attached to the suite where I could fix Carol's meals. Inocenti, an employee of the pension, was helpful watching Carol occasionally. We made friends quickly and that was a good thing because shortly after we arrived Bob had to take a trip to northern Peru, leaving me to look for a house. Diana Henderson, from England, who was also looking for a house, and a German author named Herbert Kirchhoff were a great help. We joined forces, taking Carol, along with her fold-up stroller in the trunk of the taxi. Before Bob returned I had several possibilities lined up, so a few weeks later when our furniture had arrived we moved into a big, rather plain modern house in Miraflores. We had very little furniture, but had brought the piano with us, now painted cream-colored. The first few months were difficult. I remember we had to cook on a primus stove for some time until we got our proper cooker installed. Carol had started walking at the pension, so she found new freedom in the small, walled garden, along with Linda who had been shipped from the States.

During the next few months we hired different maids—some good, some not so good. Antoinetta and her little boy didn't last too long. Then, after a disaster or two, Amanda and Maria came and things seemed to run more smoothly. Bob's work was going well and we made more friends. Diana and her husband, Harvey, were our best friends throughout our stay there and we spent much time together. Diana and I studied Spanish together; she taught me to play chess and I taught her to drive. Bob, Carol and I did a bit of exploring in the old Chevrolet we had brought from the States, sometimes going up to Chosica, above Lima, to find a few rays of sunshine. The climate in Lima is not the best—with gray days more often than not, although it never actually rained. We managed to cheer ourselves up through the worst months with fires in the fireplace and the wives entertaining with teas for friends. There were lots of parties and couples often met to exchange records and play games. By design, I never got into the bridge crowd.

Bob and I took several hiking trips up into the Andes, once driving to 10,000

feet before climbing to a small village. We also took a class in archaeology, taught by a Yale professor, and were intrigued by the different ages of pottery, fabrics and clay figures that had been found in Peru—many pre-Incan artifacts. We once went on an organized dig in northern Peru with a group of friends, which was fascinating.

One of the highlights of our travels during this time was a trip to Cuzco and Machu Picchu, the fabulous Incan ruins high in the Andes, leaving Carol in the care of Diana. In the small plane we flew in, oxygen was supplied to passengers if they needed it. Cuzco has a high altitude, over 11,000 ft., so you have to adjust even after you arrive. I was struck by the many small, uncared-for children sitting in doorways—their cheeks glowingly pink, but with extended bellies and tangled hair. Seeing them huddled there made me want to take them all home.

All the Catholic churches seemed to be filled with ornate statues and many golden objects. In such a poor country, one wonders if priorities are right. Thinking this through, I have come to realize that for these people, with so little that is beautiful or hopeful in their lives, the church brings joy and hope for a better life to come. Who could take that away? And what would be the alternative?

We wanted another child, and when I realized I was pregnant again, I decided on Dr. Tomás Díaz, a Peruvian doctor who had received his medical training in the States and who was married to an American nurse. Luckily, the months passed swiftly. Bob came home for lunch every day, so we had our main meal then. Carol was developing into a happy, loving child and the days were busy and fun. Bob's parents, Ruth and Joe, came for a visit and helped celebrate Carol's second birthday. We were all counting the days waiting for the new baby.

Peggy Ruth was born at 12 noon in the Anglo-American Clinic on May 13, 1954. It was an easy birth and she was a beautiful little baby of 8 lbs. 3 oz. The next months were fun, with two little daughters to care for. I was grateful during this time to have good help with a cook and a maid/ama, leaving me to enjoy the children but not being tied down. Marketing and planning day-to-day activities were not as simple as in the States, of course. I had to go to different places for each type of thing—butchers, bakery, milk and egg shop, as well as to the market for vegetables. I loved the big native market, however, and became quite adept at bargaining. Being able to fill the house with fresh flowers was a special joy. Diana and Harvey had a little girl, Ruth, (called Cushie), born a few months before Peggy was born, so we did a lot of things together.

When Peggy was still quite young, we took the family on a trip down the coast of Peru, taking the ama, Maria, along with us to help care for the baby. We stayed in a nice hotel, where we basked in the sunshine and played in the pool with Carol. On this trip we visited Pachacamac, Paracas, Ica, Nazca, Arequipa and Lake Titicaca, all places we had learned about in our archaeology class.

Peggy was a very active baby, lifting her head at three weeks! She was soon bouncing around in her jump seat and was always ready to go. When she was about seven months old, I noticed she was getting some tiny red spots on her body, here and there. One was near her eye and Bob and I were worried. We decided that I would return to Miami with the girls a couple of months before we were due for home leave in order to have Peggy checked. My parents, who had settled in South Miami near Coral Gables, welcomed us happily when we arrived in January 1955. A visit to a dermatologist reassured me that the spots were a type that would definitely disappear—so with relief we settled in to wait for Bob. The sunshine and beaches were a blessing after the Lima climate, and we all thrived. Mother and Dad were good to help with the children and Carol became firmly attached to Dad, following him around and learning the names of all his many exotic plants. She was not yet three—so he thought she was a genius! Peggy began crawling and climbing soon after she arrived in Miami, and got cuter every day. I was glad to have had this time to spend with my parents, but was mighty glad to welcome Bob when he arrived in March. Linda had been shipped back and this time we decided she should retire there, if agreeable with Dad. He got much pleasure from her until she was 13 years old.

After an extended vacation both in Miami and Nashville, we headed back to Lima shortly after Peggy's first birthday. This time, we decided to go by ship and arranged for the trip on a twelve-passenger freighter from New Orleans, which we visited briefly before embarking. The ship was not air-conditioned and was even hotter than we had imagined. It got cooler after we got underway and we did have an interesting trip, especially going through the Panama Canal. We stopped briefly at Guayaquil, Ecuador before arriving in Callao (Lima's port). With so few passengers aboard, there were no extras such as baby sitting services. Bob and I took turns staying with the children in the evenings, although the other passengers were not all that interesting. A carefully hoarded bottle of bourbon was appreciated. Peggy wasn't walking yet so we pushed her around the deck in her little stroller. We put a harness on Carol and sometimes she walked around pulling her squawking duck, which at least let everyone know where she was. I made a solemn vow not to take another trip by ship with babies!

Back in Lima, we went again to Ma Beech's pension, since we were changing houses and had put our things into storage while on home leave. We had ordered a new car and it was waiting for us—a pretty, blue Ford sedan. Soon we were able to get into a spacious house in San Isidro, courtesy of friends, the Cavanaughs, who were leaving the country. We now had Julia as cook and Victoria as ama, both wonderful help. The house had a lovely walled garden filled with flowers (thanks to a good gardener). We installed swings, sliding board and plastic pool for the children and settled in for some happy months.

It wasn't long before I realized I was pregnant again, something we had both hoped for. During the long months of pregnancy I kept busy with family activities, and it was during this time that I began my first formal art class—in drawing and design.

Jeanne and her husband, Charles and ten-year-old Robert came to visit after Christmas—a welcome event. The new baby was to be born exactly nine months after our sea voyage—one happy consequence of that trip! I had been sure it was to be a boy, and Steven Robert, weighing 8 lbs. 6 oz., was born at 8 p.m. on March 15, 1956 at the Anglo-American Clinic, with Dr. Díaz, as Peggy had been.

It was a busy household with three little ones to care for. I was able to arrange my day to give the children a great deal of attention, with the wonderful help of a full-time cook, the ama/maid, a part-time laundress and another woman who came in just to take care of the baby's laundry (No diaper service available). Running the house, shopping and the children's activities kept me on the go, plus planning entertainment. . It was a perfect arrangement with no drudgery and all the fun! We gave many large parties during this time in Lima, as it was easy and not expensive at that time to have them catered. Delicious anticuchos, "bocas" of ceviche and other delicacies were offered.

We put Carol briefly into a nursery school run by a German woman, but after observing the rather disorganized program and hearing Carol sing "Go 'round and 'round the WILLAGE" among other things, we decided it was not fair to make her language development even more complicated, so we withdrew her.

I stimulated the children with lots of music and by reading to them. We encouraged their artistic talents with an easel and paints, saving their "masterpieces" for years. All the children enjoyed our private garden playground. Steven learned to crawl at seven months, as had the girls, and was soon exploring every corner of the house and garden. He was precocious about building blocks and puzzles from an early age. He was obviously a bright child. Christmas that year was great fun with the children perfect ages to enjoy everything.

Bob was busy during this time getting the first National Labor Exchange set up for the Peruvian government. He worked exclusively in Spanish and became fluent in dealing with the various officials. He changed from working for the U. S. Department of Labor to work with what would later become the AID program attached to the State Department, still doing the same development work.

After Carol's fifth birthday, we arranged swimming lessons for her at a nearby private pool, and along with a small group of neighborhood children, she learned to make it across the pool alone and to dive from the side during the few months of warm weather. Movies of this accomplishment are fun to look back on.

Other early memories of the children include Peggy's habit of waking up early and while she was still in the crib, stripping the bed and "reading" her books by carefully tearing out each page as she finished it. She always loved books, but even then she was discriminating and perhaps she felt like moving on to more interesting ones! Steven had a personality different from either of the girls. He  seemed entranced by anything moving—water, wheels and such things. He developed a fascination of watching his moving legs under him as he scooted along the floor crawling with his head down, often barely escaping a collision.

Carol was more attuned to people than the other children were. She once gave her new doll to a little beggar girl who came to the door with her mother, which the ama frantically explained to me when I returned home from shopping. Victoria had been unable to dissuade her from this and I realized that this was our child beginning to think of others—something to celebrate. One of the difficulties of raising a family in an underdeveloped country is the normal questioning of children when they see so much poverty on the streets and realize they themselves have so much more—not just toys, but basic necessities of food and clothing. It is hard to explain even to ourselves, but we realized we had to maintain a healthy, safe household if we were ever going to be able to help with the development of this struggling country.

We had always wanted to see the jungle area of Peru, but kept having to postpone this trip as our family expanded. Looking forward to the end of our stay in Lima, we decided to take a week's trip over the Andes in our Jeep station wagon before we were to leave in the spring of 1957. Crossing mountain passes can become habit forming, we've found. A simple curiosity to see "the other side", if given in to, can easily develop into an obsession; soon it seems you will risk life and limb, as well as family, to gratify your desires. This trip offered a challenge we couldn't resist. I later wrote of this adventure in an article, excerpts from which bring it back vividly.

Lima lies on the Rimac River, along which the first east-west "highway" was built to afford access to the jungle area. Building a road through the mountains is more than formidable because there are two mountain ranges to cross. Nature continues to fight back every year when seasonal torrential rains attack the hard work of the previous year causing huge chunks of road to be washed out. At that time, and perhaps even today, none of the roads were paved once you got into the mountains. They were closed to any traffic until May (autumn in Peru) when the rains were supposedly finished.

We packed basic supplies in our Jeep station wagon, and along with our young daughters, Carol and Peggy, we set off in high spirits on May 1st. We had prudently left one-year-old Steven at home with the trusted ama and other household help, to be checked on regularly by a woman doctor friend.

Even though it didn't rain until we were over the first, highest pass, our spirits were a bit dampened by having to wait three times while various patches of the road were repaired. The road seemed to narrow more with each turn as it zigzagged up and around the bare mountains. Many of the lower slopes had patterned terraces carved into seemingly solid rock. There the Indians were somehow managing to subsist on produce from the scanty soil collected there, still using sharpened poles as tools—unchanged over centuries.

We found no reason to linger at the 15,889 ft. Anticona Pass without oxygen, so hurried on after quick photos. The girls had fallen asleep (or passed out), their fingernails and lips blue, while Bob and I had horrific, pulsing headaches. We drove on through the barren area between the two mountain ranges, called the "altiplano". This area is rich in minerals—copper, zinc, lead, gold and silver among the metals mined.

Between the mining towns of La Oroya (12,225 ft.) and Cerro de Pasco (14,200 ft.) the only living things we saw were several herds of llamas and alpacas, and occasionally a few Indians huddled in blankets beside the road. The beauty of the sky in the fading light contrasted with the emptiness of the landscape, making it even more desolate. We had hoped to reach the tourist hotel in Huánuco before  dark, but at dusk a sudden rain descended and the twisting road soon became muddy and treacherous. Then the windshield wiper broke and we had to creep along, straining to see a few feet ahead. The road was usually too narrow for cars to pass. When meeting another vehicle, the one descending had to back up to a wider spot. On this rainy night, with only the faint glow of the rear lights, it was frightening. In some places the drop was hundreds of feet. I'm convinced I saved our lives at one point when Bob was backing and could not see the newly formed washout just inches from the back wheels. Thanks to four-wheel drive and Bob's quick reaction to my terrified shout, we were able to continue and safely reached the hotel later that night.

The following morning we discovered the next section of road was one-way for three days of the week, the other way three days, with Sunday a free-for-all. As luck would have it, we were going to have to stay over in Huánuco. Bob disappeared and soon returned with the "good" news. Because he was working for a government ministry, he had gotten permission to travel against the traffic! That was the worst "good news" I had ever had. Sure enough, we went on the next day, expecting huge trucks and possible death around every bend. Actually, we saw five different vehicles over the side during our trip, accidents which seemed to have happened recently, although no bodies were visible. I can understand why the drivers we met were very put out with these stupid foreigners.

As we got nearer to Tingo Maria, the countryside became less threatening and increasingly tropical. Ferns appeared along the roadside, while the highway itself, still a narrow track, became a tunnel through overhanging trees. Dozens of bird nests, suspended like fruit, were silhouetted against glimpses of sky. We stopped to examine a cluster of vivid blue butterflies, some with wing spans of over six inches, lazily sunning themselves beside a small stream. Tingo Maria was an exciting "frontier" town where the government had established an agricultural station to coordinate the work involved in developing the jungle. We stayed in the tourist hotel, a group of cottages strung along the active Huallaga River. This whole area, surrounded by rain forests, lived up to all our ideas of the jungle; plants with large, oddly-shaped leaves, strange flowers and ferns grew in tangled masses. Trees, often with cascades of air-plants, twisted up and away from the cruel embrace of tropical vines. Along the river, parrots and other colorful birds mingled their sharp cries with the monotonous murmur of insects. One afternoon we watched as a horde of large ants near our cottage completely stripped a small tree of leaves, carrying their ragged green banners in a line to some unknown home. These were memories never to be forgotten.

On the way back home, we discovered another, shorter road branching off from Cerro de Pasco, joining the Pan-American highway a few miles north of

Lima. We wondered why we saw no other cars. There was good reason. We kept reassuring ourselves that it couldn't get any worse as we crept along the crumbly track at terrifying heights above the valley floor. The pass here is appropriately called the "Widow's Pass". Still, there were compensations. Where else can you discover a fantastic "bosque de piedra" (rock forest), huge rock masses rising like an ancient city of gods, silent and inscrutable? Where else can you unexpectedly come upon a series of emerald green glacial lakes, joined by waterfalls one after the other? The silence and unreal quality of the air helped create the illusion that we were the first to see these wonders.

The lights of home were a welcome sight. Relieved to be safe after our occasionally harrowing adventure, we were met with the news that little Steven had fallen from his rocking horse and broken his collarbone while waiting for us safely in Lima!

Steven mended in short order and we were soon caught up in the chaos of packing to go back to the U.S. It was difficult to finalize everything about the shipment of household effects and selling the car, while still taking care of an active family. We decided that I should go home ahead with the three children, leaving Bob to wind up things in Lima. This was not easy for either of us, but seemed the best option.

The 15-hour plane trip back was one to remember. We flew on Panagra Airlines, a branch of Pan-American, in one of the large prop-driven planes then used. We had sleepers as before, the bunks made up above the normal seats, and the children were wonderfully obedient, waiting patiently for attention in getting dressed or fed. Steven slept with me and I remember dressing him in the cramped bunk, then handing him down to a nice man across the aisle who seemed happy to watch him while I dressed. The stewardess was not at all cooperative. If anyone ever needed help, I did with the children. I decided right then to avoid Panagra or Pan-American planes in the future, whenever possible. My nice male friend helped me get the children off the plane in Miami where we were met by my parents. It was wonderful to enjoy the sun again. Bob arrived a few weeks later, and we began plans for a vacation, before returning to Washington for a tour of duty.

VI

STATESIDE LANDING

Before leaving Peru we had ordered a big Ford station wagon to accommodate our active family back in the States. After we arrived, Bob went to New Jersey to pick it up, then we began our search for a place to live. We stayed a few days in a house in D.C. lent to us by Reynolds Carlson, a former professor of Bob's from Vanderbilt, who had visited us in Lima. We were relieved to find a convenient little house we could afford in Falls Church, Virginia. It was a three-bedroom brick rambler on a slight hill with a beautifully wooded lot, backing onto more woods. The large backyard was fenced and had a swing set and barbecue. We were excited about buying our first house, even though we realized we would probably be in the States only two years, the normal tour for State Dept. officials. We painted the door red to make it a bit distinctive from the other brick houses in the Graham Road development, and began settling in.

Carol, at five and a half, was too young to be admitted to the public school, so we enrolled her in the first grade of the private Pal-Nez School in Tysons Corner. We put Peggy in the nursery school there. During this year I drove the girls to and from the school, picking them up at noon, accompanied by Steven as co-pilot in his car seat. It was a pleasant twenty minute drive cutting through leafy Gallows Road.

After having had the privilege of domestic help for the past four years, I wanted to prove to myself that I could cope with running the house and caring for the little ones without outside help. Bob left for work early with a carpool, so I was on my own during the week. It was not really a breeze, but satisfying and fun. I made simple meals and perched the children on stools and in a highchair along the kitchen-dining nook divider. We bought a large bowl with goldfish for them to watch as they ate. On weekends we took family picnics and exploring trips nearby. After a while we decided we needed a dog, and soon Sherry, a champagne-colored

47

cocker spaniel puppy, joined the family. She slept in the large basement, which also served as the laundry room, had a trampoline jumping place (old mattress and springs), and in one corner, a studio table and shelves for my art activities.

The months passed rapidly. My parents and other relatives came to visit and we later enjoyed the brilliant fall foliage then beautiful snow, particularly heavy that year, which was a novelty for the children. Bob's parents spent that

Christmas with us, great fun with the kids. Not long after this, I decided I had proved to myself that I could care for the children without help, so I relented and hired Odessa once a week, especially to do ironing, which is not my favorite chore. During the summer Bob had to take an extensive trip to several countries in South America, introducing a new technique for U. S. planning assistance programs. While he was gone, I drove to Nashville with the children, accompanied by teenage nephew, Charlie, where we spent several weeks with relatives.

In the autumn of 1958 life settled into a different schedule. Bob was still working hard in the DC office of ICA (International Cooperation Administration), but I now had more free time. Carol began attending the public elementary school, Walnut Hill, as a second-grader. She walked the few blocks to school accompanied by her friend next door, returning in the mid-afternoon. Since Steven was just old enough to enter nursery school, we put him, along with Peggy, in a wonderful private nursery, Humpty-Dumpty College. Among other activities, they studied "Shakespeare", the school's Shetland pony that was available for the children to ride. I drove them to the school each morning, and the Humpty-Dumpty bus delivered them home at noon.

This new arrangement freed me during morning hours, so I immediately looked for some part-time work. Soon I was hired to help edit a "vanity" book, entitled "Prominent Persons in Northern Virginia", promoted by a man in Warrenton, Virginia. I worked at home by the hour, and by Christmas I had managed to earn enough to buy a piano for the family—a necessity for every household, I always thought. I never did think the idea for the book was really great, however.

We drove to Miami for Christmas that year to visit my parents. They had further developed the one-acre lot they owned on one of the newly-built canals in the area, and as both loved gardening they had planted a wide variety of shrubs and fruit trees. Many of the family members gathered to celebrate the holidays together. Jeanne and her family, Cecil with her husband, Reynolds, and five-month old son, Eddie, and later Austin with her husband, John, all joined us. It was a memorable if hectic time, with the overflow people sleeping in houses of neighbors. Mother and Dad seemed to love every minute, but as my father sometimes said, "Always glad to see them come, glad to see them go."

The following months in Falls Church were full of family visits and activities. I did quite a lot of drawing during this time, putting my little basement "studio" to good use.

During the last five months of our tour in Washington, Bob was selected to attend the School of Advanced International Studies at The Johns Hopkins University, for specialized training. We knew we would be sent overseas again in the summer, so hoped for a good assignment. We soon learned we would be sent to Guatemala because of Bob's experience in Latin America, which made sense. He was to be stationed in Guatemala City as Program Officer.

We had no trouble selling our house and were soon packing to leave, excited over our new adventure. As luck would have it, in spite of the bouts of measles and chickenpox that the children had gone through during the past two years, Steven came down with the mumps just after we arrived in Miami for a brief visit before flying to Guatemala. Bob had to go on ahead while the children and I stayed with Mother and Dad until Steven recovered—about ten days, as I remember.

VII

GUATEMALAN IDYLL

The children and I, accompanied by our cocker, Sherry, arrived in Guatemala City to be met by Bob and a large welcoming committee. I was to discover that this was a tradition with the U.S. Operations Mission there, something we found nowhere else—a prophetic beginning to our stay in this beautiful country.

After a few days in a city hotel, we found a large, modern house in the suburbs near the airport. It had a patio and small garden in back, enclosed by high walls topped with broken glass fragments and bordering on a wood of trees and coffee plants. Other than the generously sized rooms and small fireplace in the living room, there was not much to recommend it except convenience. Nevertheless, we settled in and soon inherited two excellent maids, Sara and Estela, still in their teens but trained well by a German lady. They were intelligent and attractive in their spotless uniforms, always worn by the help there, and the children soon became attached to them, as did we. We had basic furniture, including the piano, and I decorated the walls with various art prints.

Our first priority, of course, was to get the children set up in school, especially Carol who was then seven years old. There was a Guatemalan bilingual school nearby, so we enrolled her there. After only a few days, however, we took her out when she was not accompanied home on the bus by a teacher, as promised, and had the traumatic experience of frantically trying to recognize our street and house as the bus driver drove up and down streets with her alone. I was standing outside by this time watching anxiously for her, and she finally directed the driver to the right street. Luckily, Carol seemed to remember enough Spanish from her early days in Peru! In fact, she was soon speaking fluently again.

This was just one indication of the disorganization of the Guatemalan school, so we investigated other possibilities and discovered that a group of American parents had just begun an experimental cooperative school, to be directed by a school board of parents and with teachers selected from the English speaking population. We joined the group enthusiastically and took an active part in the organization and growth of the Mayan School. Carol entered third grade and Peggy and Steven started in pre-school. The curriculum was based on the Calvert system of correspondence courses. Bob served on the board, while I ordered books and supplies, and helped set up a testing program.

We took lots of trips exploring the country, visiting Antigua (the old capital),

the beautiful lakes of Atitlán and Amátitlan and other places nearby. Our social life became quite active. Entertaining was easy, with the efficient domestic help. We soon had an active group of good friends and found ourselves going out to dinners and cocktail-buffets several times a week. There was not too much for foreigners to do in the city, so people formed their own groups and entertainment. You did tend to see a lot of the same people, but it was a lively group and close friendships were formed which have lasted through the years. I'll never forget the McInnises, Beckers, Dicks, Reiersons, Himebaughs and DuFlons, among others.

The children, too, had an active social life with numerous birthday parties and other activities, many of which are recorded on slides and movies. Carol began piano lessons about this time, studying with Dorothy Ascoli, a talented American teacher. Peggy took ballet lessons, which she preferred to the piano.

With more free time, I renewed my art activities, and often met with my Guatemalan friend, Maria Castillo, to paint or draw. I also began drawing political cartoons for the little newsletter put out by volunteers from the U. S. mission. My friend, Marjorie McInnis, acted as editor, and I called my cartoons "Caustics by Candi". This was a great way to poke fun at the bureaucracy as well as certain social posturing. Bob and I took another good course in archaeology, learning a lot about Mayan cultures, and I also began to do stone rubbings, making some rather good ones at the museum with an artist friend. When Jeanne and husband, Charles, visited from the States, among other excursions we went to a nearby archaeological site and did rubbings.

Shortly after Christmas, my parents came to visit. They enjoyed all the parties going on and we took several trips with them, exploring Chichicastenango as well as around the lakes. The roads were not always paved and some of the trips were quite dusty, but the scenery and native Mayan Indians in their colorful woven clothes were fascinating. In Chichicastenango, high in the mountains, there was an intermingling of Christian and pagan religions with most of the people following rituals blended from both. The short pants and distinctive headdresses of the men there were not seen anywhere else. Mother got excited about the beautiful textiles from all over the country and she enjoyed buying a lot of skirt lengths and other things to take home.

Dad was anxious to return to Miami to tend to his many plants, but Mother stayed on with us awhile after he left. She offered to supervise the children while Bob and I took a few days off for a visit to Mexico City. Bob had attended classes at Mexico City College there one summer while at Vanderbilt, but this was my first visit. It was one of the few trips that Bob and I were able to take without the children. We stayed in the charming old Hotel Géneva, a bit faded with the years but still the place of choice with most government officials and convenient to many good restaurants and shops. Before leaving home I had asked the maids to please not allow Mother to go out on the town alone, so each day they had to hurry with their chores to accompany her, as she certainly wanted to keep on the go! Dad had had his wallet taken while he was there, and for anyone not speaking the language, it was easy to get into awkward situations.

At Easter that year, my artist friend, Maria, and her family invited us all to stay in their vacation house in Antigua to see all the special ceremonies nearby. At this season, the native Indians decorate many of the streets with carpets of flower blossoms, arranged in intricate, colorful designs. Some are also made with colored sawdust, all requiring hours of dedicated work and imagination. Maria drove with us to the nearby village of Santa Maria where the Easter re-enactment of the crucifixion and resurrection story was especially realistic. Natives played the main characters, and with many decorated floats the procession moved to the church where, with loud hammering sounds, they actually "nailed" Jesus to the cross (between his fingers and toes). The colorful fiesta lasted a full day.

It was not long after that when we moved into another, much nicer house. It was large and looked over the distant mountains. There was a lovely, fenced garden and patios opening from the upstairs bedrooms. Our household help now consisted of not only Sara and Estela, who lived in, but also a cook who came one day a week to cook batches of rolls and pies to freeze, and also to teach Sara some of her culinary secrets. We always planned our dinner parties on the days Tomasa came. There was a weekly gardener who didn't particularly like to have his complicated flower beds disturbed by the children with their games.

We settled in happily to enjoy the ideal climate and interesting life. Bob was made temporary head of the educational branch of ICA, and given a driver and other perks. The permanent head arrived several months later, but it was good while it lasted. Bob did a lot to organize the group, which was one of the biggest in the mission. The Minister of Education there was so impressed with Bob's work that he organized the government Ministry along the same lines.

The second year there the children moved ahead in school, Carol to fourth grade and Peggy beginning first grade. Steven "graduated" to kindergarten. As Peggy began learning to read we realized that phonics were not taught, and as we firmly believed in both approaches to reading, we had her tutored in phonics after regular school, and also helped her at home. She soon became efficient and, amazingly, Steven also learned to read at that time (at four and half) just by joining in as Peggy learned. He also began taking elementary piano lessons from a friend, Lillian Pope, since he seemed particularly interested in learning to play after watching Carol playing.

Bob's parents came to visit in February of that year and Joe and Carol celebrated with a joint birthday party. As had other visitors, they thoroughly enjoyed the trips and social activities. We gave a particularly festive party while they were there, I remember, putting up Japanese lanterns around the patio and carport, and inviting all of our friends—about eighty people in all. It was while Ruth and Joe were visiting that I again succumbed to my love of dogs and bought a cute little Alsatian puppy. We named it "Chula" which means "cute" in Spanish. Sherry was jealous and did not enjoy playing with the energetic puppy. I didn't realize the problems we would have with Chula until later. She grew rapidly and was impossible to discipline, jumping on everyone, including five-year old Steven, who she often knocked down. The last straw was when she killed the dear little tame parakeet we had. We eventually gave her away to a family returning to their large ranch in Texas who planned to use her as a watchdog.

In early spring, we witnessed the eruption of the Pacaya volcano in Guatemala, something that hadn't happened for the past one hundred years. It was about an hour's drive from Guatemala City to the side of the adjacent mountain where we could watch the explosions and the brilliant flow of molten lava lighting up the sky as it snaked down into the valley. Luckily, the mountain was undeveloped, with very few people living there, so there were no catastrophes except for the trees and brush that the lava destroyed. The eruption lasted several weeks and we visited twice, once taking the children. Bob also made a daytime visit with a group of men friends. Looking at the volcano slides and movies became something of a family joke since they were shown so often to various people.

In April 1961, Bob received a promotion and became Economic Advisor at the U. S. Operations Mission. He was establishing good relations with the Guatemalan Ministers and other officials. In early June he was to attend a meeting in El Salvador, and since we were both curious about this neighboring country, we decided to drive down with the children. The roads were almost all unpaved. It was quite different from Guatemala, but interesting to see. We visited the capital, San Salvador, where Bob attended his meeting. Later, we refreshed ourselves with a swim in a lake nearby, and were on our way home when disaster struck! In the middle of nowhere we had a flat tire, then shortly after putting on the spare, another flat! We hoped and prayed that someone would come along, although there certainly didn't seem to be much traffic on the road that hot spring day.

We finally saw a car approaching, and as luck would have it, an acquaintance of Bob's appeared. He did not have much room in his car (a VW bug), so it was decided that I would wait with the children while Bob, along with the damaged tires, went to get help. We managed to endure a long two-hour wait in the stifling heat, having to wind up the windows whenever anyone passed. We had Sherry with us and very little to eat or drink. This was one time I called on all my ingenuity and imagination to think of things to pass the time—games, songs and stories. It was an experience I wouldn't want to repeat.

The next trip Bob and I were able to take was much more successful. We were invited to join a small group of international friends of the Minister of Finance, Meme Benefeld, to go on the large government patrol boat for a weekend out of Belize. The Director, Keith Himebaugh, who liked and relied on Bob, arranged for us to be included in the group, along with him and his wife, Mildred. We flew up in a military plane to Puerto Barrios, where we boarded the boat. It was a wonderful weekend of sightseeing, fishing and swimming in the sapphire colored water. Most of us slept on the open deck, with only a few disturbing snores!

It was about this time that the guerrilla group in the Petén became active in trying to overthrow the Ydígoras government. A state of siege was proclaimed and groups of more than four people were forbidden to meet during the dusk to dawn curfew. The radio played only martial music and official announcements, so it put quite a crimp in our social life. Luckily, Bob had ordered a Heathkit short-wave radio, which he proceeded to put together during his free evenings. This went on for several weeks. Bob was able to finish making his radio, and, believe it or not, it worked the first time he turned it on!

We were due for home leave after two years, so we saved up all our vacation time and planned a summer tour of the western U. S. before returning to Guatemala. We sold our big four-year old station wagon and ordered a new Ford Falcon station wagon that we picked up in Washington. We then drove to Nashville and Akron for visits before setting out. We practiced setting up the large, 12 by 12 ft. tent at Ruth and Joe's place on the lake, then with sleeping bags and a motley collection of other equipment, headed west.

At our first campsite, somewhere in Arkansas, Bob followed the instructions and dug a trench around the tent before we settled in under the stars. How lucky can you get? It poured rain during the night, yet we remained snug and dry. We were complete novices at camping with a family, so learned as we went along. The children were helpful, Peggy and Steven gathering wood for bonfires, and Carol helping Bob put up the tent as I prepared the meal. Some of the campsites were ideal, beside a lake or overlooking mountains. Others were less attractive, but it was all fun and different from anything we had done before.

Our itinerary sent us across several squarish states and over lots of flat country on our way to Colorado. In Boulder, Colorado, we visited an ex-WAVE friend of mine, Wicky, who lived on a small farm with her family. The children enjoyed riding their ponies and playing with the other animals. We hoped to see as many of the National parks as possible, and we camped and enjoyed the magnificent scenery of Rocky Mountain National park, the Grand Teton and the Yellowstone parks, Grand Coulee dam and other sites as we headed north.

In Montana, one of the most beautiful parks was Glacier National park. It was here that we had our adventure with the bear. We had stopped at a roadside table for lunch, and we began setting out the sandwiches and drinks while the girls went to a nearby outhouse. Steven was comfortably asleep in the car. Suddenly, a huge brown bear lumbered into sight. Frantic, I yelled at the girls to stay inside the outhouse, and as the bear came nearer, obviously looking for food, I grabbed some sandwiches and threw them as far as I could into the woods behind him. Quickly we retrieved the girls, and grabbing the rest of our lunch, we made a quick getaway. Steven was disappointed that he had slept through all the excitement.

From Montana we headed west into Washington state in order to visit the Seattle World's Fair, which was going on that summer. We arranged to rent a small apartment nearby for the few days we were there, in order to enjoy things at leisure. Also, it was a good chance to sleep in real beds for a change! I'm not sure how much the children remember, but visiting the rotating restaurant, seeing holograms for the first time and other novelties made quite an impression at the time.

We had never seen British Columbia, and since our friends from Peru days, Diana and Harvey Henderson, had moved there to live, we decided to visit them before heading south. We found that Diana was vacationing with her girls in a cottage in Horseshoe Bay, so we drove there to find her and had a good, overnight visit. It was fun exploring Victoria on Vancouver Island, as well as Vancouver itself. The totem poles and the wax museum were big hits. One special delight I'm sure everyone remembers was when I mistakenly asked a wax figure for directions to the restroom!

On the way south we followed the coast, stopping along the way to eat salmon and artichokes, among other things. We camped at beautiful campsites on the beaches and near the large dunes in Oregon. In San Francisco, we had dinner at Fisherman's Wharf, went to a Chinese restaurant, rode the cable car and saw many other well known sights. My special treat there was buying an elegant cocktail dress in one of the large stores. Dressing up for parties in those days was *de rigueur*, especially in Guatemala.

We made a detour to Glendale to visit Bob's great uncle Robert and his wife, Julia. She was completely blind, yet managed to get around easily, showing us her garden and even cooking dinner for us. Her skills and courage impressed us all.

We drove past Los Angeles on to Disneyland, which the children had been looking forward to. They were perfect ages, 5, 7, and 9 years old, and we stayed a couple of days enjoying it all. Before leaving the area, we stopped briefly to see my Aunt Hattie and her husband, John, in nearby Anaheim, then headed on down into Mexico.

I remember stopping by Mazatlán on the coast, where we stayed in a rustic cottage right on the beachfront. Our movies reflect the delight of the children playing along the edges of the surf that was quite heavy there. Carol later insists she "saved Steven's life" when the undertow caught his feet. However, we were keeping a close eye on them and as the movies show, Steven was wearing a life jacket. Still, I'm sure the feel of the water pulling against their feet was frightening.

Heading toward Mexico City, we stopped to explore the artistic community settled around Lake Chapala, with many small studios of artists, including some expatriates. It was in this area where we also saw a silkworm "farm"—mulberry trees thick with the little creatures spinning away. Beautiful, but expensive textiles were made and sold there, which we had to pass up. On to Morelia, where we spent the night at an attractive cottage complex on the hill overlooking the town. We definitely planned to return to this delightful place someday.

Our stopover in Mexico City was especially pleasant. We stayed in the zona rosa and explored a different restaurant each evening, the children getting special "cocktails" of fruit juices with fancy garnishes, all served in style. We loaded the car with various souvenirs—glasses, beautiful swirled decanters, silver items and even a guitar!

From there we went to Oaxaca, a fascinating town with many craftsmen, where we bought several beautiful small rugs. With the station wagon now packed to the roof, we drove southeast to the small station where we were to get the train on down to Guatemala. Since the regular road was impassable in certain parts beyond this point, it was necessary to put the car on a flatcar here. After a long delay, they managed to get everything loaded and we began our slow trek through the area west of the Sierra Madre, roughly following the coastline.

We had opted to pay extra for the privilege of staying in our car for the trip rather than riding in the uncomfortable, crowded passenger car. The train stopped briefly at every little village in this predominantly jungle area of the Chiapas. We were able to buy bananas and other fruit occasionally from the Mexican natives, but never had time to leave the car. Luckily, we had prepared for a long trip and had brought food and drink for several meals. The children were supplied with books, games and even comic books, a treat they were not usually allowed. Bob and I fortified ourselves with

with a supply of tranquilizers, which we certainly needed. Basic necessities had to be taken care of, and after dark Bob and Steven managed to relieve themselves from the side of the moving train, but the girls and I had to improvise with empty juice cans— quite a trick!

When we finally arrived at the border town of Tapachula, our flatcar was unhooked from the train and just left there! It took an hour and a half before we could arrange to get it unloaded. We were able to find rooms in a small hotel, and exhausted after an eighteen-hour trip, finally fell into bed. Luck was not with us that night, for it was only a couple of hours later that someone began pounding on the door. Groggily, Bob went to the door and was told he had a phone call. He stumbled down to answer it, not awake enough to realize that no one could possibly know where we were at this time. All a mistake, one which we did not appreciate! Next morning, a basic breakfast was offered in the front room of the hotel, which was proudly furnished with a shining, white refrigerator among the tables and chairs. We did not linger, as we were anxious to get over the border. There, the car was thoroughly examined, everything being taken out until the inspectors came to the guitar, which one of them proceeded to play. We tried to show our appreciation of this turn of events, and sure enough, they made no further inspection of our belongings. It was good to get back to our "home" country.

We stopped along the coast at the first opportunity to call Sara and Estela, letting them know we would be home by dinnertime. When we arrived, exhausted, but relieved to be back, we were greeted by a clean house filled with flowers, and a delicious meal topped off with a huge cake. What a welcome!

Our third year in Guatemala was filled with changes and new challenges. With the children back in school and busy with various activities, I enrolled in a course in enameling that was being taught by a young Chilean artist. He was a master in the technique and as I learned more about this new medium I became enthusiastic and began doing more and more. I ordered a kiln from the U. S. that Bob was able to install for me in my studio, converted from an extra bedroom. I was particularly interested in rather large pieces, plaques and other items limited only by the size of the kiln, rather than jewelry. It was fun working every morning producing new designs and perfecting my technique. I found a craftsman who made small attractive boxes for me that I topped with enameled pieces. Bob and the children encouraged me, especially Steven, who returned from school every day, eager to see what I had made and expressing delight in everything—good or not. I think the process of taking powdered glass and fusing it to copper to create something beautiful, intrigued him.

About this time, Sherry developed a mysterious illness. According to the vet, she was getting better until he gave her another shot of some kind, after which her heart gave out. I was terribly saddened by this and blamed the vet, I must admit. We all felt the family was not complete without a dog, and after our experience with Chula, we realized we needed one that was small and easy to manage. When a friend's beagle had puppies, we picked out "Jellybean", cute and round as her name. She was lots of fun and soon fit into the life of the family. Estela had left us by now, but Sara remained faithful and was joined by Carlota. I thought of Sara almost as an adopted daughter. I taught her the basics of sewing and lent her my sewing machine, and she was soon making new clothes for herself.

A new Ambassador arrived about this time, as well as several political appointees, who made Bob's work more complicated. Most of them had no Latin American experience and few of them even spoke Spanish. Bob had a bit of a break when he attended a planning conference in Santiago, Chile in early 1962, but working with the new people became difficult. The Director, Keith Himebaugh, whom everyone loved, was retiring, and when he left in April, Bob was named acting Director of what was now called the AID mission. With the arrival of the new Director (another political appointee), things became more and more unsatisfactory. He had no sense of the Latin American temperament, and if a meeting was called at a certain hour and the Minister, or whoever, did not arrive promptly, the Director saw no reason to wait for him. This naturally soon made him unpopular with the Guatemalans, and there was little Bob could do to improve things. We discussed this together and both could see that all Bob's good work was being undermined. He concluded that the blame for anything that went wrong would fall on his shoulders, yet he would not receive any credit for successes. There seemed nothing to do but to resign. A big decision—not entered into lightly.

The Ambassador, who was quite a nice person, tried his best to convince Bob to stay on, his wife even calling me one morning and talking about an hour about it. But Bob had already decided and could not be convinced. He sent in his resignation on June 13, which was accepted by the Secretary of State, Dean Rusk, on July 2. Meanwhile, Bob had contacted people in Washington and had been offered a job in the Commerce Department as acting Director of the

Economic Research branch of ARA (Area Redevelopment Administration)—a kind of AID for the disadvantaged areas of the U. S.

While all this was going on, I was preparing for a one-man show of my enamel art, urged on by friends, especially Margo and Temple Dick. They offered to hold the show in their penthouse apartment, and it was held there in late spring. It was a lovely show, more successful that I had hoped for, and out of the fifty-five pieces shown I sold all but about nine of them. President Ydígoras, who knew and liked Bob, honored me by coming to see the show, accompanied by his entourage. As a gift, he presented me with a picture done by a local primitive artist and I presented him with one of mine. He stayed quite a while and bought another. He later told Bob that his wife had complained that he didn't buy more! It was an exhilarating time in my life.

We were to leave Guatemala in early July. That last month, after Bob had sent in his resignation, was extremely eventful. Bob was honored by being presented with the Order of the Quetzal, the highest Guatemalan honor offered to a foreigner. He could not accept it in person (against State Department rules), so it was presented to me, for him and his work during the three years we were there.

In addition to that, the President gave a dinner in Bob's honor at the

presidential residence, to which we were permitted to invite another couple. The Dicks joined us at the fanciest dinner I have ever attended, complete with plates of gold and other festive things. I was seated next to the President—a real honor.

Bob and I were given so many *despedidas* (farewell parties) that we even had to schedule some of them for breakfast! We shipped our car to Miami, arranged to have Jellybean sent later and packed to leave. There were sad good-byes as we left for the U. S. with unforgettable memories of our exciting years in this beautiful country.

VIII

TIME OUT IN WASHINGTON

After arrival in the States we had a few days to visit my parents in Miami while waiting for our car and Jellybean. Then we were off to see Bob's parents in Nashville, where we had an air-conditioner installed in the Falcon, something we hadn't needed in spring-like Guatemala, but which was a necessity here. We planned to tour the west again, going to some of the National Parks and other sites that we had missed the previous trip. Loaded with luggage, tents and equipment, as well as the family and Jellybean, we headed west.

This time, we cut across Arkansas, Oklahoma, part of Texas and into New Mexico. We explored the Painted Desert and the Petrified Forest on our way to the Grand Canyon in Arizona. At the Grand Canyon, I remember insisting that everyone get up before dawn to stand at the edge of the canyon to watch the sun come up. It was a sight beyond description to see the fantastic colors and shadows created on the opposite canyon wall as the sun rose, even more impressive in the silence since few visitors managed to get up this early.

From there we went by Las Vegas, curious to see what it was all about. We decided to explore the simpler gambling halls, so at one place that had slot machines, we gave each of the children a handful of change to let them find out how easy it was to lose money. All of us quickly lost our nickels and quarters except Peggy, who seemed to win over and over. About this time we were ushered out, since the children were not supposed to be there. I'm not sure this was a successful teaching experience.

After driving across Death Valley into California, we camped in beautiful Yosemite National Park with its impressive Sequoia forest. And since we had all enjoyed San Francisco, we made a brief stopover there for a meal in Chinatown before going north. We camped in the redwood forest and naturally took the standard photo of our car driving through one of the giant trees.

Heading east we took the northern route as planned, camping and visiting Mount Rushmore, where we saw the Hopi Indians. In the Badlands of South Dakota, the children were "exploring" among the huge rocks scattered on the side of a valley below our campsite when Peggy, adventurous as always, fell from one of the boulders and couldn't get back up. Pandemonium! Steven alerted us and Bob finally managed to rescue her. She suffered only minor scrapes, thank goodness. In addition to worrying about the children's exploits, we often had a problem getting Jellybean to stay nearby, as she loved chasing any rabbit or other animal around. No trouble at night since she slept in the sleeping bag with Carol, both snugly warm.

A stopover at White Bear Lake near Minneapolis to visit Ellie, an ex-WAVE friend and her family was planned on an impulse. After arriving there we found they were away but with the help of a neighbor we were at least able to telephone her to say "hello". She insisted we make ourselves at home without them, so we stayed overnight and later enjoyed a motorboat ride on the lake, courtesy of the nice neighbor.

From there we drove over the Michigan peninsula into Canada to see Banff and Lake Louise, then headed toward Niagara Falls. This was as impressive as we had imagined, but we didn't linger, as everyone was now anxious to get to Washington to establish our new home. We arrived there in late August 1962.

Getting settled back in the U. S. was more of a culture shock than any we had encountered when we went overseas. We found a house we wanted fairly easily with the help of a friend, Peg Howard, who was working with a real estate company. We had known Peg and her husband, John, from early days when the men worked together at the Labor Department and when Peg and I were pregnant with our daughters, Dale and Carol. The trouble was that the house was still being built with about a month before completion. Since it was well situated for schools and in a lovely setting, we decided it was worth waiting for, so rented a furnished apartment for that time. Unfortunately, it was way across town in Silver Spring, the only one we could find for a short rental. Since we wanted to get the children started in their school near the new house, I drove two round trips across town and out to Potomac every day taking them and picking them up.

We were all getting a bit neurotic in the apartment, especially with Jellybean, who didn't take well to being left, so rode with me, but howled even if I stopped at the library for a few minutes on my trips. We finally decided we would have to find her a stable home, so following a lost dog ad in the paper were able to give her to a nice family with children and a yard. It's lucky we did, since when we finally moved to the house in Carderock Springs our yard was still torn up with digging, putting in pipes and such. Finances made it necessary for us to move in, no matter what. We didn't even have water for the first week, relying on a huge barrel in front and bottled water to drink. Quite a contrast from the comfortable, sophisticated life we had enjoyed in Guatemala!

Gradually we got settled, of course, and enjoyed planting shrubs and small trees around the house, which was on a steep hill and backed on a wood. The children soon found friends in the neighborhood and enjoyed their school. Carol was in the sixth grade, Peggy in the fourth, and Steven began the second grade. I resumed my art activities, turning one of the bedrooms into a studio where I did more enamels. My suspended "Space Web", which Bob helped me assemble, dates from this time.

October 1962 marked a dangerous development in the Cold War. The U.S. faced a treat of nuclear war when air surveillance discovered a complex of launching pads in Cuba, with potential for firing missiles to the States. Those of us who so vividly remembered the horror of Hiroshima realized what this news could mean. My first instinct was to wonder what, if anything, I could do to help avert possible catastrophe. It was a frustrating feeling, especially for those previously in the service. The school children's having to practice hiding under their desks in the event of an attack, made it all the more frightening.

Our admiration for President Kennedy was reinforced by the way he handled the crisis, causing Khrushchev to retreat from his threat after these tense days.

Almost as an echo of this traumatic event was when a pine tree from the woods fell on out house during a severe storm about this time. I was home alone and it crashed through our bedroom roof. Luckily, I was not in that area, but I remember my sense of impending doom as the storm continued to rage. All was repaired in due course and several other threatening trees were removed.

The months seemed to fly by, with visits from the family and short excursions nearby with the children. We especially enjoyed the change of seasons and the brilliant fall foliage. I remember a special visit when my mother came up around Mother's day that beautiful spring of 1963. She loved being driven around to see the masses of colorful azaleas in the Washington area, particularly lovely that year.

During the summer Carol was to attend Girl Scout camp, and Ruth and Joe agreed to keep Peggy and Steven for two weeks while Bob and I had a vacation alone, our first in a long time. My brother, Don, now living in Nashville, came to Washington occasionally on his way to Dupont headquarters in Wilmington, Delaware. He took the two younger children back to Nashville with him by plane to stay with Bob's parents. Bob and I headed for Cape Cod where we camped out—being experts at this by now! It was relaxing and fun exploring the beaches and small towns and visiting Provincetown. I was impressed with the active group of artists there.

The second year in Bethesda, Carol began junior high school at Thomas Pyle, the other two still in Potomac school. I got more deeply into my art studies, enrolling at The American University where I studied Advanced Painting with Ben Summerfield, (called "Joe" by friends). He was a good teacher, later becoming head of the art department at the University.

About this time, my youngest sister, Austin, moved to the area with her husband, John, and they rented a small house in Cabin John. It was near enough for the children to ride over on their bicycles to visit, and we saw them quite often.

I remember vividly that fateful day in November when Austin called me with the news that President Kennedy had been shot. She came over and we hovered over the TV as hopes for his life faded. Bob was away on a training session in Long Island, learning of it there. We joined the whole world in mourning the death of this young President who had rekindled the optimism of the young and who was doing so much to advance the U. S. space program. I took the children downtown near the White House to watch the impressive funeral procession, with leaders from all over the world taking part. A sad day never to be forgotten.

It was during this same autumn that we were even more shocked to learn that Mother had been diagnosed with colon cancer. She was operated on at Vanderbilt Hospital in Nashville, hastily arranged for by Jeanne, but it was suspected the malignancy had spread and her prognosis was not good. I flew immediately to see her, sitting up with her through one of the first nights, praying that she wouldn't be taken away from us. Austin generously stayed at our house to care for the children after school, making her own visit to Mother after I returned. I was deeply affected by the suddenness of this traumatic event, and grieved for my Mother, not yet sixty-nine years old and still young at heart.

Later, Rosemary, who had moved to Africa with her family, arranged to fly home to help with Mother and be with Dad, who had a hard time accepting this sad blow. She stayed several months, which was a godsend.

Mother seemed to rally during the next few months and all her children were able to spend some quality time in Miami with her and Dad before those last days the following April. With Jeanne, Cecil and Reynolds there with Dad, she went "gentle into that good night" just before Easter.

That was a sad spring. Dad came up to visit and driving him around among the lovely flowers of Washington, I had vivid memories of the previous spring when Mother and I had enjoyed them together. To cheer up Dad, we decided to visit the New York's World Fair and our cousin, Mattie G., arrived from Florida to go along with us. We made the whole trip in one day, an interesting but exhausting experience!

In early summer when life seemed to lack its usual luster, Fate offered another challenge. One day, when Bob was having lunch with his boss at a favorite restaurant in town, an old friend greeted him and seemed surprised that he was not still living overseas. He asked if he might be going out again and Bob said, "Why not?" much to the surprise of his boss. Nothing was thought of this until a few weeks later when an offer came from the Ford Foundation to go to Dar es Salaam in what was then Tanganyika to carry out a labor force survey of the country. This had never been done and they had been trying to find the right person for a couple of years, but no one had been willing to take on this difficult task. We discussed it and although we were settled and had planned to stay in the U. S. for quite awhile, the chance to see and live in that dark continent was irresistible. Also Rosemary and her family were in Tanganyika, which was a plus. Many of our friends and some of the family thought this was a rash step, as we only had a one-year contract, but practicality had seldom stopped us before, so why now? We sold the house in Carderock Springs within a few days of putting it on the market, arranged to sell the car and began packing. Steven was especially excited and was sure he would soon be swinging through the trees of the jungle!

It was at this time that we bought three lots in Montreat, North Carolina, using some of the money from the house sale. We had vague plans of building a retirement home there someday. After a short visit to Nashville where we said goodbye to Bob's parents and Dad, who was visiting Don and his family, we took off for Europe where we planned a stopover before continuing to Africa.

IX

EXPLORING AFRICA

Our introduction to Europe, on our way to Dar-es-Salaam, made one of my dreams a reality. We stopped a week in London staying in a small hotel and seeing all the famous sights that we had only read about. After a general bus tour to get oriented we explored the nooks and crannies of special places such as Westminster Abbey and St. Paul's Cathedral. Of course we wanted to sample the wonderful array of theater productions, and we managed to see five productions during the week, including The Mousetrap, Hello Dolly, The Week That Was and Oliver. We most often had to sit high up in the balcony for these, but it was a wonderful introduction to British theater.

From London we flew to Copenhagen, so different from any place we had been before. A visit to Tivoli Gardens, the busy port and later the Little Mermaid statue were highlights. The city is full of wonderful shops and we bought a few things to take to Africa. We had arranged to rent a car here to drive through Europe leaving it in Rome, so we boarded a ferry sailing to Germany. The restaurant on board offered a delicious smorgasbord with pickled fish and other meats, salads and cheeses.

In Germany we drove through Hamburg to Hanover where we stayed in a huge, old baroque hotel situated in a deer park. It was rather a mysterious place, with stuffed animals and large mirrors decorating the stairways. Deer were still to be seen in the surrounding park.

We stopped briefly in Heidelburg to see the students' tower and castle. Another notable stop was in Strasbourg, France, visiting the Cathedral and unusual clock there. We were enchanted with the city, and to celebrate we went to a famous restaurant to sample French cooking. We were sold right then on French cuisine.

Then we went on to beautiful Switzerland but we didn't have time to linger since we had to reach Rome by a certain date. We promised ourselves a return visit, however, as we headed south to the lake region. Driving over the Goddard Pass was a breathtaking experience! At Lake Como, we stayed in a small hotel high up in Moltrasio with fantastic views over the lake. Parking space was cramped, and they had to use a turntable for cars in the small front area.

After visiting Lugano we drove into Italy toward the Italian Riviera. There we stopped at several places along the coast, then at Pisa to see the leaning tower, before a brief visit to Florence.

When we arrived in Rome we had a few days for sightseeing. We visited the Coliseum (with its cats), the fountain of Trevi and Piazza España in the city, plus the fantastic gardens and fountains at Villa d'Este a short distance away. We also drove down the Appian Way, noticing all the fallen statues along the attractive wooded road. It was here we had a romantic picnic, complete with Italian bread, cheese, grapes and a bottle of Chianti, which the children were allowed to taste.

Traffic in Rome was beyond belief. The girls seemed to enjoy casually sauntering across the streets at designated crosswalks, confident that all cars would come to a screeching halt. Luckily, they did! Delivering the rental car to the proper place was a nightmare, but we finally got the car back and headed to the airport for our flight to Africa. It was a long trip, but quite comfortable in first class. During the special dinner I remember ten-year-old Peggy's insisting that she loved caviar!

We arrived in Nairobi quite early in the morning and were met by a representative from the Ford Foundation. We stayed overnight at the New Stanley Hotel, with its famous Thorn Tree outdoor café—the traditional meeting place of those making safaris. I was amazed at the size of everything in Africa. It all seemed larger than life, including the huge bathrooms in the hotel and the extremely tall domestic staff, mostly men of the Masai tribe. We were getting over the long flight so didn't have time to explore very much, but we did make a brief visit to the Nairobi game park before flying on to Dar-es-Salaam.

Our arrival there was a bit of a shock. Bob's contract had stipulated a house and car, but we soon realized that the house assigned to us was uninhabitable, having been empty for a number of months. We moved into the Oyster Bay Hotel, a former hospital that had been converted into a convenient hotel, situated right beside the Indian Ocean.

Bob had to begin his work almost immediately, so it was left to me to get the house ready to live in. This proved to be quite complicated, since I spoke no Swahili and there was no support staff in Dar to help. I insisted on some basic changes, which I felt were essential for healthy living for the family. We stayed in the hotel for six weeks while all this was taking place. Luckily, the restaurant there was quite good with everything paid for by the Ford Foundation. We bought a small record player and a few discs that we played over and over to cheer ourselves up. Years later, hearing Nelson Riddle or the Tijuana Brass brings back vivid memories of those early days in Africa.

I managed to get better basic furniture from the Public Works Department, since after the house was vacated most of the decent things had been "scavenged" by other people living in the complex. The Ford Foundation finally sent someone down to help with local contacts, and I arranged for a few things to be made. The chair cushions were covered in bright colors and new mattresses were ordered to replace the straw ones. Then I had the concrete floors covered by asphalt tiles, and individual air-conditioners installed in the bedrooms and living room. The kitchen was a disaster! The wood stove was taken out and a new gas one put in, along with a refrigerator. Shelves were built to store kitchenware. Lastly, I had the small front porch screened and screens put on all the windows, since cows were herded by our house every morning and evening with hordes of flies in attendance. This whole experience reinforced my philosophy in adjusting to overseas life. While some may take pride in going "native", I firmly believe in making basic living conditions as comfortable as possible for the family in a strange country, and then, and only then, to enjoy the new culture without complaint. There will always remain plenty of adjustments to be made.

We were able to get fairly good help, even though the cook, Mohammed, had some kind of allergy and was often heard sneezing in the kitchen (hopefully not in the food!). He spoke no English but was a nice person, supporting two wives. The houseboy, Aaron, spoke English of a sort and was a gentle young man who had walked all the way from his home in Zambia to find work. We managed to get both of these men well placed when we left. The gardener, Saidi, was rather a weird character but did keep things neat, cutting the sparse lawn with a panga (machete). The Ford Foundation arranged for an askari (guard) to watch the house from dusk to dawn, a necessary practice there, it seemed. He came complete with a tall, red fez on his head and a lethal looking panga in hand.

Getting the children enrolled in school was another project going on at the same time the house was being readied. We tried a local English language school for a few days, but soon abandoned that and put them in the International School that covered grades one through eight. This proved to be adequate for Peggy and Steven, but the eighth grade was much too easy for Carol, who had already done most of the work scheduled. After consultation, we decided to send her to Nairobi to board at Nairobi Girls School there. This was a difficult but necessary decision and called for adjustments on everyone's part. I flew up to Nairobi with her where she was tested and placed in a class. She was fitted with uniforms and after a few traumatic days, she seemed to adjust to the big change, but I had to exert pressure to have her placed in the fastest track. She had not been placed properly at first, mostly due to the fact that the entrance exam had to be taken with an old-fashioned quill pen, something Carol had certainly never used. She lived in a dormitory with only two other "Europeans" (the name given to all Caucasians)

and a dozen or so Africans, all older than she was. We were proud of the way she adapted to this arrangement.

Back in Dar we all missed Carol and tried to keep busy with regular activities. Bob's work was frustrating. He went to work at seven in the morning, working until mid-afternoon because of the debilitating heat. When he had arrived he found that his "office" was a big, open room with a table, chair and a telephone. He had to organize everything from scratch. An old circulating fan slowly rotated above, providing the only movement of air. I usually drove to work with Bob, delivering the children and doing necessary shopping before it got too hot.

Tanganyika, which changed its name to Tanzania while we were there, had declared its independence from Colonial rule a few years before. There were still many Colonial civil servants around, but changes were taking place rapidly, not always with the best results. The ordinary Tanzanian natives were not too hospitable to the Americans in Dar, and there was a strong communist presence. The only small newspaper in English constantly berated America and all it stood for. For the first time we truly understood how a minority population felt. As an American and a woman, for instance, I was always expected to step into the gutter to let an African man pass. There was also resentment toward the Indian and Pakistani population there. They were offered Tanzanian citizenship or faced being expelled from the country, even though many had lived there all their lives. At a large grocery store near Bob's office I used to perch on one of their stools each morning and talk to the Pakistani owners about the situation as I read the morning paper. They had mixed feelings about staying or trying to make a new life in their ethnic home country. I could only listen sympathetically, of course. After shopping, I often bought their fresh samozas and took them around to Bob to cheer him up in a difficult job.

Running the house was certainly not the same as in other places. Meat supply was limited and not too good, but luckily, fish was always available, often offered directly by the fishermen at the door. Papayas and other tropical fruits were plentiful, and we even had a papaya tree and a lime tree growing in our side yard. We gave up on getting good milk. The pasteurized milk that was flown in from Nairobi often was left hours in the sun before being delivered to the stores. It was usually stringy and unappetizing, so we changed to powdered milk, which wasn't too bad after being chilled in the fridge. We had fruit salad practically every night for dessert, a bit of a disappointment to Mohammed who wanted to bake cakes (not very good, from those we sampled).

At Christmas time we drove up to northern Tanzania to be with Rosemary, Bob and their three little girls who were living in Moshi. It was a good family time even though the drive up was dusty and rough over unpaved roads. The view of Mount Kilimanjaro from the Jensen house was breathtaking. The children enjoyed playing together and with the monkey, Jocko. It was a special time, too, for me to be with my sister. Together the families visited several game parks including the Serengeti National Park, Ngorongoro Crater, Lake Manyara and Amboseli, as well as nearby Mzima Springs. We saw large herds of such animals as impalas, kongoni, Thompson and Grant gazelles, giraffes and zebras, plus lions, rhinoceroses, ostriches and other birds. At Mzima Springs we saw hippopotamuses, water buffalo and different kinds of monkeys, which climbed all over the car. Later, we went on a safari together in Tsavo National Park that was an unusual and exciting experience. The Jensens had a Land Rover and camping trailer and we had our station wagon and large tent. Best of all, they took their houseboy along to prepare and cook the meals. The men, sometimes taking Steven along, went hunting, and following the license guidelines, shot one kongoni (hartebeest) for food and some "yellowneck" guinea hens. I must admit, for me, the sight of the large kongoni carcass hanging from a tree to drain off its blood was a bit off-putting. But we did enjoy the meals and the fun of sitting around the camp sipping chilled martinis along with good conversation. (We took a large part of the meat back to Moshi to share with the Jensen's friends.)

During the night, our family was peacefully sleeping in the tent when we were awakened by loud stamping sounds nearby. We were not anxious to investigate. Next morning we discovered elephant tracks and realized that we had set up our tent exactly in their usual path! Guess we were lucky that time!

Back in Dar Bob was making progress with his labor force survey, hiring interviewers and organizing their schedules. We were getting to know more people socially but we never made as many close friends as those made in Guatemala. The support group we had found there was missing in Africa, but I remember with fondness the Seals, Luckhursts and Beryl and Bill Steele. Of course there were compensations. In the late afternoons we would often drive the few blocks to the beach and either join the children in the water or sit nearby enjoying iced martinis from a thermos. The ocean there is the big attraction—deep blue fringed with white ruffled waves. Groups of Indian women in their colorful saris were often seen walking along the cliffs above the beaches. These scenes and the ocean itself inspired me to paint some of my best African paintings.

My one attempt to learn proper Swahili was not very successful. I could communicate with the servants and shopkeepers, but since the language had no relationship to any of the romance languages as far as I could recognize, it proved frustrating. After one brief course, I gave up, determined to "coast along" on my meager vocabulary. Rosemary and Bob, who spent a total of eight years in Moshi, were fluent in Swahili, of course, and we benefited from their expertise when we were with them.

While we were in Dar the children tried to influence us to get a dog. I was not keen on adding to the household at this time, even though we had succumbed to a guinea pig that turned out to be pregnant. We had enough trouble coping with the many chameleons clinging on the outside of the screens, occasionally managing to get in, and the "thousand-legged worms" (so-called Tanganyika trains) that crawled in under the doors. There was even one frog that appeared periodically in the bathroom sink, croaking and eyeing us suspiciously as we brushed our teeth. Only once did a chameleon actually join me in the shower! Aaron would go around every evening spraying the rooms to cut down on the mosquito population. Nevertheless, one day Bob and I returned from an errand to find that some kind soul had given the children a small puppy—a mixed breed dachshund, as far as we could determine. They begged for us to keep it, so of course we did and Heidi joined the family. The children enjoyed playing with her on the beach as shown by movies of that time. She stayed mostly outside the house, at night sleeping curled up in a huge clamshell by the front steps keeping the askari company.

Except for our trip to Moshi and nearby areas we had little time to do much exploring in Tanzania that year, but we did go on picnics to nearby cliffs and beaches—Ladder Cove and other places.

The year passed quickly and Bob was working hard to finish up his report of the first labor force survey ever done in Africa south of the Sahara. As his contract drew to a close, he was asked to stay on with the Ford Foundation, with a move to Nairobi where he would work with Tom Mboya, the Minister for Planning. The idea of living at 5000 feet in a lovely climate and in a more urban setting appealed to all of us, especially since Carol was already in school there. Also, Nairobi in neighboring Kenya was a bit closer to the Jensens in Moshi.

Before our move, I made a trip to Nairobi to agree on a house for us. The one offered by the Ford Foundation was an English style two-story, set among jacaranda trees in a wonderful location on Apple Tree Road looking over a small valley. I accepted it gratefully, especially since it came equipped with a huge dog, left by the previous occupants when they returned to the States. When I got back to Dar I told them all about the house; then, after a long pause and with a solemn face, I said there was just one problem to think about—a dog, half Rhodesian ridgeback and half mastiff, that was part of the package. I'll always remember the children's squeals of delight with this news! No one seemed heartbroken when we gave Heidi to a nice Indian family.

Before we left the area Bob and I wanted to see Zanzibar, which had recently been opened to foreigners, after having been closed for some years. We left the children with friends and flew over for a long day of sightseeing, feeling as if we were the first non-Africans to set foot on the island. It was an interesting place with many ornately carved doors and a mixture of architectural styles. I remember groups of old men playing checkers and other games in one of the plazas. We hired a driver to show us some of the island, visiting among other things, a place where cloves were collected and dried—millions in various stages of readiness for packaging. Another sight to remember was the speed of the young natives climbing the coconut trees to throw down the fruit.

In accepting the new assignment we had not shown any enthusiasm for driving up to Nairobi from Dar, so the Ford Foundation agreed to ship our few belongings and provide another car on arrival. This turned out to be a large Ford Zephyr, much more comfortable than the station wagon we had before. We flew to Nairobi and moved into our new house in mid-August.

Our life there was quite a contrast to our tour in Dar. The weather was the biggest change, of course, but in addition to the spring-like climate, our living arrangements improved. The house was attractive, with lovely Persian rugs on the floors, which we appreciated. I made only a few changes with new curtains and slipcovers in solid colors to complement the colors of the rugs. The garden was a delight with a variety of roses, hibiscus and other flowering shrubs, cared for by houseboy/gardener, Peter. I loved going out in late afternoons to explore the "estate" and to pick roses for the table.

Carol continued to board at the Nairobi Girl's School since there was not an opening in day school, which we had hoped for. She did come home every three weeks for regular vacations, and I drove the short distance to the school each week to pick up and deliver her laundry. I managed to send in a few bars of candy or other goodies hidden in the clothes, and almost always caught a glimpse of her since I knew her basic schedule.

Peggy was enrolled in Loretta Convent, a highly rated school run by Catholic nuns across the valley from our house. After a few days there Peggy announced at dinnertime, "Well, I know one thing. I certainly do more praying than anyone else in this family!" Whatever…she managed to adjust and was moved ahead a half year, since the school year began in January in Nairobi.

Steven's education was not as easily arranged. It proved impossible to get him in the best private boy's school since there was a long waiting list, so we enrolled him in the local Westlands school. The school was being "Africanized", a logical step in light of their new independence. This was not too good for the foreign students, however, who had to study such things as African history, instead of science and other broader subjects. They were keen on physical activities

and I remember Steven's taking swimming lessons, shivering in the unheated outdoor pool. This was supposed to toughen up the young boys (a holdover from colonial days!). We decided that changes would have to be made for the following year.

Shortly after our arrival in Nairobi, I had a brief stay in Queen Elizabeth's Hospital for a gynecological biopsy after a checkup. I imagined the worst, of course, and waited until the children were all settled in school before having this done. Rosemary and Bob drove up from Moshi to give us all moral support, which was much appreciated. To the relief of all, nothing malignant was found. Bob was so glad to hear the news that he bought me a new little car—a Ford Anglia—white with blue interior. It was small and easy to park. I can't remember a car I have enjoyed more.

Our first Christmas in Nairobi was great fun. Rosemary, Bob and children drove up to be with us, so it was a family time to remember. It was easy, with the good help of Kafna, the cook, and Peter, the houseboy. I did all the shopping and usually prepared the meat course, but left all the hard work of meals and extras to Kafna, who had been well trained by an English family. While the Jensens were there we took several excursions to nearby parks. We visited the Rift valley and Aberdare National Park north of Nairobi as well as Mt. Kenya National Park. The mountain was not as spectacular as Mt. Kilimanjaro, but nearby we were able to stand with our feet straddling the equator—being half in the northern hemisphere and half in the southern. One incident not to be forgotten happened at Lake Nakuru, home of the large flocks of pink flamingoes. The children were running and playing on the wide beach and suddenly stepped into quick sand! The younger children were too light to get in much trouble, but Peggy, always adventurous and leading the group, sank up to her knees and was terrified, as were we all. Bob, by quick action, rescued Peggy, but it was a frightening few minutes.

In February of 1966, we received the sad news of my father's death from a heart attack. This was a dreadful blow to us all, coming less than two years after Mother's death. Cecil and Reynolds and family had spent a year living with Dad

74

the previous year in Miami while Reynolds became qualified in urology, adding to his regular MD It was a blessing for them to be there, for during that time, in a sense, Dad had escaped being lonely. The Youngs had then moved to South Carolina and Dad had packed his bags ready to visit them when his attack occurred. We were all shocked and I grieved over the loss of my dad so soon after losing mother. We could only be thankful that it was swift.

After a year in Nairobi we were due home leave, so we decided to visit Europe again on the way. "This may be our last chance to see these places", I insisted. In Paris, we were all delighted to see the Arc de Triomphe, the Eiffel Tower and other sights we had heard of. We stayed in the Latin Quarter in a small hotel on Rue Bonaparte and had fun visiting the markets with huge displays of cheeses and flowers of all kinds. We also took a boat trip on the Bateau Mouche. I remember that it was unusually cold in early May that year and we had to buy coats and sweaters for the children, not having needed them in Africa.

We then flew to the States for brief visits with our relatives, stopping by Europe again on the way back to Nairobi. My sister, Austin, joined us in Madrid and together we explored Toledo and the surrounding countryside. In Toledo, we saw the cathedral and El Greco's house, and in Madrid I was especially impressed by the Prado Museum with the dramatic paintings by Goya and the wonderful collection of his drawings, which I did not even know existed.

Next we visited Greece for the first time, a place I had longed to see for many years. We rented a convenient three-room suite in the penthouse of a modest hotel off Constitution Square in Athens. As evening fell it was thrilling to sit on our little patio high above the city and watch the lights come on illuminating the Parthenon and nearby buildings. In addition to visiting the sights and seeing the museum with its famous statues and intricate gold pieces, we watched the changing of the guard in front of the palace and enjoyed the delicious ice cream served at the outdoor cafes. Later we took a day's boat trip out of the port of Piraeus to the island of Hydra. We saw other islands on the way and had several hours layover in Hydra. As we came into the small port I was impressed with the cluster of white houses forming intricate patterns up the side of this little mountainous island. We climbed the narrow streets along with the natives and their donkeys for far-reaching views over the Gulf. Later, I tried to capture the impression of all of this in a large oil painting. We promised ourselves a return visit to Greece to enjoy more of its treasures.

We wanted to visit Egypt, so stopped over in Cairo for a couple of days, staying in the center of town in a modest hotel. Cairo was one of the noisiest cities I have ever visited, before or since. We tried to avoid the rude cab drivers and outstretched hands on all sides and headed for the excellent museum. The fabulous treasures there captured our imaginations and made us appreciate the highly developed civilization that had flourished in earlier ages. The intricate gold artifacts of all kinds were magnificent, especially those of Tutankhamen, who ruled Egypt around the mid 1300s B.C. Seeing these treasures was a treat, as they had been found only earlier this century. Later, we took a tour out to the pyramids, which were even larger and more impressive than we had imagined, making us feel very small as they rose majestically before us. Naturally, we all took camel rides—*de rigueur* for tourists—and explored the halls and passageways around the huge Sphinx. It was surprising to see so much of the face disintegrating. Later, we visited Sakkara, the oldest known pyramid, a short distance away, where many of the interior walls of the burial vault are decorated. Back in Cairo, we decided we couldn't miss seeing the *souk,* which was crowded, but fascinating. We bought a few things, and in one shop that sold perfume essences, were served peppermint tea. The children, whose imaginations were stimulated by the mystery around us, became a bit anxious when I disappeared into a back room with the shop owner to see a special display, and even thought the tea they served us might be drugged! I only realized their feelings later. In the evening, we sought out a restaurant we had read about and sat around a large brass tray-table to taste some of the local specialties.

Back in Nairobi we settled into our routines. The Jensens had returned to the States, buying a house in Ashton, Maryland, near Washington, and we missed having them within visiting distance. Carol and Peggy continued in their schools, but, as previously planned, we made some changes for Steven. He finished out the last term of his Westlands school going only half-day. We ordered books and materials from the Calvert School system to enable me to tutor him. While waiting for them, Steven continued regular piano lessons and spent the afternoons practicing and playing outdoors. We had rented a piano, as we had in Dar, and his teacher, a gentle English woman, was impressed with Steven's talent and interest. Bob had built a tree house for the children and there were swings in front and back yards. Simba was a good companion for Steven during this time.

There was an excellent repertory theater, the Donovan Maule, in Nairobi, presenting different plays each month. We attended religiously, enjoying the professional productions, with occasional visiting actors. When appropriate, we took the children along.

Steven and I began our sixth grade studies In January. I allowed him to progress at his own pace (fast!) and we had fun doing studies in Greek history and Science. I must admit I learned and relearned a lot! Steven loved the workbooks for Science since workbooks of any kind seemed non-existent in Africa at that time. The students had to copy all materials by hand from lessons written on the blackboard. In addition to our regular Math lessons, Bob taught Steven New Math, just coming into vogue then.

That Christmas, Ruth and Joe visited us, and stayed over to celebrate Carol and Joe's birthdays in February. We showed them around and arranged for them to take a long excursion with a driver to Amboseli game park. Later, we drove them over into Uganda for a few days exploration, seeing lots of elephants, hippopotamuses and other animals. We visited Kampala and Entebbe, as well as Murchinson Falls, a dramatic and impressive sight. Coming back from the falls, we had to wait quite a while for a large elephant to get out of the road! It was a dusty, but memorable trip.

During our tour in Nairobi I did a lot of painting and was able to exhibit in public twice. The first was a juried show held on the grounds of the American Embassy. It was satisfying to see my "Shape of Dark" featured on the front page of the local newspaper accompanying the write-up of the show. Later, I was asked to exhibit in the New Stanley Hotel with several other artists. They chose four of my paintings to exhibit, and even though I didn't sell any of these colorful abstract expressionist works, I was pleased with the response by the professional artists around and with the write-up in the local newspaper.

That spring we decided to take the family on a vacation to the coast of Kenya. We drove to Mombasa down the main road that ran basically parallel to the rail line. It was unpaved most of the way at that time—a long, dusty drive. In Mombasa, we visited the port town before proceeding up the coast to Malindi. There, we had delightful, relaxing days at an attractive hotel right on the ocean. In the afternoons we enjoyed walking along the beach, something we had missed since leaving Dar.

As Bob's two-year contract drew to a close, we had a stroke of luck. While on a conference in Kericho, a tea-growing region northwest of Nairobi, Bob telephoned, asking first that I sit down for some unexpected news. He then wanted to know whether or not I would be interested in going to Paris! As if he needed to ask! He had been offered a position there for a year as a consultant at UNESCO's International Institute for Educational Planning. This was one of the most welcome shocks I had ever had. Paris was a place I had always wanted to see—but never dreamed we would have the opportunity to live there. Ironically, I had begun to take a course at the Alliance Française in Nairobi, simply because I wanted to refresh my basic knowledge of the language. With my art interest and background, I could hardly believe the good news.

The Ford Foundation tried to tempt Bob with an extension of his contract in Nairobi or another higher paying job in New Delhi, but we realized the children needed more challenging schools, and we planned to enroll them in the American School of Paris for the year we would be there. Besides, neither of us could rationalize turning down this chance of a lifetime—educational for all of us.

After accepting the Paris assignment, Bob and I wanted the family to see as many places as we could on our way to Paris. We ordered a VW Camperbus for delivery in Frankfurt to make touring easier. Our feelings were mixed as we said farewell to the friends we had made in Nairobi. It had been an exciting and rewarding time.

X

ON TO ROMANTIC PARIS

We left Nairobi on May 1, 1967 heading for Paris eventually, but with miles to go and sights to see, as well as taking home leave, before starting our tour there in September. Our first stop was overnight in Addis Ababa where we visited friends, the Rosenthals. Their son, Peter, had gone to school with Steven in Dar. The father was cultural attaché in Addis and his wife was a bright, attractive person. Everyone wanted to see Haile Selassie's lions, so we hired a car to see the few sites there were. The largely undeveloped city was crowded with people milling around unpaved streets. It was depressing to see so many slum areas.

Beirut, our next stop, was still a beautiful seaside city at that time. Hotels and other high-rise buildings clustered along the shore and people were enjoying the sun and beaches. We joined them to relax a bit before exploring the local market. The next day we hired a driver to take us into the mountains to see the ruins of Baalbek. Unbelievably tall columns were a dramatic reminder of a rich past. Our driver was knowledgeable and polite, offering us oranges during the dusty ride, which impressed Steven.

When we arrived in Greece we explored the countryside by car, staying only overnight in Athens since we had been there previously. Taking a circular tour of the Peloponnese Peninsula, we visited the ruins of Mycenae, with its ancient lion gates and dungeons. Then we drove to see Olympia, the site of the legendary games, and Nafplion with its graceful amphitheater of Ephesus, impressive in its grandeur. We had all studied and read novels about Greece before our trip so it was it was especially rewarding to see sites such as Marathon and the island of Salamis, knowing a bit of the history.

After driving to the Isthmus of Corinth, we took a ferry across the Gulf to the mainland then headed up the valley to Delphi, which for me is one of the jewels of Greece. The ruins of Apollo with its few remaining columns and the site of the mythical Oracle of Delphi made it truly magical. Perhaps because it was my birthday when we were there, but I'll always remember sitting alone high in the large amphitheater at sunset, looking out into the distance and feeling completely a part of nature and human history.

Our hotel had a view over the broad valley and aside from the pleasure of sitting on our balcony in the evening watching the lights come on below us, we were intrigued to see the everyday life around us. There were tourist shops, of course, and we bought a few things, but we could also look over the back yards near us where open barrels of olives were being cured and people were going about their daily tasks.

The next day we went on a romantic picnic high up the side of the mountain, Parnassus. There were masses of tiny wild flowers of all kinds around us that sunny spring day. As we sat eating our simple lunch, we had a contest to see who could count the most varieties just around where each was sitting.

Back in Athens we took a flight to Crete, an island rich in history and myth. We explored the famous ruins of the Palace of Knossos and the next day took a local bus to other ruins, those of Queen Almalfi, I believe. Getting around without a knowledge of Greek presented some interesting challenges. One incident I remember back in the capital, Iráklion, was trying to get a lunch of artichokes that we all liked. The small cafe had all their dishes displayed for customers to see. We pointed to the pile of artichokes, indicating our choice. The man seemed a bit puzzled by this, but we insisted, so he shrugged his shoulders and disappeared. We waited at our small table and soon we were served with a plate of artichokes, cut in pieces, but raw! Gales of laughter, but we finally got it sorted out.

From there we flew to the island of Rhodes, a place we all wanted to see because it was where Colossus, one of the seven wonders of the world once stood straddling the harbor. Its old port town with narrow streets and ancient buildings was fun to explore. At the local street market we bought sponges and other souvenirs and later the children had a pedal boat ride on the small bay.

The next day, wanting to explore the island as well as the city, we managed to rent a car from a private garage. It was not the greatest car, and halfway around the island one of the tires went flat. I remember the natives, who magically appeared, watching curiously as Bob changed the tire, offering comments but no help. In spite of this, we managed to see the Valley of the Butterflies, Lindos and other places, and even stopped to visit a tile factory where we bought colorful, intricately designed samples of the local work. There were very few places to buy gasoline on the island and we had qualms about getting stranded before we got back. We were literally down to our last few drops when we coasted in to return the car.

Leaving from Athens (by first class this time, courtesy of the Ford Foundation) we flew to Frankfurt to take delivery of our neat little camperbus. We were all excited about this new kind of adventure. The first thing I remember after getting the bus was when we stopped at a gas station and tried to fill the water tank over the sink. After five or more minutes it still did not seem to be full. We finally gave up and started to drive away, only to discover that we had failed to close some valve and all the water had just fallen through to the pavement below, unnoticed because of the rain. We learned a lot in the next few days! We waited until we got to Munich before buying our camping equipment. At a large store there we enjoyed picking out two tents for the children, sleeping bags, a small stove, lantern and other essentials. While in Munich we visited the old part of town, enjoying hot chocolate in a tea shop overlooking the famous glockenspiel clock. A visit to the Deutsch Museum, (a huge science museum) was a highlight for everyone, especially Steven, who loved to push all the buttons to see things move. We somehow never found time to visit the art museum that I had hoped to see, so had to save it for a future visit.

We headed for Austria, driving and camping through the beautiful countryside. Our first city stop was in Salzburg to see Mozart's birthplace. We stayed in a small hotel, the White Dove, in the center of town, and wandered around the picturesque streets admiring the houses and tasting some of the local knockwursts, which were sold from open carts. For dinner we selected a restaurant that our guidebook said had a certain delicious specialty, called Salzburger nockerel, I believe. We settled in for a feast, with Bob ordering the specialty and the rest of us ordering such things as weinersnitzel, which the children liked. Everyone except Bob was served and after waiting awhile, we started eating, sure that his order would soon arrive. He shared some of our food while he waited, but we were really puzzled by the delay until the waiter finally came out with a platter filled with a large soufflé-type dessert! It seemed that Salzburger nockerel was not a main course at all. Chagrined, we laughed about our mistake and all enjoyed the delicious specialty. That incident remains a family joke, and we realized that our lack of the language sometimes got us into trouble. One thing we noticed in both Germany and Austria were the huge portions of food they served—especially potatoes. Also, we discovered that at most of the restaurants they counted the rolls they served and charged you accordingly. Steven, who loved to hoard a few rolls in his pockets for later, would often ask, "Is this a restaurant that counts the bread?" I cleaned out many crumbs from his jacket pockets during these years.

Vienna was a highlight for all of us. We camped a short distance out of the city, setting up the two tents and then driving in to see the famous "Ring", the cathedral and other sights. The children were keen on seeing the Lippizaner horses there, so we got them settled in the balcony overlooking the indoor exhibition arena then Bob and I hurried across the street to the art museum to see their unique collection of Brueghel landscapes. It was fun wandering around the romantic city, hearing snatches of Viennese waltzes here and there. The city is a music lover's delight. We saw the famous opera house, but alas, did not hear a performance. It was here that we bought a clarinet for Steven, as he had expressed a strong interest in learning to play it. I was also reminded of my violin that had been made here almost two hundred years earlier.

Heading west, we went through tiny Liechtenstein into Switzerland. Some of the campsites we found were delightful, but near the cities many of them seemed to be situated by train tracks. A bit noisy, but at least if we couldn't locate a particular camp, we knew where to look! High on our list of places to see was Lucerne, and there we found the perfect campsite just out of town near the lake, complete with pool and convenient snack bar. Lucerne is almost too Swiss to be real. Covered bridges, painted houses, gleaming lake, flowers, cheeses, chocolates and cheerful people—plus the well-praised efficiency and vitality of a thriving town—all inspire admiration and perhaps a touch of envy. Small wonder it tops the tourists' lists. We wandered around the old town, marveling at the fanciful architecture and colorful decorations on the steep-roofed houses. Just walking around in all that sparkling cleanliness after three years in Africa was like a champagne bath! This idyll was soon shaken up, if not broken, by the news that Bob was summoned urgently to Paris for advance planning for his job there. None of us wanted to leave just then, so we agreed that the children and I

would wait there in Lucerne until Bob returned.

I wasn't exactly thrilled to be stranded with a new camperbus (How do you drive it?) and three teenagers unable to suppress their energy and enthusiasms. We MUST see everything, they stated, unequivocally. So, in spite of a thunderstorm during the night, which resulted in abandoned tents and four people cuddled together cozily in the camperbus, we made our plans. Is there anyone besides an eleven-year old boy who opts to see the Transport Museum two days in a row? Lucerne was explored *ad exhaustium* until finally the children retired to the swimming pool to "rest". I remember that the Israeli seven-day war took place during this time, reported by the man in the next campsite, who said I looked like Doris Day, and who was becoming quite friendly before Bob returned!

Together again, we drove to lovely Geneva, where we admired the flower clock and the Jet d'Eau and bought watches for all who wanted them (everyone except Bob). We would have liked to linger here, but it was time to get to Holland if we wanted to see any of that country before flying home for leave. We drove up along the Rhine, stopping overnight at Karlsruhe, and taking a day's boat trip admiring the castles and vineyards along the river. We returned by train, arriving late that night. Then we drove through Luxembourg into Belgium. There, along the coast, we arrived at one campsite after dark. Most of the sites seemed occupied, but we finally found an open space in the sand dunes. All went well, but in the morning light we realized that we had tied one of our ropes to a post with a sign that read *Défense de Camping*. We packed up and left in a hurry! Outside Amsterdam we found a nice legal campsite and while set up there, we had time to see the Rijksmuseum and other sights of the city and also took a ride on a canal boat. Another memorable event was attending a Dutch flower auction. It was fascinating to see masses of all kinds of flowers wheeled in to be bid on by dealers. We were a bit anxious that the children might accidentally push one of the buttons on the panel in front of them, committing us to buy hundreds of red tulips, but we made it through without incident. We waited to see most of the country outside Amsterdam after our return from the States. After a bit of a hassle, Bob found a garage where we could leave the camperbus while we were gone.

Home leave was rather hectic. We stopped over with Rosemary, Bob and their three girls, Janet, Kathy and Tova in Ashton, Maryland. In Washington, we went into our storage, which had been paid for by the Ford Foundation while we were in Africa. Now, going to Paris on a consultant's flat fee, it was our responsibility. I remember the intense summer heat the day we sorted out things left from Carderock Spring days. We wanted to get rid of things we didn't really need, and since the Jensens needed furniture after their long stay in Africa, it all worked out well. Bob even gave up his handmade workbench, which was a bit of a sacrifice, I think. I gave Rosemary a large picture of jacaranda trees I had painted in Nairobi, knowing it would remind her of our time together in Africa.

In Nashville, we enjoyed a visit with Bob's parents and day trips on their cruiser, the Chosica. We also saw Don, Bette and their children, Beverly, Barbara, Bonnie and Don, before flying back to Europe. Jeanne and her husband, Lee, who had been traveling in Europe, met us in Amsterdam to explore the country together for a few days. We shopped for antique cookie molds and other things, and saw the cheese market at Alkmaar, the villages of Edam, Hoorn and the large dike across the Wadden Zee. We also visited the wonderful Kröller-Muller museum near Utrecht. Later, when we took the Thunes to the Schipol airport for their flight home, Peggy and Steven clomped around the departure lounge in wooden shoes they had bought. A bit embarrassing to Lee, I'm afraid, but delightful fun for the children.

Everyone was eager to reach Paris and get settled after many weeks of traveling. We found a temporary home in a new campsite north of the city near Maisons-Laffitte. It was conveniently located beside the Seine and even equipped with hot showers. We were tempted to just relax and watch the barges

go by on the river, but soon realized we had to find a place to rent for the coming year. We drove in each day to follow up leads we got from the UNESCO and OECD headquarters. Since it was August, the perfect time, if ever, to drive in Paris, we managed to get around quite efficiently— aside from a minor confrontation at a traffic circle. I remember looking at quite a few cramped dark apartments and we were getting increasingly discouraged when we lucked into a place across the Seine in the small town of Suresnes. This was a large, three-bedroom apartment on the upper floor of a house on Ave. de Londres that gave glimpses of the Paris skyline. Transportation was good for both school and work since the train stopped several blocks down the hill, going both to St. Cloud for the American School, and in the opposite direction into the city. The landlady, Mme. Poirier, lived downstairs, a disadvantage, but since no one planned to stay there during the daytime, we decided to rent it. It was fully furnished in a manner of speaking, so we soon moved in with our few belongings and made plans for the year. The children were enrolled in grades 7, 9 and 11, and were shown where to take the train and how to make the one change necessary to get to school. Carol assumed the responsibility of getting everyone home safely.

Bob and I took the train in the opposite direction to Gare St. Lazare; Bob went on to his job at the International Institute for Educational Planning near the Trocadero in the 16th arrondissement, and I to my classes at Alliance Française on Blvd. Raspail. The children were given a full lunch at the American School (part of the tuition), so I was free of responsibility all day. French classes were enjoyable and it was there I met Gretchen Chinal, who was to become a dear friend over the years. Once a week we would have lunch together and visit a museum. We managed to see all the major shows and were often amused to see exhibitions of the highly creative artists of the *avant-garde* flourishing at the time.

In addition to French classes, I did research and found a place where I could study oil painting again. To be able to study art in Paris was something I had never dreamed would come true. Excited and determined to make the best of this opportunity, I enrolled for afternoon sessions at the Goetz Academy in Montparnasse. The Academy had been started by the well-known artist, André L' Hôte. One of his students, Henri Goetz, was an American expatriate who had been in Paris many years. He and his artist wife had been friends of Picasso, Miro and others. There were students of all ages working at the Academy, and M. Goetz gave criticism twice a week going around to each individually. Although he was not extravagant with praise for any of his students, I was encouraged when he said to me, *"Tu as quelque chose à dire."* (You have something to say.), which I interpreted to mean that I was becoming more successful in expressing my emotions in my art—my principal aim in learning to paint. This was an advanced painting class working from models—a new experience for me. All was in French, of course, so I was glad I was becoming a bit more proficient in the language. I worked hard and learned a lot during that year. I also enjoyed wandering around the streets of the Latin Quarter, practicing my French and stopping for a coffee at Café Flore or Brasserie Lipp, to remember Ernest Hemingway, F. Scott Fitzgerald and others who had frequented these places years before. My romantic nature thrived!

Not long after we got settled, we added a cheerful blue parakeet, Pierre, to our family. We couldn't resist him when we visited the bird market held on Sundays on the Ile de la Cité. Markets are always fun; we also enjoyed visiting the *Marché aux Puces* (flea market) in the suburb of Porte de Montreuil. I had a hard time resisting some of the unusual items collected there, especially the lovely old jewelry.

The house in Suresnes was on a hill and had a small garden in front where the children could play. Steven once set up his tent in the garden and later in the winter, the children made an impressive snowman. Activities were a bit restricted since Mme. Poirier was not too tolerant of balls going into her flower beds, but we managed, knowing it was not to last long. All the children seemed to thrive in the American-type school, so different from those they had attended in Africa. Steven began taking clarinet lessons and looked forward to playing in a school group. It was during this time that Carol got her contact lenses (paid for with some of the money I had inherited from my Dad). I went with her periodically for fittings in the area around Parc Monceau, where we would walk around waiting until her eyes were dilated.

We took several short trips out of Paris. One weekend we drove through thick patches of fog north into Belgium to visit the attractive towns of Ghent and Brugge. Another early trip was over into Brittany where we followed the coast, stopping at Mont-St-Michel and St. Malo, then to Quimper where some of the native women still wear the distinctive starched hats of that region. Then on to Carnac to see the ancient megoliths we had read about. After exploring that region, we stayed one night in Vannes in a hotel converted from a castle and surrounded by a large moat. There are interesting old towns and forts scattered throughout the area.

On the way home we went by Chartres to see the fabulous stained glass windows. Later, during the Christmas holidays when my sister, Austin, came to visit, we returned there and afterward drove along the Loire valley to see several of the large chateaux. She was the only one of our relatives to visit us during our year in Paris. I really enjoyed showing her around and we shopped and did a lot of sightseeing.

Her arrival, however, had been a bit traumatic. The plane she was on had to overfly Paris because of the weather and flew to Rome instead. We found out about that but couldn't locate Austin, who did not arrive on the next plane from Rome. It seems that she had decided to stay over for a few hours to see the city! But we didn't know that, as it was a weekend and she didn't know our home number to call us. Getting increasingly worried, I decided that I would go out to the airport and just wait, since we knew she would be in sometime. Miracles of miracles, she arrived on the first plane that arrived after I got there. A wire she had sent arrived a day later!

During this time, the Viet Nam War was still raging on, with more and more American young men losing their lives. I, along with many others, thought the whole war was a big mistake, a conflict in which the US should never have gotten involved. There were student protests and marches all over the country calling for an end to the conflict.

The spring of 1968 was also the time of the dramatic student revolution in Paris, and living there we were able to see this first hand. It was quite tumultuous at times, with numerous violent demonstrations, pavement blocks torn from some of the streets and other destructive acts. In the Latin Quarter where many of these things took place, I was able to witness a lot of this—even though from a respectful distance. The unrest was noticeable in all the streets that students frequented. On my way to my art academy in Montparnasse one day, I saw a young student in the metro with a bloody bandage around his head, presumably after a clash with the police. For a few days at the height of the uprising there was no public transportation into town. I could not get to my classes and I remember that Bob had to walk to work and back—a long trek from Suresnes. Much of this student unrest spread to the U. S. and other countries, as we all know from history.

The uprising affected our family in a roundabout way. One weekend Steven was scheduled to go to a party given by his clarinet teacher for his students. Since he was now a mature twelve-year old, we decided he could go by metro that stopped near his destination. He had traveled on the metro with us and knew the system, so we drove him to the center of Suresnes where a group taxi left to join the end of the metro line at Porte Maillot. We gave him a detailed map and money, so we were surprised to get a call from him not long after he left. It seems he was stranded at the Etoile by the Arc de Triomphe because the line was not running due to the uprising. Luckily, he understood the French announcement but didn't know what to do next—his dilemma expressed in his wavering voice. We told him to go out of the station and become oriented as to the surrounding streets using his map, and then to follow the avenue that led back to Porte Maillot where he could get the group taxi home. It was a bit of a walk, but he managed perfectly and got the taxi. Unfortunately, on the drive back to Suresnes through the Bois de Boulogne, the taxi had a minor accident. You can imagine the hullabaloo with everyone screaming French insults back and forth! Some kind woman, seeing Steven alone and uncertain what to do, took him in hand and they got another taxi, thank goodness. We had become increasingly worried as we waited in Suresnes, and eyes were damp with relief when he finally arrived safely.

I remember one evening during this turbulent spring when a group of students from the American School had a get together near the Etoile. We were to pick the girls up at a certain time and were waiting at the crosswalk when suddenly I heard, "Hi, Mom!" I looked around and there was Peggy tearing around the Arc de Triomphe on the back of a friend's motorbike in the midst of all the chaotic traffic! What next?

Another moment of worry was when Steven went to visit a school friend who lived with his parents on a houseboat on the Seine. This friend was a bright, inquisitive boy, and we only learned later that he liked to experiment with various chemical reactions. Not long after that we heard he had blown off several of his fingers. Perhaps it was timely that our tour in Paris was coming to a close.

During the year Bob had been called to Geneva several times to give lectures at the International Institute for Labour Studies at the ILO. In the spring he was offered a position there, and since living in beautiful Switzerland appealed to all of us, he accepted.

It had cost us several thousand dollars more than Bob's consultant fee to cover living expenses that year. Still, for a family of five to have such an experience, it was a bargain. We did want to take home leave, even though only Bob got his fare home paid for. Since I was classified as a student because of my art studies, I was able to arrange an inexpensive charter flight for myself and dependents. Bob took the four of us to the terminal meeting point and then left to arrange for the storage of the camperbus before taking his scheduled flight.

Then began one hectic trip for the rest of us, involving a long bus ride to Belgium with few stops, then hours of waiting with crowds of students in the airport, due to canceled flights. The children didn't seem to mind the wait as much as I did.

We finally arrived in New York and took the next shuttle to Washington where Bob was getting more and more worried as he waited. It was quite awhile before I got over that traumatic experience, which lasted over twenty-four hours!

After visiting family, we flew back to Paris, this time our flights being paid for by the ILO, thank goodness.

We retrieved the camperbus and the budgie Pierre, who had been cared for by our French cleaning woman, then we headed for Switzerland.

XI

LIVING BY LAKE GENEVA

Driving through the Jura Mountains over the pass into Switzerland was an exciting time in the late summer of 1968. The camperbus was loaded down with the few things we had accumulated in Paris, including my paintings and Pierre, who was "sneaked" over the border with his cage covered. As we drove down the mountain, the thrill of seeing the Alps above Lake Geneva that beautifully clear day made us sure that we would love living in this magnificent country.

The children had been accepted in the International School of Geneva, so we were anxious to find something to rent on the same side of the lake. After a few days at a pension near the school, we found what seemed to be something we could enjoy. It was an apartment recently converted from part of a barn in the small village of Chevrens a few miles out from the city. Built on four levels, it had three bedrooms and a large loft where Steven seemed happy to settle. All the rooms were small with crooked walls following the sides of the original barn, and it did have a bit of character, which was more than we had found in other places we saw. When we first moved in we had no furniture, so used camping chairs and slept on air mattresses, and for Bob and me, the bed from the camperbus. Our household goods were being shipped from the States. In light of the limited space, we were glad we had given away a lot of furniture. We bought a small table and chairs and since the kitchen was furnished, we managed for the several weeks until the shipment from the U.S. arrived.

Almost as soon as we got settled, Bob at work at ILO headquarters, and the children in grades 8, 10 and 12 of the school, we began exploring different parts of Switzerland, since we had not seen much of it previously. The area around the lake and the Jura Mountains drew us first. Our village and others nearby were picturesque, especially Hermance, on the French border just two kilometers farther around the lake. Due to the way France crowds around Switzerland on that side of the lake, our village also was just along the border, separated only by a small stream behind our apartment. You could easily wade across or throw a stone into another country! We were the only non-Swiss family in the village, which had a population of about 100, and it did not even have a post office or *épicerie*. None of us had had the experience of living in a small village, so it was interesting to see a different kind of life up close. It was easy to make friends. One I kept up with many years was an American artist married to a Swiss who lived nearby in Hermance. We still had the camperbus and soon bought a white Triumph 1300 which I used for errands and shopping.

Our first year in Switzerland was crowded with new experiences. Something new for all of us was learning to ski. Early in the season we went for a weekend to Les Gets, nearby in France. Everyone took lessons but the children soon passed us, and they loved the sport, heading for the slopes whenever possible from then on. After a few years of downhill skiing, Bob and I switched to ski de fond (cross country), mainly because I hated going on some of the wobbly ski lifts, and we enjoyed that for a number of years.

The annual *vendange* was especially fun for us, as we had never seen the grapes being picked and processed before. We watched the activities in the nearby vineyards and later went to the local co-op to see the grapes crushed and the juice collected. This first juice, called *moût*, is rather bland, but many good wines came from nearby vineyards. We took several trips to the wine regions of France, stopping for brief "tastings" while the children waited in the camperbus. They did not think this was the greatest idea, so we did most of our serious tasting later when they were not with us. We especially enjoyed the wines from Côte de Rhone vineyards. That winter I decided to go to a conference with Bob at Sussex University. Since Carol was a responsible high school senior and all the children got along well together, we decided to leave them on their own. Bob and I drove over taking the hovercraft and stopping briefly to see Canterbury on the way to Brighton. After the conference, we made a day's trip to see a few sights, including Stonehenge. This was the first time we had left the children alone and they seemed to manage well.

In early spring, we went with the family to the French Riviera, driving down over the mountains in a late snowstorm. Along the coast we explored Cannes, Antibes and Nice, then went up into the foothills to see Matisse's masterpiece of a chapel in Vence, and the picturesque village of St. Paul de Vence. Just out of the village we visited what became one of our favorite museums, La Fondation de Maight. While we were there, Alexander Calder was supervising the setting up of one of his stabiles in the garden. He was easily recognized with his white hair and his favorite red flannel shirt. The children approached him and were able to get an autograph—a thrill for all of us. On around the coast, we visited Monaco, going up to see the palace with its colorfully dressed guards, and the outstanding view over the Mediterranean, then on over to Menton, the border town with Italy. This spring trip started a precedent, and every spring after that we tried to explore a different part of southern Europe, welcoming the season before it reached Geneva.

Later that year, we added Tania, a miniature black poodle, to our household. She was a gift from a casual acquaintance I had met on the street, who, when I asked where she had gotten the cute puppy, mentioned that she was hoping to give it to a good home as she was having trouble caring for it in her city apartment. We all enjoyed Tania, taking her on walks, picnics and even camping with us. I remember a camping trip one summer in the valley of Saas Fee followed by a visit to Zermatt, where she went with us in the cable car as far as it went up the Matterhorn. The Swiss are much more tolerant of well behaved dogs in public places, so it was not unusual to see them beneath the tables of restaurants and other places.

As Carol's senior year at the International School was coming to a close, she took a trip to Russia with some of her classmates. While there, she got a terrible flu-like virus, and accompanied by a friend, had to go to a Russian hospital for antibiotics. This was traumatic for Carol, and made us realize again how lucky we were to live in Geneva.

In June, we discovered the fields of wild narcissi that bloomed in the Jura Mountains above Vevey and Blonay. White fields covered the hillsides and we picked masses of the fragrant flowers to take home for ourselves and friends. This became something to look forward to every June, one of the most beautiful months in Switzerland, when many of the wild flowers bloom.

There was much activity around graduation time, including senior picnics and parties. Carol made both her graduation dress and her prom dress, having learned to sew first from my mother years before. At this time she was dating a nice boy, Gordon McKechnie, who was editor of the school newspaper, and she went to the prom with him. She looked young and beautiful and I was sad knowing that she would soon be leaving for college.

It was in July of 1969 that man first walked on the moon. We had all been looking forward to this historic event and I remember waking up the children in the middle of the night to witness it on the TV, then the thrill of hearing Alan Shephard's "One small step for man, one giant leap for mankind." I thought of President Kennedy's 1962 promise to accomplish this before the end of the decade. Unfortunately, he did not live to see what was undeniably the highlight of the century.

Jeanne and Lee visited us that first summer and together we visited the village of Yvoire farther along the lake, and Gruyere, the cheese center, where we often went to indulge in the delicious strawberries and thick cream. One of the highlights of that visit was camping together in Lauterbrunnen, a small town with an impressive waterfall and gorges in the valley below Mürren. From there we took the train up to visit the Jungfrau, the highest mountain around, which is always covered with snow. At the summit, in addition to admiring the 360-degree view, you can go through ice tunnels and even take a dog-sled ride. Later we rode the cable car up to Mürren, high on the opposite mountain, returning by funicular to our camp in the valley below.

In the autumn, Carol left for the U. S. to attend Ohio Wesleyan University. We hated sending her back to the States alone, but she wanted to continue her education there. After she left, I was depressed for quite awhile, knowing our family would never be quite the same. I volunteered for work at the International Red Cross about this time, working one afternoon a week to coordinate and help set up a file of NGOs (non-governmental organizations).

The family kept busy with various activities. Earlier we had bought a piano, and Steven began taking lessons again. He also played the clarinet in the school orchestra. Peggy was doing some drawing at this time and showed a lot of talent. I also got back into my art activities, and earned a bit of money restoring an oil painting owned by the landlord.

In November, Bob took a rather lengthy trip to Mexico and several other Latin American countries for the Institute. During this time, I was driving Peggy and Steven to school, and I remember keeping them guessing by varying my route each day, both to explore the neighborhoods and to make it a more interesting trip. We took several excursions nearby, including a few hikes. One evening, we "chased the sunset" over and around the hills of the Voirons in nearby France, which they may remember.

My brother, Don, visited us briefly while Bob was gone, extending a business trip from Luxembourg, I believe. It was great fun showing him Geneva and nearby villages. One day we drove all the way around the lake, stopping at the castle of Chillon, which we had seen before but which is always interesting. I recall Don's enjoyment and his reciting from Byron's, "The Prisoner of Chillon". Shortly after that we had our first big snowfall, which turned Chevrens into a fairyland. This was a thrill for us, since we had seen only light snow in Paris, and of course, none in the years we were in Africa.

The children had a small inflatable boat which they enjoyed paddling around on the lake near the shore below Chevrens. They also had bicycles and occasionally took excursions with their friends. Once, Peggy and two friends went all the way around the lake, staying at a hotel in Evian, France (where we made reservations for them), then at a hostel in Lausanne. I think they made the last leg of the journey by lake steamer—completely exhausted by then! The three girls had different nationalities and each displayed her country's flag on her bike. The International School was a wonderful place to learn to live with people from diverse cultures, as the students came from about sixty different countries. There was both an English and a French section, with many activities bi-lingual. It was here that Peggy joined the International Baccalaureate program that was just being offered. It was an ambitious program, basically made up of advanced placement level courses, with many student graduates being able to enter university in the sophomore year in the U. S. Unfortunately, Carol had missed this opportunity, but Steven was able to take advantage of it during his last three years of highschool.

Our Christmas that year was not the same with Carol away, since we were not able, financially, to have her fly home. She spent the holidays with Bob's parents, Ruth and Joe, but I'm afraid she deeply missed the usual activities of home. We made it as festive as we could in Chevrens, with a big tree, stockings hung by the fireplace, turkey and the usual traditions, such as reading "The Night Before Christmas" aloud—with our private family joke and laughter.

During the winter months we went on several ski trips, once going to Les Gets again for the day, Another time, we took a visiting cousin, Steve Harris, to the nearby mountains to learn to ski. Our most memorable ski trip that year, however, was the week we spent in Villars, high up in the mountains around the lake. We stayed in an attractive chalet-type inn overlooking the valley, having our meals there as well. There was a group of young teachers there at the same time, and the raclette supper with them was fun, with competition to see who could eat the most servings of potatoes and hot, scraped cheese. One of the teachers won, eating an amazing amount, although Steven made a good showing! This was our introduction to raclette, although we already enjoyed fondue, the other cheese favorite of the Swiss. We took ski lessons each morning and in the afternoons we skied on our own. We all improved, but I do remember my sore ankles! I later did a large oil painting of the mountains across the valley, from sketches made from our balcony. Carol has that painting because I was thinking of her then and wishing she could be with us.

In early spring, Bob joined me in taking a class in etching at the Centre d'Arts Contemporain de Genève. It was fun to learn about a medium I had always admired, as we experimented with methods and colors. I later developed more expertise and produced a few creditable things.

Just before Easter, 1970, we went with Peggy and Steven to Florence for a week's vacation, driving along the Italian Riviera with another brief stop at Pisa. In Florence, we stayed in an interesting pension, inexplicably named the Monna Lisa that was made up of many small rooms on different levels, all decorated with unusual antiques. Bob and I stayed in what was once a monk's cell, with the children up a couple of levels in a room overlooking the trees of the small back garden. It was well located and within easy walking distance of everything.

We enjoyed seeing the Duomo and especially the Baptistery with its intricately carved Paradise doors by Ghiberti. But it was the wonderful works by

Michelangelo all over the city, especially in the Accademia, with the David and the emotionally moving "Prisoners" statues, so symbolic of man's struggle as they remain half formed in the marble, that impressed me most deeply. We saw the treasures of the Uffizi Gallery, with Botticelli's "Birth of Venus", and in the Pitti Palace, Raphael's wonderful circular-framed Madonna. The ancient Annunciation fresco of Fra Angelico on the walls in the Museum San Marco was wonderful to behold! What a pleasure to see these masterpieces that I had only read about.

In addition to such touristy sites as Ponte Vecchio, which was crowded with small shops, we explored the ancient city of Fiesole above Florence, to see the Roman theater ruins and other archaeological sites there. Before heading home we took a short trip south to see Siena with its unique curved plaza and distinctive campanile. All together this spring trip was a delight, with perfect weather and not quite as many people around as would be found there at Easter.

We welcomed Carol home from college in June of 1970. It seemed to be a short summer—time for short trips exploring Switzerland, driving across various passes and doing a bit of camping before Carol had to return to the U.S. for her second year at Ohio Wesleyan.

When Bob and I realized that we would be staying in Geneva for the foreseeable future, we wanted to have a house of our own. International personnel did not have all the restrictions that other foreigners had on buying land, so we started looking around. We wanted to build on the right rather than left side of the lake, since the ILO was located there and Bob would not have to continue to cross the Mont Blanc bridge twice a day—a real bottleneck. Also, the children would soon be leaving the International School, which had influenced our decision to rent on the left bank when we had first arrived. I spent many weeks scouting around and then together Bob and I would check the best possibilities. We finally found a lot on an open field outside the small village of Founex, which had wonderful views over the lake to the Alps and views to the Jura Mountains in the other direction. After financial juggling we were able to buy it in September of 1970, then settled in to wait until we could save the money to build.

In November that year Bob went to Sri Lanka (Ceylon, as it was then called) to lecture and take part in a two-week conference. He came back with lots of fascinating photos, making me hope to visit there someday. On the way home, he stopped by to visit Cecil, Reynolds and family in Pakistan, where Reynolds was serving as a medical missionary. They welcomed him warmly in Montgomery (later called Sahiwal) and showed him a bit of the country.

We decided to spend the Christmas holidays in the U.S. in 1970, so we could all be together. There, we enjoyed a big celebration with Ruth and Joe at their house, the Anchorage, on the lake outside of Nashville.

Back in Geneva, Peggy was in her senior year of highschool and Steven was in the tenth grade. Peggy worked hard to finish her International Baccalaureate in just two years, rather than three that was later recommended. We were proud of her, because in addition to her studies and socializing with friends, she tutored two young Hungarian children for some months. She had decided to go to England for her university studies, and I went over with her for her interview at Sussex University, near Brighton. She wanted to major in art history and philosophy and was accepted to begin in the autumn as the youngest freshman they had enrolled—just seventeen.

Before Easter that year, we decided to go to Venice for our spring trip. We took the train instead of driving, knowing that we couldn't take a car on the watery streets of the city. It was a long, tedious trip, unfortunately, since we got caught up in a large group of the Italian military on the move, and with no reservations, had to stand for several hours before finding a place to sit. Once we arrived in Venice, however, there was a magical transformation. It was a night of the full moon and as we left the train station we were met by the sight of glittering water in front of us and the sound of serenading gondoliers. You couldn't have asked for a more romantic introduction to a fascinating city. Our hotel was in an ideal location, with a glimpse of Piazza San Marcos from the small balcony. Peggy and Steven enjoyed feeding the pigeons that gathered by the hundreds, swooping and cooing around the tourists on the Piazza. I was impressed by the beautiful mosaics and gold ornaments in the Duomo and the romantic cafés around the piazza, where we had minute cups of coffee and thought of all the great writers who had once lingered there.

We saw the usual tourist sights, such as the Bridge of Sighs, the Doge's Palace, the Rialto Bridge and old houses along the canals. Naturally, we took a ride in a gondola—overpriced, but fun. Peggy and Steven were intrigued by tales of the spies who used to roam around the narrow streets and alleys off the canals. One evening, the four of us explored some of these rather eerie places, feeling very daring, but seeing more cats than spies, or even people. Later, we took a boat to the resort island of Lido and on the way back we stopped to see the multicolored glass articles being made in Murano. It was on this boat trip that we saw the funeral barges of Stravinsky pass by, all decorated with flowers. He had just died and was being buried on one of the islands off Venice.

Peggy's graduation in June 1971 was a special event, since hers was the first class to graduate from the International Baccalaureate program at the school. Lord Montbatten from England presented the diplomas, and a picture of Peggy taken as she was receiving hers was featured in publicity material sent out for years afterward. We were proud of the high marks she had made on her exams and her enthusiasm for continuing her education. Meanwhile, Carol had expressed a desire to leave Ohio Wesleyan and go to England, as well. We were delighted and encouraged her in this, since she would be closer to us, and with the many social changes going on in the U.S. colleges, we were a bit concerned about some of the influences there. Carol was accepted at Queen Mary College, University of London, where she was to major in Comparative Zoology, so both girls made plans to go to England in the autumn.

The summer of 1971 was active. There was more camping, and several of Carol's classmates from the States turned up from time to time, looking for a place to sleep and somewhere to wash clothes (mostly the girls!). Perhaps the most memorable surprise visit was when two young men arrived on their motorcycles before breakfast. They had flown over and bought the bikes so they could tour around Europe. I shocked the people of the village a bit when I rode up and down the road on the back of one of the boy's motorcycles, a new experience for me.

An unpleasant experience that summer was the accident we had while Bob's parents were visiting. One evening as we drove them over to see our lot in Founex, a speeding car hit us from behind, knocking us into an electricity pole, which was completely lopped off. There were a few cuts and some bad bruises, but no one was seriously hurt, thank goodness. The car, however, was a total write-off. After months getting the insurance settled, we bought a new car, a Renault, which served us well for years.

Jeanne and Lee visited again that summer and asked me to go part way with them later as they headed to Germany. We crowded into the little rental Volkswagen and drove over to Visp where we took the train up to Zermatt. It was fun spending the night there and at sunrise from our balconies to view the sun dramatically light up the top of the Matterhorn (Mont Cervin). We left early to drive through the beautiful scenery on over to St. Moritz. After staying overnight there, I took the train back to Geneva, and they drove on to Germany. On the way home the train went through the dramatic Engadine valley, cutting across high in the mountains to Chur. I was so impressed with the perfect little villages nestled in the valley that I was determined to show this part of Switzerland to the rest of the family.

Everyone was enthusiastic, so soon afterward we took an extensive trip to the northeastern part of the country, camping near picturesque villages, sometimes beside rushing streams and at times getting permission to set up our tents in a farmer's field. We crossed several passes and went over into Italy to Bolzano and Cortina, then drove into the Dolomite area to see the huge, strangely shaped formations that were scattered around. They seemed fashioned by some whimsical nature god, completely different from anything we had seen before. On the way home we went by St. Anton, St. Gallen, Appenzell and on down through Lucerne and Bern to Geneva.

In the autumn of 1971 it was sad to see our family continuing to shrink as both girls left for their universities. To avoid being too depressed, we kept very busy and made plans for a big Christmas. It turned out to be even bigger than we had planned—really a Christmas to remember. Cecil and her six children arrived in Geneva unexpectedly from Pakistan, where there was a lot of unrest going on. They had finally gotten a flight out and Reynolds was to meet them in the States. We received their telegram on the very Sunday they were to arrive in the afternoon. Much rushing around to get groceries and other essentials, since at that time the Swiss stores did not open on Sunday (except the bakeries!). I managed to get a chicken from my friend in Hermance, who also lent us a crib, and we got milk and a few other things across the French border. Seeing Cecil arrive after hours and hours on the plane with all the children—little Matthew only three months old—made tears of relief come to my eyes. We convinced her to stay over with us for

Christmas, and it was the most fun we had had for ages. The girls had arrived home from England and it was a full house, including the dog! We managed to double up all the children and fit everyone in. We took turns taking the children Christmas shopping, and I remember when Bob and I took Mason (then seven years old) to pick out his presents. He decided to get different kinds of loose candies for each person, and really went wild choosing from the many bins in Grand Passage department store. Since they were all different prices, the salesgirl was also going a bit wild, until Bob got things organized. It was a great celebration, complete with all the trimmings. We hated to say goodbye to all the Youngs, who were anxious to get home. After a bit of finagling, Bob was able to get them reservations on to the States.

During the cold winter that year, Austin and Art came in their camperbus for a visit on their way to Morocco. We enjoyed showing them around and took some trips up into the snowy mountains before they went south.

All during these months Bob and I had been actively looking for an architect to build a house for us on the lot in Founex. We finally located a company that constructed Techbuilt houses from designs developed in the States at MIT. After complicated negotiations, the foundation was laid in early 1972, and gradually the house began taking shape. I kept a close eye on the process, and with almost daily trips around the lake, was able to keep certain disasters from occurring, all this taking place in French, of course. The contractor was quite good but there was not enough supervision of the workmen. I remember one near disaster when I discovered a half-built fireplace completely different from the one we had specified, even after Bob had made a model for them to go by. I insisted the mason tear it out and begin over, which he did, with a bit of grumbling. Later he had the audacity to ask if he could take a picture of the finished product to show his future clients!

During Easter vacation we took a trip to Barcelona. The girls, home from their universities, had a rather short break, so we decided to save time by going by train, and we reserved couchettes to the border of Spain. The bunks were not very comfortable, and unfortunately, the train arrived at the border at some ungodly hour in the morning, so the whole experience was memorable in more ways than one. But, it was a good vacation and we were able to see all the sights and enjoy the delicious seafood and sangria.

In the Picasso museum we saw many of his very early works, things we hadn't even known about. There was one he painted when he was nine years old! We also enjoyed watching the Catalonian dances performed in front of the city hall by anyone who wanted to join (and knew the dances!). It was also fun walking down the famous avenue, Ramblas, near our small hotel, people watching. One sight never to be forgotten was the Gaudi cathedral, an unfinished "drip-castle", with fantastic shapes and formations.

In the summer of 1972, our house in Founex was finished. None of the yard work had been done, but we were able to move in. We taped over the windows and left for home leave shortly after our move. In Bonclarken, North Carolina, a big family reunion had been planned. All my sisters and brother were there with most of their children. It was an ideal time for everyone to get reacquainted.

Back in Switzerland, we got the girls off to their universities again, and we began settling into our new home.

Soon after we moved to Founex Steven bought a small sailboat, a snipe. He and I had scouted around the lake and finally found one we could afford. It needed some work, which turned out to be an ongoing project to keep it in shape for sailing. But Bob and Steven worked hard, affording some good times, and Steven learned a lot about sailing, even in a leaky boat!

Steven was in eleventh grade at the International School, taking the IB program and planning to continue through grade thirteen, as recommended. He was now licensed to drive a motorbike, so usually drove in with Bob to the ILO headquarters (located on the lake at that time), with his bike in the camperbus, then drove it home after school. I was concerned about his driving through heavy traffic over the Mt. Blanc bridge, but knew he had good judgment and needed this new independence.

Earlier, I had joined the American Women's Club of Geneva, going to a few of the monthly luncheons, and now I became more active by attending the Country Living group in the Coppet-Nyon area. I still stay in touch with some of the friends made there.

We began improving our lot as soon as we could that autumn, first putting in a hedge around three sides. On the remaining side we were next to an apple orchard owned by the neighboring farmer, M. Polencent. I tried to "rent" an apple tree from him so we could pick fruit whenever we wanted, but evidently that is not done. His explanation was that all the apples had to be picked at

about the same time. I guess that makes sense, but it would have been convenient!

We continued to improve our home and garden by planting trees and shrubs, and made a small pool and waterfall near a weeping willow given to us by friends. Steven was a great help in all this. Once when Bob was away, the nursery delivered a large birch tree and some shrubs that we had ordered. It was pouring rain, but Steven and I sloshed through the mud for hours to plant them. It was all worth the effort, and the first Christmas in our own home with all the family together was festive and fun.

During the February break at school that year, Bob, Steven and I took a skiing vacation to Montana-Crans where we enjoyed the beautiful scenery as well as the skiing and fondue suppers. Bob and I were doing ski de fond at this time, but we often took the lifts up the slopes to watch Steven perfect his various turns and other maneuvers. It was here that we saw a one-legged man zooming down one of the more difficult slopes! Later in the spring, Charlie, Kathy and their children, Christina, Elizabeth and Deborah drove down for a visit from Heidelburg where they were living. It was fun having little ones around.

After a busy autumn, we went to the States for a family Christmas celebration with Ruth, Joe, Dan, Joanne and Cindy. This was a good chance for the Ray cousins to get acquainted. Unfortunately, it was during this vacation that Tania died. My hairdresser friend, who loved Tania, had asked to keep her while we were away. He and his wife took her skiing with them and spoiled her, but the night before we arrived back home, she was accidentally run over in the lane by their house after she had inadvertently been let out while the gate was open. This was a hard blow to all of us, including the Niselles. We were sad for a long time, and not anxious to have another dog.

Shortly after this I went in to the American Women's Club and volunteered to work on the monthly magazine, the Courier. I did editing and soon began writing, as well. This was the part of the club that interested me most, and something I seemed to fall into naturally. I had many articles published during this time, and during the coming years got great enjoyment from writing.

Our first extended visit to Provençe in the spring of 1974 was an eye-opener. We were enchanted by the old monuments and picturesque villages scattered over the varying terrain. Avignon and San Rémy, with the nearby ruins of Les Baux, high on a hill above olive groves were favorites, and we returned to Provençe every spring we could manage to take a few days off. The roads lined with the typical slender cypress trees, and the masses of yellow wild stock in spring make this an ideal place to explore.

When Steven became eighteen in 1974, he was required to register for the draft for duty in Viet Nam, which was still going on. At the Embassy in Bern he was told there was little chance he would be called. I realized how lucky it was that Carol and Peggy were not males, and that Steven was our third child instead of the first. Now, he could look forward to an education without interruption.

Steven graduated with high marks from the International School in June 1974. He wanted to major in physics at university and we drove over to England for interviews at places he was interested in. He was accepted at all those where he had interviews, and he chose Bristol University with its top-notch physics department, to enter in the autumn.

After graduation, Steven took an extended trip with two of his good friends. One was from Pakistan, and the other of French-Nigerian background. A real mixture of nationalities, but they got along well. With rail passes they toured through France then into Italy, Austria and Germany. They slept on a beach in Italy, visiting Capri and other sites. One night in Vienna, two of them STOOD all through an opera, Steven reported.

Meanwhile, Peggy graduated with high honors from Sussex University, and we went over to celebrate this event. She was anxious to be on her own and decided to take a job in Lincoln, England as a town planner, beginning in the fall.

That summer we toured around the Cotswolds in England with the Thunes and Peggy and Steven. Carol, who was getting settled in a new house, could not come along. For our exploring, we used a book on mysterious sites of England, following clues and sometimes vague directions to unusual areas. We sought out such things as the Long Man of Wilmington, Hetty Pegler's Tump and the Uffington White Horse. It was great fun, giving a focus to the vacation.

Politics in the U.S. was particularly fascinating at this time. Through the International Herald Tribune and news magazines, we had kept up with the rumors of the Watergate break in. When President Nixon was forced to resign in 1974, we were reassured that justice was still alive. While this reaffirmed my belief that our democracy was strong, it also was a psychological blow to all thinking Americans. Ironically, our Swiss friends could not understand why our president had been forced from office, and probably don't to this day.

We made frequent trips to England. One I will never forget was when we drove over, and after a good visit, were faced with an unexpected shock as we were to leave. While in line to take the hovercraft back across the channel to France, I glanced at my passport and discovered, to my horror, that it was not mine, but Peggy's! Somehow, while we were comparing passports, they had become mixed up. Now, with tickets and reservations, we were faced with this!

The customs man agreed to let us out of England, but couldn't promise what would happen when we tried to enter France. We decided to chance it, since we had special identification cards, which would allow us into Switzerland. What a traumatic trip! Nevertheless, we did manage to bluff our way through French customs by waving our identification cards and acting as if we didn't understand French. We must have looked fairly harmless, since the poor frustrated man just waved us on. I never want to repeat that adventure!

XII

BROADENING HORIZONS

During the years we lived in Switzerland we explored as many parts of that beautiful country as possible, also taking advantage of any free time to see other parts of Europe and farther afield. So, when Bob was sent to Mexico City to direct a two-week course in October 1974, I immediately made plans to join him the last week. All went well in spite of losing my luggage on the long flight over. After several days trying to get something to wear in a country of short people, I flew up to San Antonio, Texas, where Rosemary and her family were living. It was not an ideal visit with my sister, but it was good to see her and she was certainly helpful in shopping for necessary clothes. When I arrived back in Mexico City, I discovered that my suitcase had finally turned up! So, it seemed I had acquired several new outfits, plus a new suitcase, courtesy of the airline.

During free time from Bob's responsibilities we wandered around the city. We visited the Mercado Sábado (Saturday market) and had lunch at the Inn des Angeles. After the course was over, we drove to Taxco, then to see the Axtec ruins at Toluca, with their huge stelae.

When we stopped to see the lake at Pátzcuano, famous for its butterfly fishing nets, we were "adopted" by a group of retired Americans touring the area in their Airstream trailers. They invited us to accompany them on a tour they had arranged to an island in the middle of the lake to see the Tarascan dances performed. The group could not have been friendlier, and it was an interesting experience, but we decided we preferred traveling on our own.

From there we drove on to Morelia, which we had wanted to revisit. Again we stayed at a hotel on the hill above the city—a group of small cottages clustered amidst the bougainvillea and other flowering shrubs. Our cottage was delightfully romantic, with fresh flowers, a view over the valley and the added luxury of having someone come in early to light a fire in our small fireplace.

Leaving Morelia, we drove to Guanajuato to visit Margo and Temple Dick, friends from Guatemala days. They had rented a house for a number of years and were gracious in showing us around the city—one of the loveliest in the Mexican highlands. We rather regretted leaving this idyllic place, as we headed back to Mexico City and on home to Switzerland.

At Christmas time, with the children home from England, we opted for a skiing vacation, renting an apartment in Montana-Crans again. The children were becoming good downhill skiers by then, although Bob and I had more or less reached our "plateau" of skill—about the second grade up. We also enjoyed the less challenging ski du fond.

For our spring trip that year Bob and I went to Majorca for a week. We stayed at a large hotel by the sea out of the capitol, Palma, and rented a tiny Siat (Spanish Fiat) to explore the island. The countryside away from the coast was lovely; with fruit trees in blossom while we were there. I was surprised at the variety of terrain—hilly and green in places, yet flat and bare in others. One of the reasons I had wanted to go to Majorca was to see where George Sand and Chopin lived during their liaison in the 18th century. Their relationship seemed so romantic to me, yet it was evidently less than serene. George Sand had taken Chopin to Majorca to try to help him recover from tuberculosis, and there she encouraged him to continue his composing.

We explored Palma, and drove around the southern coast to visit the pearl factory where the high-quality Majorica pearls are made. (Bob bought a lovely, double strand for me.)

An interesting sidelight during this stay was getting acquainted with a cheerful middle-aged couple from Switzerland during dinner. They were each married to someone else, but having worked together in previous days, they met every year, one place or another, to renew and enjoy their friendship. They volunteered this information and it seemed to be a satisfactory arrangement for them, although of course we didn't know the details.

The following summer, friends from Guatemala and Peru stopped over, as well as some of the children's friends. A lot of people were touring Europe at this time it seemed, and since Geneva is centrally located, it was a logical stop. We always welcomed our friends and relatives, but sometimes we would get a phone call from people we had never seen—children of friends, or friends of relatives, who had given no advance notice of arriving. Some even called from the Geneva train station, asking innocently if we knew of a youth hostel nearby. We didn't really mind putting up all these guests, but feeding them was sometimes a chore. Our only solution to these situations was, after a few days, to ask the young people if they would mind mowing the lawn or helping a bit in the garden. Few of them lingered for long.

Meanwhile, we built a rockery around the patio and enlisted anyone visiting to help collect interesting rocks from the Jura Mountains. The camperbus was perfect for this, but it got so that every time we would start on a picnic or short trip, everyone became suspicious as to what they might be getting into!

The camperbus was now eight years old, and even though it was running well with a new motor we had put in, we decided its usefulness for us was nearing an end. We sold it to a young man who took it to India for a camping trip. Meanwhile we arranged to buy a sporty little MGB-GT in England for Bob. (I was still happy with my trusty Renault.) With the help of Peggy, we ordered the new car to be picked up in Lincoln during the summer. There, in addition to seeing Peggy, we saw the lovely cathedral and other sights. In the new car, we then drove down to the southwest, stopping to visit Steven in Bristol and to see Bath.

In exploring Cornwall, we drove through incredibly narrow roads with hedgerows on both sides, making driving in a small, low car a bit challenging. But we didn't want to miss seeing Mousehole, Penzance and Land's End, which we had often heard about. We sampled the Cornish pasties and indulged in afternoon teas with scones and clotted cream without a bit of guilt!

Carol met us in Taunton on the way back, and insisted on scrunching up in the small back seat of the MG to ride with us over to Wimborne in Dorset, where we were to meet Mark Lewis's parents for the first time. Carol and Mark, who had come to know each other at Queen Mary, had decided to get married. They planned the wedding for that September (1975) in Poole, and we were happy for them since we liked Mark and they seemed very much in love.

Before the wedding, we flew back to England in order to have some time with Carol alone. We stayed briefly in the New Forest in Lyndhurst, a small village where wild horses wandered through the streets. During this time, students felt it was almost a sacrilege to worry about clothes, and Carol needed a lot of things (even if she didn't think so), so we spent a lot of time shopping. Later we three settled in a hotel in Bournemouth where Peggy and Steven joined us.

The wedding was held in the Poole Registry Office, nearby. It was raining on the morning of the wedding, but everyone seemed happy. I may have been the only one who had a lump in her throat all during this time— intellectually happy for Carol, but emotionally not so happy. The reception luncheon was a big success with delicious food well served at a nearby Inn. For a wedding present, Bob and I gave them two tickets to the U.S., to use the following summer. After a brief honeymoon, they settled into a small house on a farm in Barton St. David in Somerset, near the town of Street where Mark had a job teaching.

Earlier in 1975, Bob's father, Joe, had been diagnosed with prostate cancer. In spite of treatments, he was getting progressively worse. In late December he was taken to the hospital in Nashville. We felt it was important for Bob to fly over to see him immediately, and he was glad he did, even though all our children were coming for Christmas. He was able to say good-bye to his father before he died, just a day after Bob had returned to Switzerland. Joe was a wonderful person and always a perfect father-in-law to me. He was almost 82 years old and even though he had lived a full, productive life, we all wished he could have been with us longer. He will always be remembered with love.

In March, Bob and I drove to Paris to visit our niece, Miriam, her husband, Bill, and their children, Corina, Matthew and Maggie. Bill was taking a sabbatical there, and it was fun doing a bit of sightseeing with them. I remember going to the Rodin museum and having lunch at Café de Beaux Arts on Rue

Bonaparte, a place we used to frequent with our own children. Matthew loved the escargots! Later in the year, when Miriam and family visited us in Founex, we took them exploring around the lake and up into the mountains to our favorite valley above Vevey. It was a magical time, one I remember with pleasure, especially since Bill later sent me some poems he had written, inspired by the beautiful landscape.

In early Spring of 1976 during Easter vacation, Bob, Steven and I traveled to the States. The girls, busy with their own activities, couldn't accompany us, but we thought that Steven should see a bit of the U.S. since he had spent so many years of his life overseas. It was the 200th anniversary of our country's independence—an especially appropriate time to take the trip. After flying into Miami, we rented a car and drove down the Florida Keys to Key West, stopping on the way to enjoy the warmth and rejuvenating sunshine. In Key West, we saw the usual sights, including Ernest Hemmingway's house and where President Harry Truman used to stay. We found it all a bit touristy, but did enjoy looking around and eating Key lime pie. Back in Miami we stopped by to see the house on the canal where Mother and Dad had lived for eleven years. Driving north, we stopped at many of the places I had remembered, including one of those "All the orange juice you can drink for ten cents" places. After a busy and exhausting day at Disney World, we headed for the Kennedy Space Center at Cape Canaveral, which we all wanted to see. It was fun touring around the huge silos, seeing the rockets and other things. The timing was not right to see a space flight, however.

I remember stopping in Gainesville for lunch with my friend from early days, Rae Pattishall Egger, whom I hadn't seen for many years. She was now a widow and worked as a librarian. She had a weak heart, due to a bout with rheumatic fever, and had recently had a pacemaker installed. We had a good visit reminiscing about olden days, and I was saddened to hear that Rae died just a few months after we were there—only in her mid-fifties.

We visited my old home on the St. John's river near Jacksonville, stopping to see Mother and Dad's graves in Arlington on the way, wishing sadly that they could have shared a few more years with us. Our place had been bought by another family with a lot of children, which pleased us all. No one was at home, but we took photos and I roamed around remembering many good years there.

In South Carolina, we visited Cecil, Reynolds and their children at their big ante-bellum house in Due West. It was the perfect time for flowering of the azaleas and we marveled at the profuse beauty of nearby gardens. From there, we stopped briefly in Montreat, North Carolina to see our lots on the side of the mountain, then drove over to Nashville by way of Gatlinburg, where we showed Steven the cottage where Bob and I had stayed during our honeymoon—way back in 1949. After a visit with relatives in Nashville, we headed back home to Switzerland with new respect for our wonderful home country.

We had a chance to have an interesting trip with Peggy in June when we met her in England and drove her home with us, touring through the Loire valley. We stopped at several of the imposing chateaux there and marveled at the ornate cathedral at Bourges. We sometimes drove out of our way to search for special restaurants recommended by the Michelin guide. This was becoming a delightful hobby with us. I remember one meal where we had the most delicious fresh, white asparagus—served wrapped in a steaming linen napkin with two different dipping sauces. Again I realized that French cuisine may never be surpassed.

I had continued writing articles for the Courier and in 1976 I was asked to be the editor of the magazine. I looked forward to working with an energetic and creative group of women, and the combined July-August issue celebrating the 200th anniversary of the U.S. was my first effort. For the cover we had obtained a special drawing by Hank Ketchem of Dennis the Menace fame, who was living in Geneva then. During the next two years I was responsible for the monthly magazine, which at that time, was the only English language magazine being published in Geneva, with a circulation of over 1500. We covered local  cultural news, travel articles and thought provoking discussions of UN and world affairs, in addition to humorous pieces and news of the American Women's Club. I formed strong friendships with the women I worked with, many talented and experienced writers, as well as the others who did layout, advertising and other jobs to get out the magazine. We all learned a lot doing this concentrated work, gaining skills, as well as confidence in dealing with the printer and advertisers. I up-graded the office with carpets, new furniture, light boxes and later installed a computer to make the process more efficient and pleasant. Writing the editorials and arranging for the Courier covers each month were among my favorite jobs. I was proud of some of the strikingly original photos and other designs.

At the club, we also published two booklets—Living in Geneva, put out for many years by friend, Barbara Bishop, and one I originated and edited called Coping, with advice for foreign woman facing certain of life's milestones and crises in Geneva. All in all, it was a satisfying two years, and as a team we developed a first-class magazine, widely admired. The principal responsibilities at the club were changed every two years. After I left as editor of the Courier, they had a series of short-term editors, no one seemingly wanting to take on the demanding job for very long. Later, I was asked to step in as Vice President of

Publications, which I did, naming friend Chris Maller as managing editor of the Courier. Together, we continued to edit the magazine for two more years. A group of editors sharing in the responsibilities took over after that.

About this time, Peggy was becoming less enamored with her job in Lincoln and wanted to change to something more challenging. She had been volunteering at the Citizen's Advice Bureau one evening a week and had gotten to know a lawyer who was helping there. After discussions with us, she decided to go back to the university to prepare for the more demanding career of law. We agreed to finance this if she could get accepted with her Art History degree. She was accepted at University of Sussex for a one-year course, to be followed by a two years of study to pass exams, and then apprenticeship. We were proud of her decision. Carol, also, found she needed special qualifications in addition to her degree in order to teach. We knew she would be a wonderful teacher, so offered to help her, and she attended a teacher's training course at the University of Bath, and later got a job teaching Biology in Yeovil, south of Butleigh.

In March of 1977, I flew to England for a week while Bob was in Kuwait for the Institute. Immediately afterward, we left together for a short vacation in southern Spain, flying in to Málaga. With a rented car, we explored the coast, going over to the Rock of Gibraltar and visiting Cadiz. Driving inland, we stayed in beautiful Seville, a favorite with me, then over the rolling hills to Granada. There, at the Alhambra, we marveled at the courtyards with their graceful arches and pools, and the profusion of gorgeous mosaics. Returning to the coast across the Sierra Nevada, we saw few people but an impressive landscape with acres of olive trees covering the hills. After a brief look at Málaga, we visited nearby Nerja to see the caves. I have always been drawn to caves, and those at Nerja were special since they played classical music as the visitors walked through. We arrived early and it was truly magical listening to Beethoven as we walked alone through these fanciful underground spaces formed by nature.

The highlight of May was the honor of meeting President Carter when he came to Geneva. As editor of the Courier, I was able to attend his news conference with President Assad of Syria. The thing I remember most of that conference was President Carter's remarks about how the Palestinians deserved a homeland, something that has not come about to this day.

Highlights of President Carter's visit were shown on the local TV and our neighbors in Founex were impressed to see me being greeted by him FIRST in a small group of American community leaders at the Intercontinental Hotel. From this experience, the farmers of Founex seemed to get the impression that I knew all of the U.S. presidents, and several years later when President Reagan came to Geneva one of them asked me when I was going to meet him!

Later in the spring, we took a short trip to Milan to see the famous cathedral there as well as the fading remains of the Leonardo da Vinci's Last Supper mural.

Time and the elements have done a lot of damage, but it was still worth seeing, and efforts are being made to save it. Milan is a cosmopolitan city—a shoppers paradise (if you are wealthy and into haute couture). We enjoyed looking and wandering around through the huge, high-ceilinged Galleria, and admiring the masses of flowers at the street markets around the *piazza* by the cathedral.

Steven passed an important milestone in the summer of 1977 when he graduated from Bristol University with a degree in Physics. All the family attended the ceremony and we were very proud of him. Meanwhile, he had been applying for graduate school in the U.S. and we were all thrilled when he was offered full fellowships at both MIT and Princeton. He chose Princeton and planned to enter in the autumn. To celebrate this, we took Steven with us on a trip to Ireland after his graduation.

The three of us took a train to Fishguard, on the coast, and then ferried over to Rosslare where we had arranged a car rental. It was our first trip to Ireland and we explored all kinds of castles, various ruins, churches with their Celtic crosses, and interesting villages.

The traffic was light and some of the roads were extremely narrow. Of course, since Steven was navigating, we often drove on little lanes with grass growing down the middle, or had to wait for sheep or donkeys to amble across. We went by Cork then Blarney Castle, and particularly enjoyed the isolated coves and lakes around the southern

peninsula. Near Glengariff, we stayed in a huge old hotel that had formerly been a castle. The headboard in our room was painted with a pastoral scene, the floor was uneven, and we had a magnificent, wide view over the water. I didn't want to leave, but was overruled, so we continued to explore, covering a lot of territory and falling in love with Ireland.

A new experience for Bob and me was attending a big Fête de Campagne in Stourbridge, England while visiting Carol and Mark in Butleigh. This annual affair is held on a beautifully landscaped estate, complete with lakes, gazebos, and paths, interspersed with waterfalls leading through trees and flowering shrubs. Everyone takes a picnic to enjoy while listening to the musical events. Mark's sister, Annabelle, and her husband were among those performing—playing in a string quartet. Small groups of musicians, puppeteers and clowns wandered around entertaining the crowd. It was a good family time with all our children there.

Switzerland was a perfect place to visit, and during various summers we were able to see several of our nieces. Among these, in addition to Miriam, they included Mayhoward, Janet, Bonnie, Cindy, as well as nephews Charlie and Robert. I would have loved to have had more of them visit and we always enjoyed showing them around.

Too soon it was time for Steven to leave, and Bob and I were alone again. To keep from feeling too lonely, we decided to revisit Paris to see the new Pompidou Center (Beaubourg), which had opened after we left. They were having a large exhibition of Impressionist paintings—some done by Frenchmen who had worked in Russia, and others by Russians who studied in Paris. While in Paris, we went to a "vernissage" of gravures done by my old art teacher, M. Goetz. It was good to see him again and we bought one of his etchings and one done by his artist wife.

Christmas 1977 was a particularly good time with all the children at home. We went skiing nearby and had parties with friends, but this was a time for big changes in all our lives. Except for holidays, the girls were busy with their studies and activities in England, and Steven was now away at Princeton. It was a new phase for Bob and me as we adjusted to our "empty nest".

Bob continued to make trips to Latin America, Africa and the Middle East. I began teaching a course in Design for a small group of artist friends. We met every week to explore different methods of artistic expression, covering such facets of design as line, shapes and tensions in creating space and form, and experiments with texture and color. I had the students use various media to explore these concepts—with drawing, painting and three-dimensional paper constructions. I also taught them the basic techniques of printing and making enamels. This was convenient since I had my own studio in the house, complete with an enamel kiln and a simple press. The approach was based mainly on experimentation and self-discovery. I gave two consecutive courses and enjoyed them both, although they did require a lot of work. Later, mostly for my own satisfaction, I wrote a book based on my teaching, which I called Creative by Design, but I will probably never try to it get published, since there is a lot of competition out there!

Early in 1978 Bob and I flew to the States for home leave, stopping by England to see the girls on the way, then visiting Steven in Princeton. He was sharing a suite in the Graduate Hall, a lovely old building with a huge Katsura tree in the courtyard. He enjoyed showing us around, in spite of the snowy February weather, then went with us by train to Washington where we had a few days of sightseeing. We saw the Space Museum for the first time, a place that later became one of Steven's favorite museums. From Washington, Bob and I visited his mother and other relatives, before returning to Switzerland.

Bob continued to travel, going to Argentina to direct another course, and later lecturing in Nigeria. This proved to be a traumatic few days for him, dealing with prevalent corruption on all sides, especially at the airport in Lagos.

He arrived home with his suit stained and the handle of his attaché case hanging loose, after having to bribe officials and fight his way through at every stage of the boarding process just to get his confirmed seat on the plane. He vowed never to return under those conditions.

In May 1978, Bob and I went to Yugoslavia for a week. We got a flight and hotel package, then rented a car rather than taking any of the tours offered. Everyday, we headed in opposite directions from the tour buses—by design. Our attractive hotel looking over the sea was in Cavtat just south of Dubrovnik.

The weather was ideal as we explored the city as well as the coastal area, seeing parts of the country not usually visited by foreigners. The natural beauty of the scenery, with twisted trees framing breathtaking views over the water and the small towns clustered around inlets or scattered up the foothills, made each day a delightful surprise. I cherish the memory of a delicious lunch at an outdoor restaurant looking over the port in a small southern town. Dubrovnik was unique of course, the walls of the fortress city jutting into the sea. In addition to visiting numerous churches, we followed the steep steps angling up the hill above the main part of town to find lively plazas with markets and small shops. At that time, Yugoslavia was still a communist country ruled by Tito, but there seemed to be a lot of private enterprise going on, and the atmosphere was optimistic and friendly. It is sad to think of the later years of turmoil and horrible bloodshed that ripped the country apart.

After I stopped spending so much of my time editing the Courier, I had strong withdrawal symptoms for awhile, and to counteract this touch of depression, I turned again to my violin, which had been more or less neglected for some years. I took it to the expert luthier (violin maker) in Geneva for repairs and to have the bow rehaired, then began a routine of practicing everyday. After some months I regained confidence and gradually reestablished some of my technique. This experience taught me, once again, the importance of music making in my life, and I've enjoyed playing the violin through the years— especially when I need a lift of spirits.

Summer is a lovely time in Switzerland. In June, Carol, Mark, Peggy and a friend from Lewes drove over from England. The lilacs were in full bloom and cascades of clematis draped over the sides of the deck of the house to the terrace below. A small larch which Steven and I had brought back from a mountain hike and planted a year or two before, already reached above the deck.

During the visit, we went up into the mountains to pick wild narcissus again and to appreciate the wildflowers carpeting the slopes. What is so rare as those days in June—perfect days to remember.

Later in the year, while Bob was on an extended trip, I flew to London and rented a small mews house in the Kensington area for a week. Peggy was taking a special law course in Guilford and she managed to commute to stay with me when she didn't have lectures. We both appreciated how nice it was to have a place of our own instead of staying at a hotel. I was enamoured with the British theater and wanted to see as many plays as I could during the time I was there. When I offered to treat any of the children who could go with me, amazingly, they arranged things beautifully! I figured that I bought a total of 18 play tickets during that week, for Peggy and myself and also for Carol and Mark who managed to come over from Butleigh. It was an expensive, but fabulous week!

Next spring we had a nice surprise when Peggy managed to come to Geneva during Easter vacation, joining us for a "gourmet" trip to Provençe that we had planned. We drove around to many of our favorite places and as usual sought out Michelin star restaurants. I remember delicious meals in Avignon (especially the *boule de neige*), in Nice and elsewhere. We wandered around the hillside market in Nice and enjoyed the warm sunshine of the waterfront promenade in the Jardin Anglais. We could only admire the courage of the few sunbathers on the beaches, as it was quite cool that spring. Having Peggy with us made it more fun, and together we explored Antibes, and some of the small towns above the coast.

The island of Corfu had always captured my imagination (as most islands do). In May 1979 Bob and I flew down to explore this part of Greece. As usual, we rented a small car and spent a delightful week driving through small villages and following narrow roads through groves of twisted olive trees. We found ourselves on the opposite side of the island at one point where we came upon graceful crescent beaches and rocky cliffs. There was a boatman nearby who took us to see some of the dramatic caves and rock formations extending around the coast. Turquoise water contrasted with the varied earth colors of the rock walls, creating another of Nature's masterpieces.

It was on one of these isolated beaches that we saw an older woman swimming energetically in the chilly sea. A woman friend was waiting on the shore and in a conversation with her I learned that her English companion swam everyday no matter where she was and in all kinds of weather, even in the English Channel in winter! I must admit she looked quite fit although she must have been well into her sixties.

Corfu is quite close to Albania, and although we would have liked to visit there, it was completely closed to tourists at that time. Instead, we decided to explore a bit of the coast of Greece opposite the island. We took a ferry to the mainland, and then boarded a bus south to the small town of Párga. The bus driver blared the current music at full volume all the way, which dimmed our enthusiasm for this part of the trip.

After a short stop in Párga, we took a boat to the nearby island of Paxoi. A day trip was all the time we needed to explore this small island. It had much natural beauty, however, with old olive trees and pines forming unforgettable views over the clear sea. That part of the world must be a delight for private cruising. After a rather basic country lunch, we headed back to the mainland and on to Corfu—just making the last ferry departure. After an overnight there, we flew back over the Alps to our Swiss home with our souls refreshed.

When Steven arrived home from Princeton, we asked him to name three things he would like best for us to do during the summer. He chose a balloon ride over the Alps, a return trip to Paris and a trip to the Riviera. Quite a choice!

We had often dreamed of sailing gently up over fields and hills watching people, animals and houses get smaller and smaller; and we arranged to fly from

Château-dOex, a few hours drive from Geneva. Our balloon ride lived up to all our dreams, and as we lifted up, our spirits also rose. I admit I was a little taken aback when I first saw the rather rickety wicker basket which was to hold the three of us, plus the pilot, tanks of gas and the propane heater.

When we were given crash helmets it was too late to back out! After the balloon was inflated, we boarded quickly and soon rose, catching a gentle breeze that carried us down the valley. The pilot seemed to know all about air currents, sometimes skimming tops of trees a breath away as we passed over farm houses, frightened cows and curious people. I will never forget the extraordinary beauty of green fields sparkling with stars of Queen Anne's lace below us—a fanciful reflection of an emerald sky—impossible to see from any other vantage point.

The pilot had arranged for the balloon to be tracked as nearly as possible from a car on the ground in case the winds did not cooperate and we had to land in an inconvenient spot. Luckily, we set down safely right in the middle of a campsite, much to the delight of all, especially the pilot, who was offered a drink to celebrate his success, in good Swiss fashion.

Following Steven's other choices, we revisited favorite places in Paris one sunny weekend, bringing back pleasant memories of the year we had lived there. The trip to Provençe and the Riviera also more than lived up to expectations, since this time we visited some of the hill villages above Cannes and the Maritime Alps, seeing dramatic gorges and streams we had not seen before.

After Peggy finished her law exams she continued her apprenticeship as an articled clerk (as they are called in England) in the attractive town of Lewes in Sussex. She had rented a small apartment in a private house, but this was not too satisfactory, so we considered buying a place in Lewes for her to use and as an investment for us. We found a tiny town house, with three floors and rooms only 10 ft. wide, across from the wooded park looking up to the castle on the hill in the center of town. To get a bit more space, we had an architect add a hall and kitchen to extend back from the large room. With new banisters, fresh paint and carpeting, it was an attractive place. A small garden behind the house rose up the hill to trees and shrubs. Peggy moved in happily with her black cat, Titch.

In the autumn, Bob was asked to take another trip to Argentina. Since he would be there for quite awhile, I decided to fly to the U. S., stay in New York for a short while, then meet Bob later in Nashville. Steven came up from Princeton for the weekend and stayed with me at the Elysee, a small hotel famous for one of its previous occupants, Tennessee Williams. I later heard he had committed suicide there! Steven and I explored the major sights, going to the Trade Center Towers (new at that time), Chinatown, Greenwich Village, Rockefeller Center and other places.

From New York, I took the train to Baltimore where I visited an old friend from WAVE days, Marjorie Foley. She insisted on driving me to Washington where I was to fly on to North Carolina to see my sisters before meeting Bob in Nashville. We reminisced and drank John Collins as we waited for my delayed plane. Later, when Marjorie came to visit us in Switzerland, we were able to repay her for her kindness by taking her for a short visit to Provençe.

In late summer of 1979 we invited Carol to join us for a trip to the Lake District of England, which I had long wanted to see. These few days were precious to us, as we had not had much time with Carol alone for a number of years. I was excited to be visiting where the Romantic poets, Wordsworth and Coleridge had centered their lives, as I had always been drawn to them when studying literature earlier. We drove through Windermere, along the lake and up to Grasmere where in Dove Cottage, Wordsworth had lived for some years with his sister, Dorothy. It was a small, modest house, bringing forth images of life during those years of the early nineteenth century. Later, when we were visiting another of Wordsworth's houses, now a museum, in Ambleside, we were thrilled to meet a direct descendant of his, Mary Wordsworth, who graciously signed a copy of Dorothy Wordsworth's Journals for us.

From Grasmere, we took long walks in the hills around the lakes and I felt close to the Romantic poets, realizing how they could have been inspired by the natural beauty of the countryside. Before driving Carol back to Somerset, we also visited the home of Beatrix Potter, high above one of the lakes. It was not hard to visualize Peter Rabbit and his little friends scampering around the garden.

In the autumn of 1979 Bob had to direct a two-week course at Trinity College in Dublin. I flew over to Lewes for a short visit with Peggy, then flew to Dublin to meet Bob for the last days of his course. It was my first visit there and I loved wandering around the city, seeing the Book of Kells at Trinity College and the numerous second-hand bookstores nearby. I stayed by myself in a small hotel near the campus, since Bob was housed elsewhere. The weather at that time was typically "Irish". There was an almost imperceptible mist in the air most days, much like the weather I remembered in Lima. The Irish, always friendly, would say, "Isn't it a lovely, soft day?" To use an umbrella was considered strange.

Bob and I enjoyed trying various Irish dishes and one night we went to see a John Synge play at the famous Abbey Theater, where "The Playboy of the Western World" was first produced early in the century—causing a riot at that time. After Bob's course was over, we rented a car and drove west to visit the area around Galway. It was an interesting, and at times beautiful, drive, but I decided that I preferred the southern peninsula, which we had explored with Steven. But both of us loved Ireland and the Irish people and promised ourselves a return visit.

XIII

AROUND THE WORLD

The high point of 1980 was our round-the-world trip. Since the children were more or less on their own, Bob and I felt that we deserved this trip that we had dreamed of. We saved up all our leave and began making plans, choosing and arranging for hotels and side-trips. Because of Bob's work, we had to go in the summer and we left Geneva in mid-July.

We boarded our Pan Am plane in England to start our adventure, flying first to Frankfurt then to Bahrain. Food and seating arrangements were quite good. I was amused to overhear a comment by one young, harassed flight attendant as he balanced a pile of snack trays: "Mother said to become a doctor, but no, I wanted to see the world!"

Our first layover was in New Delhi. Not an auspicious beginning, in the 109-degree heat at 2 a.m. after 12 hours on the plane. It took us an hour and a half to get our two suitcases through customs. Luckily, we had booked a suite in an air-conditioned hotel and were greeted "warmly" with fresh flowers. The next day we hired a car and guide for a tour of Old Delhi. High points were the huge Red Fort and the intricately carved minaret called Quth Minar standing in a park of ruins, columns and arches. The local people insisted I reach back to touch my hands together around the iron obelisk there, which never rusts although it is ages old. This is supposed to bring good luck. With much stretching of my arms by "helpers" I managed it (with only a few bruises later).

In Delhi we saw many beautiful palaces and homes—but also many hovels. There were more people than one can imagine—on bicycles, buses, cars, walking or riding in small "honeymoon" cabs or rickshaws. The sacred cows wandered through the crowds and we even saw an elephant being used for advertising of some kind. The heat was intense, so we got out of the mildly air-conditioned car only for short periods. There was unbelievable poverty on all sides—squatters living in appalling conditions, tiny children running freely everywhere. All kinds of items were sold from carts lining the streets. Pineapple and other fruit, cut in pieces, looked refreshing—not safe enough to chance, however.

We visited various craft shops and bought a well-made oriental rug in one of them (probably from a cousin of our guide!).

The next day we took an all-day trip to Agra. The bus, supposedly air-conditioned, was barely tolerable as it was jammed with people. The road, though

117

mostly paved, was rough and full of holes—some of which were being repaired. The driver blew his horn constantly during the long trip. Most of the trucks on the road had names painted on them and were decorated with tinsel, pictures of Jesus and other things. We stopped briefly for a snack at an oasis-type restaurant after about two hours. There we were entertained by a monkey, bears and a huge python wrapped around a man's neck!

After driving through the town of Agra, we arrived at the Taj Mahal, stopping on the way to see several mosques and palaces built by earlier moguls (military rulers). The Taj itself was a fabulous sight and not too crowded when we were there. I can understand why people recommend seeing it in the moonlight. Unfortunately, we were there at noon in 115-degree heat! With the aid of a hat and umbrella, however, I managed. It is truly a unique monument, both in its beauty and inspiration—a jewel, built by mogul Emperor Shahjahan for his beloved queen, Mumtaz Mahal. Later we visited the Agra Red Fort, center of the mogul dynasty, with its beautiful inlaid marble, carvings in relief, painted ceiling and graceful arches. The mausoleum of Akbar was another fabulous structure. The drive back to New Delhi was not too uncomfortable, becoming cooler as the day faded. On the way, we saw many women on the horizon in colorful saris carrying jugs on their heads, coming from the communal wells in the countryside—an affecting sight against the afterglow of the sunset.

The following day, Bob had to fly to Bombay for some Institute business. I opted to rest in the air-conditioned hotel after our trip to Agra. I remember when I told the houseboys, as they serviced the room, that my husband had gone away, they thought I had been abandoned, and expressed sincere sympathy! Happily, he returned in the evening and we had a typical Indian dinner, accompanied by Indian musicians playing sitars, violins, drums and other instruments—rather haunting songs, perfect for the setting. We left two days later, our minds and hearts touched by the beauty and the poverty of India. We are happy to hear that conditions have improved somewhat in recent years.

In Bangkok, we found the customs people to be more gracious than the officious ones in New Delhi. Since it was mid-summer, we opted for the best hotels we could manage on our trip, especially in countries where it would be more difficult to cope with second-rate accommodations. We had chosen the famous Oriental Hotel in Bangkok, and had lucked into a room on an upper floor overlooking the canal. This represented the high point of our choices in more ways than one, as it had such extras as candy, fruit and flowers in the room and perfect service.

There were so many things to see that it was hard to decide where to begin. We started at the Grand Palace grounds with its ornately decorated temples. Among the treasures, we saw the Temple of the Emerald Buddha with carvings of animals and monsters in unusual settings. There was a lot of gold leaf, with every surface decorated in some way. Near the huge reclining Buddha, the saffron-robed priests and novices wandering around added to the unique atmosphere. The whole complex was a mixture of religion and on-going fair.

Of course we had to take a canal tour to the floating market. It was a colorful and interesting excursion if a bit touristy. In the afternoon, we went to see Jim Thompson's house (now a museum of his treasures). He was the American who settled there and became famous for developing the raw silk trade in the region. A leafy garden, lush plants, shady walks and a small patio surround the wooden structure he had made by joining four old houses. Everything was beautifully fashioned from teak—a delightful place. We bought a few samples of the colorful elegant silk before heading back to the hotel in one of the little three-wheeled carts we had seen scooting around. A Siamese dinner in the hotel's restaurant by the river was followed by a performance of Thai dancers.

In Hong Kong we stayed in a big, modern hotel (The Hong Kong), which is in Kowloon just next to the ferry going over to Hong Kong Island. We managed to arrange for a room overlooking the bay.

It was impossible to resist some of the bargains at the huge shopping complex next to the hotel. Bob bought a camera and bought me a beautiful ring with small emeralds and diamonds, as souvenirs of our trip. Later, we found an antique intricately carved wooden wall hanging, illustrating a Chinese couple's fiftieth anniversary. We had this shipped home, along with an old Chinese print and other things. We finished our busy day with good Indonesian food at a restaurant overlooking the mosaic of lights in the harbor.

While exploring some of the busy streets, and visiting the famous Peninsula Hotel the next day, we chanced upon a puppet show in the concourse, with almost life-sized puppets. We couldn't understand a bit of what was going on, but it was interesting to see. That evening as we relaxed in our happi coats and watched the changing view over the harbor, we realized how fortunate we were to be in a part of the world we had only dreamed about.

Both of us wanted to see a bit of nearby China, so we arranged a day tour into Canton offered by the hotel travel office. During the train trip to the border, we managed to communicate with a few of the friendly native Chinese, who were returning home loaded down with electric fans and other appliances not available in China. We did not have our passports stamped in or out of China, to avoid complications when we went to Taiwan, which we had arranged as a side trip from Hong Kong.

In Canton, we drove with a small group to the town of Shum Chun City, one of the "show places" being developed near the border to attract tourists. There was only one street and one traffic light for the population of over 300,000. People were much poorer than in Hong Kong. We saw women wearing the typical straw hat with a black, ruffled band hanging down around the edge. Whether this was to protect from the dust or the flies, we didn't know.

Our lunch at a modern circular restaurant was Cantonese cooking and very good, as was the beer. At the Friendship store (open only to foreigners) we couldn't resist the beautiful jade, and bought a few pendants as souvenirs.

The tour stopped at a kindergarten, where the little children were like precious dolls as they danced and played a few games for us. On all sides, we noticed that the children seemed to be cherished. They begin school at 7 yrs. and are educated until they are 16, with the bright ones able to go on to the University. In contrast, all through the area we saw men and women carrying heavy loads balanced on the ends of bamboo poles over the shoulders, just as in pictures we had seen. This brief tour gave us an enlightening glimpse of China, even between the staged events.

Thai Airlines was quite a change from Pan Am. Their planes were violet colored and were brightly decorated inside. Hostesses wore Thai silk uniforms and the women passengers were given small orchid corsages. In Taipei we had reserved a room in the Grand Hotel, where to our delight, we were installed in a luxurious suite, since no normal rooms were available until the next day. The Grand Hotel, a huge, square structure on a hill overlooking the city, had been built by Madame Chiang Kai-shek. The architecture is unusual, with large red and gold columns; and the lobby, three or four stories high, is lavishly decorated with carved wooden panels and gilt decorations. From our suite, we looked out from a balcony flanked by columns to the winding Kee Lung River. There are five large restaurants in the hotel, as well as the usual shops. A bookstore in the basement was especially intriguing, since there we found all the latest books in English as well as such things as sets of Encyclopedia Britannica and other publications from both the U.S and England. They were priced fabulously low, since it seems they don't pay any royalties for these books. The paper some of them were printed on was not of first quality, but we could not resist a few of the bargains. After an inexpensive but delicious dinner in one of the hotel restaurants, we were able to listen to classical and semi-classical music on the radio in our room. The TV was all in Chinese, in contrast to Hong Kong, which has several English stations.

We were up early the next day to visit the National Palace Museum—the main reason we chose to fly over to Taiwan. We took a taxi to the museum, and since we spoke no Chinese, we had the hotel clerk write down the name of our destination, also taking a hotel card to show the driver on the way back. This worked quite well, except the taxi gave out of gas halfway! After a bit of gesturing and displaying indignation (in English, which of course he didn't understand) he helped us get another cab on to the museum. We spent a long morning marveling at the fabulous treasures found there. All the best art works of mainland China had been brought over by Chiang Kai-shek at the time of the communist takeover. Early porcelain—delicate, with lovely glazes, intricately carved jade of all kinds, and other things took our breath away. There were many minute objects carved from ivory—whole little city scenes, which are viewed through a magnifying glass. The paintings and scrolls are beautiful with all the important Chinese artists represented, and the calligraphy exhibit was especially interesting. We bought several reproductions of scroll paintings and other things, and had them sent home to Switzerland.

During the afternoon we explored a bit of downtown Taipei. In an antique shop in "Haggler's Alley" we found a lovely old carved pendant and a small green porcelain brush bowl from the Ching Dynasty. With our treasures, we walked around some of the other busy streets, observing the normal life, and buying some carved signature seals. On the way back to the hotel, we noticed that most of the people riding bicycles or motorbikes wore masks over their faces because of the heavy pollution, which we had also noticed when walking around.

Before leaving Taiwan we wanted to see more of the island, so arranged and early flight to see the Taroko Gorge to the east of Taipei. We joined a small group of tourists, mostly Chinese, and flew to the town of Hualien just 20 minutes away. There, we joined others in an air-conditioned bus for the 12-mile drive up the gorge.

It was a dramatic trip, through beautiful marble cliffs alongside a rushing stream. The narrow road twisted back and forth, going through more than 30 tunnels. The driver stopped occasionally for photos of the steep drops to waterfalls and colorful rocks below. At lunch time, we had a Cantonese meal with some friendly Chinese at Tien Hsiang Lodge. We wished, again, that we could speak a bit of their language. Afterward, we walked over a suspension bridge and climbed the hill to the shrine high above the valley. We were told this is a memorial to Tien Hsiang, a scholar warrior of the 13th century, who was executed when he refused allegiance to his mogul captors.

On the drive back, we stopped to see a demonstration of dances by the Ami aborigines who live in that area. The beautiful young girls dancing wore bells on their ankles and sometimes on their arms. As in so many things all over China, the predominant colors, red and gold, were used almost exclusively in the costumes. Back in Taipei, at dinner we found carrots cut in the shape of goldfish!

On July 1 we drove to the airport for our short flight back to Hong Kong, passing several unusual temples on the way. Back on the mainland, we found they had reserved our same room for us, overlooking the harbor. It was a bit like getting home. Since it was still early, we decided to explore the island of Hong Kong, so took the Star ferry across, then took a taxi ride around the island and up to the top of the Peak funicular. The drive was beautiful in the late afternoon light, curving through the leafy roads of the residential sections. At the top, we took a long walk near Peak station taking photos, then stopped for tea at the top of the tower to watch the sun set over the harbor. It was one of those perfect times that will remain in my memory. We lingered until dusk, then took the funicular down the mountain. On the way to the ferry, we stopped to see the famous Mandarin Hotel. I didn't find it exceptional, but the ladies room there is the most elaborate I have ever come across—even the porcelain toilets had blue flower decorations.

Back in our hotel, we found fresh fruit in our room—a nice ending to our stay in Hong Kong. The next day, we flew to Tokyo, arriving at Narika airport in early evening.

Our hotel, the Ginza Dai Ichi, was a large, business-type hotel, well located for exploring the city center. We planned to see Tokyo on our own, so with maps in hand we set out early the next day. We first explored the main Ginza area, which has all kinds of elegant shops as well as smaller, more interesting ones, displaying fine fabrics and delicate porcelain, along with more ordinary objects. We bought some small household items in a large department store and marveled over the array of every kind of food you could imagine on sale in the basement there, including sun-dried meats, fruits, salads and fish. Many of the cafés we saw along the streets had plastic models in the windows of all their menu offerings. When trying one of these places, we found the food did not live up to the plastic model.

Later we had a taxi driver take us to the Museum of Modern Art, with a slight detour since he had never heard of it and spoke no English. We had marked our maps, however, and with a bit of help from another Japanese, we finally got there. The museum was showing a special textile exhibition that was outstanding, although I didn't find the other things shown to be exceptional. Across from the museum we visited the Imperial Palace Gardens. I remember shady walks, huge trees and unusual shaped hedges—undulating in artistic ways around the shrubbery and small trees.

There were many things to remember from our first day in Tokyo. We had seen a man walking on stilted sandals, had found "salad bowel" listed on a menu, and noticed the tiny cream servers and the half-full glasses of water always served us. The sidewalks of the main streets were very wide in the Ginza area, and everyone was extremely polite. In the smaller streets, many of the houses had short cloth "banners" hanging in the doorways—most inviting.

Breakfast next day was in a busy Japanese place called Café Endless. We sat at a low table with coffee, a dish of fried egg salad and very thick toast. It was all good and inexpensive. Afterwards we visited the Riccar Art Museum, which had some wonderful block prints on display.

Later, we left for our trip to Kyoto, which was high on our list of places to see in Japan. We had reserved seats on the fast Shinkansen "bullet" train—an experience in itself. It was well equipped with carpeted footrests, a side table and lots of room. There was a western style W.C., as well as the usual oriental one. Bob and I had bought sandwiches and juice before boarding the train, so we relaxed and enjoyed watching the countryside as we sped south. Most of the houses we saw seemed to have a two-tiered roof with the top floor smaller— quite attractive.

In Kyoto, we stayed in a tiny Japanese hotel, Three Sisters Inn, which had been recommended to us. We entered through a small gate and followed a winding path through the trees and shrubs. Halfway to the house itself, there was an inviting bench with a basin of water and a wooden ladle beside it. Rocks and ferns were in artistic groupings along the way. Inside, we removed our shoes before stepping on the tatami mats, and were welcomed by the couple that owned the inn. They offered us Japanese "cider" (rather like 7-Up, but welcome), then gave us a map and explained a bit about the city.

Our suite was a delight—opening out into a small, private garden, beautifully arranged yet still natural looking. Stepping-stones led one through the peaceful setting. The room was equipped with a low table with a tea set and a thermos of hot water (tea on demand!). Flowered happi coats and slippers were provided for each guest, and our mattresses were on the floor, Japanese style. The adjoining bathroom was small, but spotlessly clean and had a sunken tub. All this was a unique experience for us—ideal for a relaxing stay.

Later we explored nearby handicraft places and had a truly Japanese meal at an attractive restaurant on a canal. Everything was served in tiny, different shaped dishes, with such things as two little olives arranged on a porcelain leaf. Back in our room, we closed the paper-paneled sliding doors to the garden and the filtered light added to the peaceful atmosphere as we fell asleep.

The beauties of the many temples and shrines in Kyoto are too numerous to mention in detail. At the Nijojo Castle, after removing our shoes, we were allowed to see all the ornately decorated rooms with painted ceilings and beautiful carved sections. There was a large reception area where the old Shogun sat when receiving visitors.

In the extensive gardens, everything was perfectly placed for the overall effect. Wherever you looked you saw a balanced arrangement of natural things—composed with thought for detail and beauty of the changing seasons. The azaleas, clipped in flowering hedges, were still holding a few blossoms here and there—as if forgotten by the passing spring.

We had to get permission to visit the Imperial Palace grounds (not allowed inside the Palace itself). The huge carved gateways, different ones for people of different status—one for the Emperor, another for high officials, were most impressive.

We both wanted to see Nara, not far from Kyoto, so early the next day, we managed to take a local train—happily surprised when it arrived at the proper destination. There, we wandered around the large park, mingling with the tame deer as well as with the masses of people. We were stopped several times by students who wished to practice their English. The highlight of this visit was seeing the mammoth bronze Buddha built in 745-749. This must have been a tremendous undertaking, impossible to imagine. We also saw the golden bell tower and the beautiful Kasuga-taisha shrine. The small streets nearby were interesting, and I bought some Japanese brushes, a brush rack and a water holder before we took the express train back to Kyoto. There, since it was still early, we visited the Higashiyama-ku area, a large, park-like setting on a hill overlooking Kyoto. It has many shrines—both Buddhist and Shinto—the old, wooden structures with pointed roof corners, weathered and lovely.

On July 7, the day before we were to leave, we went to the Katsura Imperial Villa on the other side of Kyoto. We had to get permission ahead of time to visit, as we had done for the Imperial Palace. The gardens were even more beautiful, set around a small lake with little islands, stone lanterns and a tea house. The graceful Golden Pavilion, opposite, was reflected in the lake.

When we visited the Shinto Gion Shrine, we noticed paper prayers had been twisted onto small trees and shrubs around the central area. Huge bell pulls hung down before some of the images and we saw several people come to ring the bell and offer a prayer. As in most of the Shinto shrines, the Gion had an orange-red entrance gate, with this same color combination used in the other buildings.

On the way back to the hotel, we visited downtown Kyoto—a real contrast to the serene gardens we had seen, but interesting even so. There I saw a young Geisha girl, with her elaborate dress and hairdo, her powdered white face showing no emotion as she waited to cross the street.

The next day we got ready to leave, carrying with us many impressions—the bird calls at street crossings when the lights change, each one different; the hot wash cloths handed to us before every meal; the way the men are usually served first in the restaurants; and the very small cups of tea that are always placed before you when you arrive to eat, rather like the glasses of water they serve in the U.S. I also noted that the taxi doors pop out at you automatically and don't open when you arrive at your destination until you've paid the fare. Perhaps the most lasting memory, however, was the politeness of everyone we encountered.

After taking the fast train back to Tokyo, we had only a few hours before our flight to Hawaii. As we boarded our plane, we were both glad that even in a short visit, we had been able to learn a bit about Japan and Japanese life.

The flight to Hawaii was long, but not too bad since we had extra seat space and were able to get some sleep. Crossing the date line meant that when we arrived at 9 a.m. it was the same day we had left Tokyo the evening before!

In Honolulu we stayed in a small apartment that had been recommended to us by a friend. It was a bit depressing, but was in a perfect location and quite inexpensive. Also, it was only a short walk to Waikiki beach, where we took a dip in the ocean the first morning. We only ate breakfast in the apartment, opting for some of the good restaurants nearby for our other meals.

No need to describe Honolulu, which is a bit like Disneyland with every kind of shop or restaurant you can imagine—many shopping arcades, with such things as fountains or banyan trees. Our main pleasure in Honolulu was going to the big hotels for meals or to have a cocktail while looking out over Waikiki beach and Diamond Head. One evening, we took a "pedicart" (bicycle driven) to the Hilton's Hawaiian Village, and another night we had dinner in the Oceanarium Restaurant, looking out and up to a two-story water tank filled with unusual fish. Naturally we ordered the fish platter!

Our most interesting days in Hawaii, however, were spent out of Honolulu. One day, we rented a small car and explored the whole island of Oahu. We saw lovely little beaches between rocky outcroppings—the jade-green water breaking into foamy white sprays as it reached the shore. The small towns were not unlike those found in other parts of the U.S., except for the lush tropical foliage on all sides—bougainvillea, hibiscus, oleander hedges, yellow flowering canaris, "flamboyantes", palm trees and other things we couldn't identify. We also saw papayas, mangoes, sugarcane and coffee growing on all sides. Mother and Dad would have loved it.

In the afternoon we visited beautiful Wainea Falls, then drove through the center of the island, which was more mountainous than the hilly areas along the coast. In the central plateau there are huge plantations of pineapple (Libby and Del Monte) extending for miles. As we neared Honolulu again, we passed Pearl Harbor, but didn't stop since it was getting late.

Another wonderful day on this trip was our airplane excursion over all the major islands. We joined a small group and took off in three small planes. There were about 8 or 9 passengers in each one, with 2 pilots accompanying (and offering informative comments). Our plane led the group in a Cessena 404, with each of us having a window seat to enjoy the dramatic scenery. We flew over Oahu, then Lanai, the principal pineapple island. Next was the completely deserted island of Kahoolawe (being used for bombing practice by the military—with some opposition). We landed on Hawaii, called the Big Island by most people and the Orchid Island by others. Before landing there, we flew low over the fascinating volcano area—smoking and dangerous looking in places. Here the world's largest active volcano, the Mauna Loa, is found. There were numerous narrow waterfalls along the coast, formed because the rain cannot be absorbed in the large volcanic area inland. While on Hawaii, we visited an orchid "farm", with a fantastic display of a multi-colored blooms.

On the isle of Maui, we saw the famous Seven Pools at the base of the inactive volcano, Haleakala. We landed at Hana, a remote area where many people, including Ann Lindbergh, had established hideaways. (Charles Lindbergh is buried there.) After lunch at a ranch-type restaurant, we flew over the "leper island" of Molokai, one peninsula of which is still inhabited by these unfortunate people.

We flew back over Oahu and on over Nilhau, an island that allows only native Hawaiians to live there, and where no visitors are admitted unless personally invited. We were able to land on the "garden" island of Kauai with its magnificent canyon area of red rocks dropping in a jagged line to form the "Grand Canyon of the Pacific". Its spectacular cliffs overlooked attractive beaches.

After landing at Lihue airport, we drove to the Wailua River where we took a short boat ride to the Fern Grotto—beautiful, but too touristy, we thought (including the hula dancers performing on the boat). Back in the plane, we flew low over Pearl Harbor as we came in to land on Oahu, ending our last day in this unique part of the U.S.

We arrived back on mainland U.S. on July 13th, and were met by Austin and Art at the Los Angeles airport (a truly hectic place!). We had a brief visit with them at their attractive house in Claremont, where they both worked. They spoiled us with a champagne breakfast the next morning before showing us around Claremont and Pasadena.

We wanted to see all the relatives we could on this trip, and our next stop was to visit Rosemary, Bob and family in San Antonio. It was good to see them again and catch up on family news. We visited the site the Bible Study Fellowship was developing outside San Antonio. Rosemary served as Director of this large organization, which made it particularly interesting to see.

We stopped over in Nashville to visit Bob's mother and the other relatives there. We saw Don and Bette's houseboat, and I had an exciting ride in Don's speedboat, while Don, Jr. demonstrated his expertise on water skis.

From Nashville, we stopped briefly in the Carolinas to see the Thunes and the Youngs, then following a rather tight schedule, we flew to New York and drove to Princeton, where we had a joyful reunion with Steven. We saw his lab and met his housemate, Andy, and some of his other friends.

While in Princeton, we were able to stay in a nice apartment by offering a swap for accommodations in Switzerland the following summer. This was arranged with the reluctant help of Steven, ("Mom, no-one will be interested in swapping a place!"). Several people called, as I had thought they would. We stayed in Lisa Smith's apartment right in the center of town. She was an attractive young woman, a free-lance journalist and editor who was working in New York City.

While with Steven, we took a trip to the Pocano Mountains of Pennsylvania, driving through beautiful woodland areas and spending the night at a resort on a small lake. On the way back, we followed the Delaware River to visit Buskill Falls.

After returning to New York, we boarded the plane for England, arriving there on July 30th. Then we flew on to Switzerland, finishing our unforgettable round-the-world adventure 46 days after we started.

XIV

YEARS OF CHANGE

Events seemed to move even more rapidly during the 1980s. The children were leading active lives following their careers and Bob was working hard at the ILO Institute. In addition to other activities, I had started a study group of fellow artists living nearby. We met every week, either to see a video of an art related subject or to discuss some particular exhibition. Occasionally we took excursions to see art shows in nearby towns. I have kept in touch with many of these women through the years.

We arranged our busy lives to take trips whenever possible. After Peggy finished her legal studies and became a qualified solicitor in the autumn of 1980, she vacationed in Provençe with friends, then called us saying she would like to visit before returning to England, if I could drive her back. It appealed to me as a fun adventure with my daughter alone, so after a short stay in Founex, she and I took off, stopping overnight before we skirted around Paris. We managed to see Versailles on the way, as well as eating some delicious meals, guided by starred Michelin recommendations. We lingered over our last lunch before going on to Dieppe to take the ferry to Newhaven. We had no reservation and drove up just as the last car was boarding, by luck managing to squeeze on instead of waiting several hours.

It was a great trip and it was only when I realized that I would have to drive back alone that I had a few misgivings. Bob was too busy to fly over, so I set out, prepared to take things as they came. The ferry trip went well, but the weather worsened as I approached Paris. I planned to go around the *peripherique,* but as short a distance as possible. It was a nightmare in the rain with huge trucks speeding along on both sides. I had counted how many exits before I was to get off, and since I couldn't see any of the exit signs (blocked by trucks in the right lane), I just hoped I had made the right decision when I crossed over to get off. My guardian angel was with me, as it was the exit I wanted. The rest of the trip was less traumatic, although I did have an unpleasant experience when some guy kept following me on the autoroute, then passing and slowing down while gesturing for me to stop and have a drink with him. I decided to outwit him, so indicated a turn off at the next exit, and at the last minute I switched lanes and sped away. I'm sure he must have had bad eyesight or else was desperate for company. I was relieved to get home to Geneva, proud that I had made the trip alone but convinced that was not an experience I would repeat.

Bob and I toured Portugal in the early spring of 1981, flying over to Lisbon and renting a car for a week. There, after exploring the old Alfama section of the city and the castle high on the hill overlooking the harbor, we drove around the peninsula to the attractive city of Cascais where the black and white cobblestone sidewalks are arranged in undulating patterns. Continuing around the dramatic coastline, we were impressed with the huge cliffs and crashing waves alternating with crescent beaches, a contrast to the hills around Sintra.

Before continuing our explorations north, we stopped on the outskirts of Lisbon to see the fabulous Hieronymite Monastery—the most ornate, overly decorated building I have ever seen. A real hodgepodge of styles, it had been developed over many centuries of seafaring explorers, beginning way back when Vasco da Gama was exploring India in the early 1500s.

Going north, we visited the fortified city of Obidos, then Alcobaca with its more classical monastery and cloister. When we arrived in the small fishing

village of Nazaré, the fishermen had returned from their early expeditions and had their nets stretched out and also had numerous racks of small fish arranged on screens to dry. Their boats of different colors with pointed bows and graceful shapes were beached along the sand—an inspiring sight for an artist and reminiscent of a particular Van Gogh painting I grew up with at home in Florida.

We stayed in several *posadas* in Portugal and found all of them pleasant. Many were established in interesting old abbeys or other historic structures. Oporto was our northernmost point of exploration, but we were a bit disappointed in that city, finding it too commercial. We did manage to see the Baroque cathedral there. It was dark inside and while looking at the Rose window, I stepped off a narrow step and fell flat on my face. Don't really have good memories of that town. We soon left and drove through attractive hills to Viseu. This was of particular interest because it was the site of one of the early painting schools in the 16th century.

Looping back toward Lisbon, we visited the fabulous gardens and hunting lodge in Bucaco forest. The lodge is now a hotel and we had a delicious lunch there, although we could not get rooms for the night. The gardens were full of huge shrubs—camellias, rhododendron of all colors and other flowering plants as big as small trees, arranged along twisting paths interspersed with small fountains and ponds. We would have liked to linger in this restful spot.

One vivid memory was when we wandered into the Convent of Christ church in Tomar late in the day. The afternoon light through the stained glass windows cast a multicolored glow on the interior arches, creating a unique masterpiece of color beyond the talent of an artist.

It was in Coimbra, once the capitol of Portugal and the site of an ancient university, where we stayed in an attractive *posada* that had been originally been an old abbey. It was easy to imagine silent monks wandering through the cloistered halls repeating their prayers.

We flew home from Lisbon with pleasant memories of Portugal to add to our collection of travel experiences.

Another trip we won't forget was one to Norway in July 1981. We especially wanted to see the "top of the world" at North Cape. From England, we flew to the interesting coastal town of Bergen, and then boarded the train to cross the mountain range to Oslo. The scenery during this trip was fantastic—views of snowy mountains mixed with lakes and broad plains.

Oslo impressed us with its sophistication and handsome young people, the majority of them tall and blond, as expected. Near Oslo we saw a huge, oddly shaped church, almost as large as a cathedral, dating from long ago and made entirely of wood. Our two days there gave us an overall view of the Norwegian life and a bit of the history as we visited some of their museums.

We then joined a small tour to fly up to the northernmost airport in Norway. From there, we took a bus on up to the Cape where we spent the night—if you can call it that! It makes for an eerie feeling when we are tuned to expect nightfall and it never gets dark, only a bit less light for an hour or so. Then, dramatic sunrise colors stained the sky, with the sun remaining quite close to the horizon. Quite a sight!

On the bus trip to and from the Cape, we saw groups of Laplanders beside the road, some with their reindeer, selling hides and other souvenirs. Our stops were brief as this was the season for numerous mosquitoes. After another day in Oslo, we flew back to England, then Switzerland—a short trip but one to remember.

A major event of 1981 was Steven's graduation from Princeton in late summer. He finished at the top of his group and we were very proud of him. After graduation, he was offered a post-doctoral fellowship at the National Bureau of Standards in Gaithersburg, Maryland near Washington, and began working there in the autumn. They wanted him enough to pay for a huge shipment of his things from Switzerland.

Another big event of 1981 was Peggy's marriage in late December. Allen Jones, a bright, attractive young graduate of Sussex seemed to be a good match for Peggy. They were married in Lewes with all the family congregating there, including Bob's mother, Ruth. Steven came over from the States with his current girlfriend. It was a civil ceremony, but solemn and proper. Peggy was radiant and lovely in her white wedding dress. I was happy for Peggy, but feeling sad at the same time. We celebrated the marriage with a reception luncheon and later there was a large dance and dinner at the community hall in Lewes Park with many friends of the couple joining the party.

After Peggy's marriage, she left the law firm in Lewes and joined one in London, where Allen was working as a systems analyst at British Petroleum. We kept the little house in Lewes for awhile, but eventually sold it to a widowed schoolteacher who taught nearby. I have fond memories of the time we spent there and remember the fun of exploring the Sussex countryside—wandering over the downs, visiting Brighton and the cliffs of the Seven Sisters. Another interesting visit was to Charleston, the farmhouse that was the home of some of the literary and artistic Bloomsbury circle. The rooms there are fancifully decorated with their paintings, including every surface of the walls, doors and fireplaces. It is truly an original museum of an era in British history and art.

It was a busy spring that year. When Peggy and Allen came over in March, we took them to Grindelwald to catch some of the last snow of the season. Allen had never skied before, but with Peggy's help was soon scooting down the easy slopes. In May, Bob was off on a trip to Caracas, and when he returned, we went to London for a joint birthday celebration for Peggy and me. Later that month, Lisa Smith, the young woman whose apartment we had used in Princeton earlier, arrived for a visit with her new husband, John Nielson, an editor for Time magazine. We enjoyed having them for a week and they managed to see a bit of Swiss life.

Our home leave in the summer of 1982 was special since another family reunion had been planned. The Thunes generously hosted the group in Black Mountain in July. Quite a few family members came, including most of the siblings, spouses and several of their children. Among the younger generation were Miriam and daughter, Maggie, Tova, Matthew, Don Jr., Ed and Steven, who drove down from Washington together. Peggy and Allen were also able to stop by, as they took

advantage of our wedding present trip to the States. We missed having Carol with us.

I had long wanted to visit the USSR, especially Russia, but even though I had been invited to accompany Bob when he went to Moscow and Alma Ata, Kazakhstan in 1980 to direct a course, I had refused because I was so incensed that the Soviet Union had invaded Afghanistan. Under the circumstances I felt I couldn't accept their hospitality with good grace. Two years later, however, I was able to rise above my principles when I was again invited to go with Bob to Tallinn, Estonia where he was to direct a three-week course. There was to be a stopover in Moscow, and later several days in Leningrad (as St. Petersburg was then called). This was too tempting to resist and I realized that this could well be my only chance to see this part of the world. In September 1982 the Iron Curtain was very much in evidence. My experiences were revealing and gave me a chance to realize how different life can be under a repressive regime.

During our one-day stay in Moscow, we were taken on an extensive tour of the city by private limousine, visiting the Kremlin's Red Square, Lenin's Tomb and the Tomb of the Unknown Soldier (where Bob was asked to lay a wreath, since the U.S. was a World War II ally). We visited the colorful, ornately domed jewel of St. Basil's Cathedral with its beautiful frescos, and viewed many other impressive cathedrals and towers, rising in splendor on all sides—imposing monuments to Russian art and architecture. Among other sights, I remember especially the Bell Tower of Ivan the Great. In addition to bells in the tower, the huge Tsar bell, largest in the world, stands at its base. Our visit was truly a feast for the eyes.

We were driven around Moscow with a stop to view Moscow State University from a nearby hill. I soon realized that in contrast to the magnificent older buildings in the Kremlin and elsewhere, the city's modern high-rise buildings showed little grace or imagination. There was no lightness or color anywhere. Huge pictures and statues of Lenin were on all sides in this depressing metropolis.

Driving down the broad boulevards, I saw that we were using the solitary center lane, with normal traffic on both sides. I was told that Government cars and VIPs had special privileges, which was a bit of a shock in what was supposedly an egalitarian society. Since we were guests of the government, we experienced this preferential treatment, just taken for granted by those in power. Unfortunately, we were not able to talk to any average people while in Moscow.

From Moscow, we had a special overnight train ride to Tallinn in Estonia. The trip was an unusual experience in itself. We had a fairly comfortable compartment and a good, light meal was brought to us. Our Russian host director was extremely friendly and kept offering alcoholic beverages. I was amazed at the amount of vodka that the Russians drank, both young and old, and practically everyone smoked one cigarette after another. Non-smoking areas were unheard of. We got to bed as early as we could manage graciously and did not see much of the countryside until the next morning as we arrived in Tallinn.

There we were greeted with bouquets of flowers and treated as objets d'art everywhere we went. Our luxurious suite in the 22-story Viru Hotel was supplied with fruit, wine and soft drinks daily and had a large TV with stations of Moscow, Leningrad, Estonia and Helsinki (without sound) available. We abandoned any attempt to get English news. Meals were copious and well served, our hosts thoughtful and friendly. Nothing to be desired, I thought, except independence and access to information—luxuries we take for granted. The woman floor attendant seated near the elevator seemingly checked each arrival and departure. The fire escape door at the end of the corridor was locked. The two small English-language newspapers available in the lobby (Moscow

News and Morning Star) were over a week old and politically biased beyond belief.

The mystery behind this stage set intrigued me. During the first few days, as we were driven around the Estonian countryside to state farms, collective farms, fish farms, agricultural research stations, *ad infinitum*, I had tantalizing glimpses of the past. Imposing old mansions in neglected estates were frequently seen. Some of these are kept as museums and also used as meeting places for the surrounding farm workers. In Tallinn, the larger churches, most of them architectural treasures, are also now museums. Driving back through the city I was especially touched by the sight of lovely old wooden houses—standing in dignified disrepair behind newer, built-up areas. Some hid their age behind fans of trees; others, their paint peeling, posed proud and defiant in the soft lens of the afternoon sunlight. The beauty of old Tallinn cannot be suppressed. What was needed was an opportunity to see and appreciate it. To do this required strategic planning on my part.

We were provided with young Russian guides, and Katia had shown me many of the public sights, including a former vacation home of Peter the Great. There was a feeling of resentment in the air at some of the museums as these young people went around in a proprietary way among the older Estonians in charge. Even though the Soviet Union had taken over the country, the people had clung to their own Estonian language. One old woman museum attendant, to my amusement, insisted she only spoke Estonian and absolutely refused to communicate with the young Muscovite guide when asked a question. Since I attended only a few of the meetings Bob was directing, I had free time and was determined to go exploring on my own. Every time I attempted to get out, however, I would be waylaid with insistent offers of a guide. One day, I just walked briskly out of the hotel, ignoring a questioning attendant with a smile and wave of my camera. "Just a few photos", I said, leaving him with a worried look. Alone at last, I worked my way in the general direction of the 13th century Oleviste Church with its distinctive green spire rising above the narrow streets of the old town. I thought back to what this community must have been like in earlier days.

To read Estonian history is to become fascinated by the story of courageous, independent people who, through the centuries, have found themselves manipulated and used, sometimes tragically, by different foreign powers. Estonia's strategic importance comes mainly from its location, jutting out into the Baltic Sea about 80 kilometers from Finland. It is about the size of Switzerland, but what a different history! Tallinn is one of the oldest cities in what was then the Soviet Union and came under the hammer and sickle for the second time in 1944. (I rejoiced for them when they again gained their independence after the fall of the Soviet Union.)

Exploring Tallinn in 1982, I followed small alleys and arcades and came upon the square where the medieval Town Hall stands—a solid, rather awkwardly placed building dating from the 1300s. Inside, there were beautifully carved wooden benches and impressive biblical paintings and tapestries. A small door led down to the dungeons below, now used as a museum. Outside, I noticed one of the characteristic weathervanes of Tallinn on the roof. This, a figure of a warrior, was nicknamed "Vana Thomas" (old Thomas) and still looked down on the square after well over 400 years. In the narrow streets of the old town I passed many medieval houses of a style I had never seen. Merchants of the Middle Ages lived in the lower stories, while the upper part of the house was used as a warehouse, with large hatches opening to receive goods. Some of the houses have retained their original form; others, altered, still show scars of their original storage openings.

We were able to see many of Estonia's treasures, as well as the port of Tallinn, which seen from a distance seemed busy and crowded, but with spacious park lands along the waterfront leading out to the attractive suburb of Pirita. My impressions of Estonia after our ten-day stay are only impressions, naturally, but as I became acquainted with some of the people, attended their concerts and other activities, I was impressed by their warm friendliness. The men of Tallinn were extremely gallant (that romantic custom of kissing a woman's hand a definite plus!) and they are justly proud of being Estonians. Our visit, as official guests, meant a structured schedule of activities, but it was the time I had alone wandering in the old parts of Tallinn that made me appreciate its indestructible beauty, and make me want to return someday. I also gained a renewed appreciation of freedom.

As a reward for the outstanding work Bob had done directing the course, we were delighted to be offered an extension of four days to see Leningrad. From Tallinn, we were provided with car and driver and private guide for the all-day trip over. It was an opportunity to see the real countryside, mostly rural and far from prosperous. We stopped in a small city for a meal where we were eyed curiously, perhaps the first Americans to come that way. One slightly inebriated man came up to our table, mumbling "American", and offered to buy me a drink. I refused with a smile, as the guide asked him to leave. Coming in to Leningrad, there were blocks and blocks of grim, depressing high-rise apartment blocks. But the city itself along the Neva River is magnificent, with many canals, impressive buildings and statues. After our arrival, we checked into the large, centrally located Hotel Astoria, famous because it was where Hitler stated that he would establish himself when he conquered Russia during World War II. He never conquered the city, and the huge cemetery with thousands of graves attest to the bloody siege that lives in the memories of the people there. Seeing this cemetery was an absolute must for us, according to the new guide who took us over upon arrival in the city. It was terribly depressing, another reminder of the insane tragedies of war. They play classical music as a background for visits, making it even more poignant. *Ars longa, vita brevis.*

Across from our hotel was St. Nicholas Cathedral, then the largest functioning church in the city. Most of the other cathedrals had been turned into museums. One, which we didn't visit, had been turned into a museum of the history of religion and atheism. Of the cathedrals, St. Isaac's is probably the most outstanding—the third highest domed building in the world—renowned for its past glory and pageantry. Many older people still frequent this solemn sanctuary.

I have more memories of our few days in Leningrad than I can mention here. The highlight of our visit, for me, was a visit to the Hermitage Museum in the Winter Palace. We saw a treasure of paintings from all periods of art (except contemporary, which we now know they had but were not displaying). There were rooms full of intricately crafted treasures of silver, gold and objects decorated with precious and semi-precious jewels—an array beyond belief. The main staircase to the museum is a masterpiece in itself, one of the most imposing features of the Winter Palace. We could not see everything, of course, but I had done some research, so carefully influenced our guide to go to those rooms I had read about. We saw some of the medieval artists, many from the Dutch school, (Rembrandt, Van Dyck), Renaissance works, Impressionists and others.

Another highlight was a visit to Peterhof, the home of Peter the Great some miles outside of Leningrad. The palace and gardens were carefully designed with cascades and fountains on the hill leading up to the main building. We had to take off our shoes and wear special slippers to protect the floors as we visited the palace. For this visit we enjoyed the luxury of our private car and were ushered to the head of the long line of visitors. I felt a bit guilty about this, even though the guide assured us that this was common practice. I realized how easily one could get used to this kind of treatment!

Back in Leningrad, we saw the Summer Palace of Peter the Great, with its extensive gardens, and another place I especially remember was the ancient cemetery, where Dostoevski, Tchaikovsky and Rimski-Korsakov are buried. Cemeteries have always intrigued me and that was a special thrill.

One incident in Leningrad made us realize again how closed the society was in 1982. We had been given a comfortable suite in the Astoria Hotel and in it we were delighted to find a large short-wave radio. Since we enjoyed listening to the BBC while in Switzerland, Bob searched the airways and was successful in locating the station the first evening we were there. How wonderful to get some news, we thought! There was a music quiz program on in English and then they announced the news. As we listened intently we heard "Israel has ...." followed by the loud noise of jamming. That was the end of any hope for world news of the past weeks.

It was a wonderful trip in many ways but we were both glad to be flying back to Switzerland, first on Aeroflot to Vienna, then on a SwissAir plane to Geneva.

During the stopover in Vienna, I was able to borrow a copy of the International Herald Tribune that some kind man had finished reading. I "devoured" it, learning of the Israeli invasion of Lebanon, which caused such widespread devastation, and also of the untimely accidental death of Grace Kelly of Monaco. It was with great relief that we boarded SwissAir after the austere Aeroflot flight. Music was playing and all passengers were greeted with smiles and chocolates. Geneva looked beautiful, even in the rain, as we flew in and were able to breath the air of freedom again.

The last months of 1982 were filled with activities. In early December we saw the Chinals again when they came from Bonn to meet us in Munich for the annual Christmas market. We had several days together exploring the market and trying out specialties at the local restaurants. We couldn't resist the beautiful hand-made ornaments and among other things we bought the Christmas carousel, which is now part of our celebration every year. On the way home, we stopped briefly to visit Charlie, Kathy and their children in Augsberg. Christmas in Geneva was a festive event, as usual, with all the young ones coming over from England and the States.

We wanted to see Berlin while in Europe, so over the Easter holidays we joined a small group from the American Women's Club (with spouses) for a short tour. At this time, the wall was very much in place and it would have been difficult to see as much of East Germany as we did without special arrangements. By bus we were able to visit the Potsdam country house where Churchill, Truman and Stalin met after World War II. It is now a museum and I noticed many German tourists examining the displays. We also visited some of the ornate palaces open to the public, which were full of pictures and artifacts.

When entering or leaving East Germany all passports were checked carefully at "Checkpoint Charlie" gate. The contrast between the East and West parts of the city was striking. The people on the streets east of the wall seemed rather depressed—rightly so—although a few of them waved at us. From our bus we saw streets lined with ruins or partially ruined buildings, many of which had been large, impressive structures, now showing mere remnants of their former beauty. By contrast, in West Berlin, commercial development was seen on all sides. One huge, dramatic ruin was left standing in the center of the city, and with the development all around it, it created a heart-rending reminder of the horrors of war.

XV

GOOD AND BAD TIMES

The big event in the spring of 1983 was the birth of our first grandchild, Ryan Fairhurst Lewis, born on May 20th. It was a joyous time for all of us, and the baby was beautiful and healthy although Carol had a difficult delivery. We planned a visit to England after the birth, and the Thunes, who were touring Europe, came by to join us in the drive over. We stopped overnight at Fontainebleau, then went by Bayeaux to see the famous tapestry. Before crossing the channel we visited Omaha beach and thought of all the brave men who had died there on D-Day.

After welcoming our first grandson, we left for a canal boat trip we had planned with Jeanne and Lee. It was a first for all of us and we had an exciting week together exploring the Avon and the canal at Stratford-upon-Avon. This was an extremely narrow canal in disrepair and with dozens of locks. We started out as complete novices (with goof-ups to prove it!), but soon became quite good at operating the locks and all the other tasks involved. All in all, it was lots of fun.

In September, again Bob and I felt the need for a break from the routine, so decided to revisit Lucerne, which we hadn't seen for fifteen years. The city with its painted buildings and narrow streets, plus the famous covered bridge, was as attractive as ever. In contrast to our previous visit when we had camped on the outskirts with the children, we stayed in a wonderful hotel, the Waldhaas, just outside Lucerne. Our room was literally perched high over the slope to the lake—a corner room with balcony and a view to capture your heart. The changing light on the mountains and lake in early morning and at sunset could easily inspire a sonnet. Instead, we took photos and relaxed with chilled white wine, letting the poetry of the scene take over. The hotel was famous for its restaurant with nouvelle cuisine—many small portions served with great flair from under large silver covers. There were so many courses we couldn't eat another bite by the time the coffee and chocolates arrived. The next day after exploring around the lake, we drove on to Meiringen to visit the "Sherlock Holmes" (Reichenbach) falls—a spooky place when thinking of Conan Doyle's dramatic tales.

We tried to take short trips whenever we could. In October, we had a few days in Provençe, then a long weekend in England. One date to remember about this time was November 19th, which, according to my notes, was when Steven took his flying test for a private license—following his parents in this love of flying. Later, during our home leave, he took each of us up for a brief flight over the Montgomery County countryside in a two-place Cessna. We were proud of his competence and careful attention to details—essentials for a good pilot.

Christmas was spent in London that year. We rented an apartment near Portman Square and Steven flew over to be with us. The girls joined us with their husbands and with adorable little Ryan, now seven months old. It was a good time together, but unfortunately, Peggy and Allen seemed to be having some problems with their relationship, which was worrying to all of us.

The year of 1984 started out well—days filled with writing and editing at the Courier, leading my Thursday Art Group, and taking part in many other activities with friends. In February, we welcomed Peggy and Allen for a visit and went skiing with them on nearby slopes. We were glad to see they seemed to be getting along better.

Our home leave that spring was especially important, because, while visiting Steven in Washington, we had a chance to meet Barbara Chow, who would later become our daughter-in-law. She seemed extremely nice and they were obviously in love. We looked forward to getting to know her.

Back at home, Carol and Mark came over for Easter with Ryan, now an active ten-month bundle of energy. Later I flew to England to help celebrate his first birthday. But, it seemed that Peggy and Allen were no longer together. Peggy was now in her own apartment in Islington, sans Allen, who, unfortunately, had been engaging in various extra-marital adventures, and showed no signs of commitment to their marriage. It was not a happy time.

During the summer, our niece Cindy celebrated her twenty-third birthday with us. Then later Steven brought Barbara over for a visit, and Peggy flew in to join them. It was good to get to know Barbara better and Steven loved introducing her to Switzerland and showing her around his old haunts. They were all going back via Paris, so Bob and I drove them over as far as Barbizon, the attractive town where a group of painters, namely Corot, Millet and Rousseau, had gathered in the 19th century. The next day we all took the train into Paris, Steven and Barbara then going off on their own. Peggy spent the day with us exploring the Pompidou Center among other things. We all enjoyed being in Paris again.

Bob had to go to Turkey in September, so I went with him to Istanbul for a few days before his conference. We stayed in a large hotel overlooking the Bosphorus and explored the city, marveling at the beautiful mosaics of the Blue Mosque, the treasures of the Topkapi Museum and other sights. A colleague of Bob's who lived in Istanbul drove us along the coast of the Bosphorus and to parts of the city we hadn't seen, later introducing us to some of the local specialties at dinner. Since Bob had to go on to his meeting in the capital, Ankara, I flew over to London for a few days before we both returned home.

Shortly after watching the 1984 presidential elections results when Reagan was re-elected, we prepared for our family Christmas. Unfortunately, Peggy was now separated from Allen. It was not nearly as happy an occasion as usual.

There were two joyous events in 1985. In April, Steven and Barbara were married. We treasure the memory of a beautiful wedding and welcoming our delightful new daughter-in-law.

Then, on the 25th of June, our first granddaughter, Anika Marguerite Lewis, was born, adding a beautiful baby girl to the family, thanks to Carol and Mark. I flew to Colchester to help take care of Ryan when Carol went to the hospital to give birth to Anika. The baby was beautiful and I loved pushing Ryan in his stroller everyday to visit mother and baby in the hospital nearby. Bob flew over a few days after the birth to join in celebrating the happy event.

A sadder event of that year was having to put Bob's mother in a retirement home after she was found unconscious in her home by the lake. Ruth, in her late 80's and fiercely independent, had refused to leave her home earlier, but now the doctor where she had been taken insisted she have more care. Bob flew to the States, and he and Dan found a place for her in a retirement community in Hendersonville, not far from where she had lived for twenty-odd years. She agreed to sell the place by the lake, but was really upset when her car was sold, although it was not safe for her to drive anymore.

In April, Ruth did manage to join us in Washington for Steven and Barbara's wedding, as did Jeanne. Later, Bob flew back to Nashville with Ruth and I drove Jeanne home to Black Mountain, then on over to meet Bob. Dan joined us there and we cleared out Ruth's house and disposed of all the things that she had not wanted in her retirement apartment. It was a hectic and traumatic time—both physically and psychologically exhausting— stress adding to stress.

Home in Switzerland, we tried to pick up our lives, and were helped by a pleasant visit from Miriam and her husband, John. Later, we went to Brussels for a few days, where Bob had to attend a meeting. I wandered around the city alone and was especially impressed with the unique Museum of Modern Art, which is built underground, angling down with an open court in the center. The town centers around the attractive town square with its impressive architecture.

On the way home we had a most unusual experience. For some reason, the Swissair flight we had booked for a late evening departure put us on an extra plane they needed to take to Geneva for a flight scheduled to leave early the next day. We boarded the large jetliner to find that there was only one other passenger on the flight! Having a private jetliner was quite an experience.

In late summer Bob and I decided to try boating again in England. We rented a small cruiser this time, a bit more comfortable, especially as it could be piloted from inside the cabin, a plus considering the uncertain weather of England. We took over the boat near Wallingford on the river Thames and headed toward Oxford, visiting small towns and riverside pubs along the way. It was fun cruising along watching the swans and ducks and waving at the fishermen on shore. Lock keepers were on hand to operate the locks, with still plenty of other activities for us, such as attaching and releasing lines. Most of the locks presented a cheerful sight with colorful flowers and sometimes a dog welcoming us. We chatted with other boaters along the way, locals as well as many from overseas. In Oxford, we explored the historic city, and especially enjoyed the bookstores in the University area. There were many convenient places to tie up along the river. We did some cooking on board, but ate in pubs when they were nearby. Later, Peggy joined us for the weekend, which made it even more enjoyable. She brought along a hibachi, which we used one evening for a cookout. After Peggy left, Bob and I continued west on the Thames a bit, then went back east beyond Oxford and Wallingford as far as Windsor. The fun of that week made us anxious to cruise again.

It was during the same summer that Bob and I bought a small flat in London to use for our frequent visits. We found a fifth floor one-bedroom place on Eton College Road within walking distance of Belsize Park, Hampstead and Primrose Hill. We looked forward to spending Christmas in our new London "home".

Bob was finishing his last year at the ILO Institute, and we faced this milestone with mixed feelings. We planned to stay in Founex awhile, as we had to sell the house, but we also knew we wanted to retire back in our own country. Our plans went through some unexpected and unwelcome changes, beginning with an accident Dec. 17th, just before Bob's birthday, when he slipped on our entry steps and broke a couple of ribs. Due to this, we were not able to go over to England until the day after Christmas and missed sharing it with the children for the first time. Steven had come over from the States and we looked forward to having as much time as possible with him.

Our lives were affected even more drastically when I discovered a lump in my breast about the same time as Bob's accident. After a trip to the gynecologist, I promised him I would have a mammogram in England, as I was going over in just a few days. After we got there, a little later than planned, I had that test done and it was suspected that the lump was malignant. I did not want to ruin our Christmas holiday, so I decided to wait until Steven had returned to the U.S. before going in for final evaluation. The surgeon, Mr. Gilmore (more prestigious than a doctor in England), examined my x-rays and said I needed to have an operation right away. Two days later, on Jan. 15th, I underwent a sectional mastectomy (called a lumpectomy in the U. S.) at the Princess Grace Hospital. The lump was cancerous and unfortunately had spread to one lymph node. This meant I needed to follow up with radiation treatment, which I arranged to have back in Geneva. We were lucky to have the flat in London where I could recuperate two weeks before going home. It is hard to write about my feelings at this time, but the support of Bob and the girls, as well as long distance support of Steven and my brother and sisters, helped me to face the future with hope.

Back in Switzerland, our lives were changed in more ways than one. In addition to the stress of my six weeks of daily radiation therapy, we had the shocking news that Carol's marriage was breaking up. This was a real blow to all of us, especially because the children were so small. Anika was only nine months old, and Ryan not quite three years. Mark had been carrying on an affair for some months, it seems. Even though Carol tried to hold the marriage together, and they went to counseling, Mark chose not to stay with the family. My heart ached for Carol, and I wished that I could bear some of her pain (in addition to that I was personally going through). It was one of the most depressing times of my life. I appreciated the wonderful support of Bob throughout these dark days, and I tried to maintain a certain equilibrium with relaxation and visualization exercises, facing each day as a challenge and somehow knowing that things were bound to get better.

When my radiation treatment was finished in April, Bob and I wanted to get away for awhile. We hadn't been to Italy for years, so we set out to visit Ravenna and other towns we had not seen along the northeastern coast. After some hectic hours driving in and out of the numerous Italian tunnels with most drivers going at breakneck speeds, we decided it would be our last trip on that route!

It was a relief to reach the relative calm of Ravenna, where the famous mosaics in the modest Catholic church there lived up to their reputation. Exploring on down the coast we were in a hotel looking over the water and were puzzled when the waitress in the restaurant said they couldn't serve any salads. We soon learned of the nuclear catastrophe in Chernobyl, and since some of the nuclear clouds were thought to be drifting toward Italy, all precautions were being taken with the food supply. We headed for home in a hurry, since more radiation was something I certainly didn't need!

All of us were still having difficulty getting over the breakup of Carol and Mark's marriage and what it meant for the innocent children. Bob and I went to England as often as possible to offer support. It was a stressful time, but I managed to get through the summer with the help of Bob and friends, especially my group of EX-EX women (made up of eight of us who had held executive positions in the American Women's Club of Geneva). These women were of different nationalities—Swiss, Canadian and British, as well as American. Their friendship and support was a real lifesaver to me at that time, and throughout the years they have remained treasured friends.

During these months Bob and I worked to get the house and garden ready to sell. We had spent fourteen years creating a beautiful home looking over the lake and mountains and we had mixed feelings about leaving it. The deciduous trees, colorful in the autumn, flowering shrubs and evergreens, plus the pool and waterfall shaded by the graceful weeping willow had given us much pleasure as well as a feeling of security. But now we realized we had to be practical, and in September the house was sold for a good price.

Steven and Barbara had come over during the summer and after a tour into the lake district of Switzerland in Bob's car, they agreed to drive it over to Colchester for us, since we wanted Carol to have it.

After a hasty goodbye to friends, we left Switzerland with mixed feelings of sadness and anticipation of things to come. We drove to England, spending a few days in Colchester where we left the Mazda, since Carol agreed to keep it for us to use when visiting the country. It was a rush getting things organized before we left for Washington to look for a new home.

Our arrival back in the States was not as happy as we had hoped, due to a crisis with Ruth. She had not been doing well in her retirement apartment and needed more care. Dan and Joanne had been taking most of the ongoing responsibility for her, since we were overseas and trying to wrap things up there. With all the things that were going on in our lives at that time—my sickness, selling the house and the need to offer Carol as much support as possible during her difficult readjustment to becoming a single mother, there was little we could do to help with Ruth. This situation was resented by Joanne and Dan, I'm afraid, which didn't make things easier for any of us.

As soon as we got to the States, Bob and I postponed looking for a home to fly to Nashville to help get Ruth re-settled somewhere. It was a traumatic time. After several depressing days of visiting possible retirement homes in Nashville, where Ruth preferred to stay, we learned that Joanne and Dan had suddenly decided to drive her back to Ohio with them. They first tried to care for her in their home—an impractical idea from the start—and later put her in a nursing home in Aurora, not too far from where they lived. Tensions were high between the two families at this time, with stress building up on all sides, and resistance by Ruth for any and all decisions.

Since we needed a car, Bob and I decided to buy one in Nashville and drive back to Washington. With our new Honda, we went back through the Blue Ridge Mountains that were ablaze with autumn colors. Seeing this wonder of nature again—something we had missed during our many years out of the country—did a lot to restore our spirits.

In Washington, Steven and Barbara graciously put us up for a couple of weeks while we were looking for our own place. We knew approximately the

area where we wanted to live, and lucked into our townhouse on Crescent Street just over the border into Maryland from DC. It was smaller than we had been looking for, but with its convenient location—near public transportation and not too far from Steven and Barbara—it seemed a good choice. We moved in the last day of October. Much work had to be done to make the house more livable, including replacing all the appliances. The townhouse was two levels in front and three in back opening to the garden. The patio had to be completely rebuilt and the garden shrubs given some TLC. Bob and I were looking forward to our retirement years and we were still settling in when we welcomed all the children for Christmas. Everyone seemed to approve of our new home.

XVI

HOME IN BETHESDA

It was an exciting and challenging period of our lives settling back in the U.S. after living the last twenty-two years overseas in different countries. We were amazed at the changes that had taken place in the Washington area. Bethesda had become a thriving center instead of a rather dull crossroad out Wisconsin Avenue. Downtown Washington had added the Kennedy Center, the Space Museum, the new East Wing of the National Gallery, the Hirshorn Museum and other buildings as well as the Metro. All in all, the city had become much more alive—an exciting cultural as well as political metropolis.

Another startling change was how much more integrated the city had become. In the streets many well-dressed Afro-American men and women were seen going to various offices, along with those of other ethnic backgrounds. The Washington Post was full of pictures and news of the black community— something that was not usual when we had last lived in the area. We welcomed these changes and looked forward to getting re-oriented in a city we both loved.

It was fun getting used to the different choices in the grocery stores, but it was a long time before I stopped converting the prices to Swiss francs! Nothing seemed very expensive after our eighteen years in Geneva. We missed some of the Swiss specialties, but enjoyed exploring the numerous ethnic restaurants in Bethesda and elsewhere.

Shortly after we settled in, Bob bought his first personal computer. He had enjoyed using those at the ILO so he was eager to become acquainted with all the newest technology offered. This has proved to be an absorbing avocation for him, with frequent refining and upgrading which has made our records more organized, as well as offering an amazing amount of information in various fields. Personally, I resisted the allure of this fast-developing electronic tool for some years, finally giving in when I wanted to do more writing. I gradually branched out from word processing to enjoy e-mail and the seemingly endless expansion of the Internet.

We wasted no time in getting acquainted with the Kennedy Center, going to a variety of events, and we visited the museums as often as possible. I especially enjoyed a comprehensive Matisse exhibition soon after we got back. In addition to concerts of the National Symphony, it was a real pleasure having good music radio stations and a wide choice of CDs to enjoy on our own stereo player. People in the States take these things for granted, but having the TV in English, and later cable TV, is quite a change from the two or three French language stations we had in Geneva. Our life style definitely changed, but we soon reestablished old friendships and made new acquaintances.

Settled into our townhouse in Bethesda, we were thrilled to see the wonders of spring after many years away. We could only look at life more optimistically as we saw this renewal of nature in such dramatic form—flowering cherry trees and azaleas bringing beauty to the whole area. Our little garden put on a show of its own with the star magnolia, then the pink dogwood bringing surprises.

Early in April that first year back we went to Montreat, North Carolina and sold our three lots on the side of the mountain, realizing we would never retire there as we had once thought we might. We still owned the flat in London and the apartment in Gaithersburg that we had bought for Steven to live in, which was now rented.

The birth of Kathryn Austin Hua Ray on May 28th was the happiest event of 1987. Barbara had an easy delivery, giving birth to a beautiful, healthy baby of 6 pounds 13 ounces. Steven and Barbara were thrilled to begin their new life as first-time parents, and Bob and I looked forward to being near our little granddaughter through her early development—always a wonder and joy.

That first summer we went over to Europe for three months—first to visit friends in Geneva, then to London, where we now had our flat to stay in. We spent a lot of time with the girls and grandchildren, having picnics and exploring the beaches.

Later, inviting them to join us, we rented a cottage in Yorkshire on a large farm. The little ones loved riding the ponies, and Ryan was thrilled with his first ride on a tractor. One day we took a long hike along a rocky wooded cavern with several lacy waterfalls. Anika, just two, was carried in a backpack. Another day Bob and I took them to board a train going north over the moors (the grandchildren's first train ride). We met them at the next station, stopping on the way to admire the rolling heaths covered with flowering purple sage as far as we could see.

Back in Washington, I started going to Georgetown University's Lombardi Cancer Center for my oncology check-ups. Dr. Paul Woolley provided wonderful support and prescribed a new follow-up treatment, tamoxifen, to guard against recurrence of my breast cancer. This was reassuring because my malignancy had been an invasive type with a rather poor prognosis. I continued with various tests and felt more energetic day by day.

That autumn we joined a group of seniors at the Institute for Learning in Retirement, associated with the American University. Several hundred retirees take part in some fifty different classes led by volunteers from the group. These people had been leaders in various fields of academia, government and business. We selected different classes according to our individual interests for the next several years. Later, Bob taught a few courses—one on genealogy and one on computers for beginners.

Our periodic visits to Aurora to offer support to Bob's mother, Ruth, were depressing. She had refused to live in the retirement apartment and although we all understood her fierce determination to remain independent, she wouldn't go halfway, so had to be moved to the nursing home section of the facility. There seemed no easy answer to this sad situation.

There were many places in North America Bob and I had not seen, even with our extensive travels elsewhere, so we set out to see some of them. We began by flying to Mexico in late February to explore the Yucatán Peninsula.

After arriving in Cancún, we left immediately for the more interesting parts of the area, although the turquoise blue water and white beaches were hard to resist. We wanted to see as many of the Mayan ruins as possible and started at Chichén-Itzá where we stayed in a cottage of the Hacienda Hotel. It was set in a tropical forest, with orchids hanging from the trees, and numerous parrots and

other exotic birds around. One morning on the way to breakfast, we saw a large iguana casually wandering along our front walk. We had to brave the heat and sun to admire the Chitchén-Itzá ruins where we saw the Temple of the Warriors, the beautiful stone carvings on the Igleslia and other monuments of the Mayan civilization. I wasted no time in buying a straw hat before we continued.

At Uxmal the pyramids and smaller ruins were impressive with their intricate carvings and unique architecture. We marveled at how the Mayans could have had the techniques to construct such monuments.

We had to drive slowly along the narrow roads between the various sites since our rental car was not too well equipped, and there were many man-made *tumulos* as well as natural obstacles. Since we both spoke Spanish, we had no trouble finding places to stay or eat. One day we passed a young boy beside the road offering a live armadillo for sale, and we wondered if this was something that appeared on native menus! We felt a special kinship with the Mexicans, after our many happy years living in Latin America.

On the way back to Cancún we stopped over in the charming colonial town of Mérida, where we reveled in a cool, comfortable hotel and enjoyed tasting the local specialties (not armadillos!). Back on the eastern coast we visited the ruins of Tulum before flying home.

In England that year, we joined our good friends, Jill and Ron Neath, for a week's cruise on the Norfolk Broads. We stopped often at riverside pubs and were surprised by the number of windmills and the many small sailboats in the area, obviously a regatta of a popular sailing school.

Later in the summer, we decided to go to Scotland, which we had not seen. We had left the Mazda in England, so we put it on the overnight train to Edinburgh, then spent a week driving around the country. From Aberdeen we cut across and along the northern coast. There many areas were sparsely developed and had a lonely, rather brooding beauty.

Back in the West Highlands—more varied with lakes and rolling hills—we visited several castles, some of which were still occupied by descendants of the original families. We ferried over to the Isle of Skye, where some of my paternal ancestors were supposed to have come from. This was a fascinating area, complete with skeletons of castles and small croft houses. Later, along the lower peninsula of mainland Scotland, we came across a huge castle in the McDonald Center. Since the McEacherns are a branch of the McDonald clan, I was sure that some of my forebears must have lived there! Nearby in an old cemetery, we even discovered some gravestones marked with the McEachern name. I wondered about the lives of these people who might well have been an ancient branch of the family.

Driving back to Edinburgh, we stopped by Ft. William and saw Loch Ness (but no monster), then back to Edinburgh where we boarded the train with our car to return to London.

All the family gathered in Washington for Christmas of 1988, the first time the grandchildren had been together. It was a holiday to remember, but sad saying goodbye to those going back. Life was good in Bethesda, however, and we felt lucky to be near Steven, Barbara and Katie to share birthdays and other holidays.

In the summer of 1989 we went to Europe earlier than usual in order to be in Geneva for the seventieth anniversary of the ILO. We saw many of our friends and revisited favorite places. A highlight during this time was the few glorious days we enjoyed in Grindelwald, staying in a picturesque Swiss chalet looking out at mountains, and again appreciating the unique beauty of the country we still thought of as our second home.

Sadly, shortly after we had left for England that summer Bob's mother had died of congestive heart failure. She had fallen and broken her hip earlier and never regained the ability to walk. Bob and Dan had visited her just a few weeks before. At that visit, after saying good-bye, Ruth had called Bob back, and as he gave her a special hug, he said he somehow felt it was a final parting and that he would not see his mother again. Perhaps she, too, realized it. We were all very sad when hearing the news, but knew she had lived a full, productive life during her ninety-one years. A memorial service was scheduled for October in Nashville.

Continuing our determination to see more of our home continent, we traveled to Alaska in early autumn. After flying to Anchorage via Seattle, we stayed in a small apartment and rented a car to see the surrounding glaciers and other sights. We even went to the state fair in Palmer one day, which was a different experience for both of us. There I bought an interesting handmade pendant with a polished piece of mammoth tusk, thousands of years old, in its center.

Taking the train from Anchorage to Denali National Park on one of its last trips for the season, we stopped over at the park headquarters for a bus tour into the park. Snow-covered Mt. McKinley was out in all its glory in the afternoon sunshine. The rolling hills around were covered with a low growing red shrub called bear berry—a unique show of nature accented by patches of evergreens. We stopped often to take pictures and to watch bears, moose and other wild animals.

The next day we continued over to Fairbanks by train, enjoying unforgettable views of white birches bright in their autumn yellow, mixed with evergreens along the river and distant hills. Fairbanks was a rather ordinary town, yet with a definite frontier atmosphere. We took a boat tour on the Tanano River nearby, where it joined tributaries of the Yukon, and stopped along the way to see restored Eskimo settlements and an exhibition of dogs and dog sleds used in the well-known Iditerod races. The woman showing the dogs had actually taken part in one of the races.

We flew back to Anchorage and on south to Juneau. There we wandered around the thriving town, seeing the old Russian church and other sights. The broad, white Mendenhall Glacier just out of town was especially impressive, framed with snow-capped mountains.

We felt lucky to get one of the last trips up into the Glacier National Park, and we took a small plane up to the lodge there to spend the night. Next day, we went on an extensive boat trip through the two main passages and various inlets. The experienced pilot seemed to know all the best places to see the awe-inspiring glaciers rising on all sides. Some had moved down toward the water and we witnessed several episodes of "calving" as huge sections collapsed into the water.

The lodge was closing for the season, so we flew directly back to Juneau where we boarded the coastal ferry north to Skagway.

That old gold rush town was fascinating, with boardwalks instead of sidewalks in many places, and original wooden houses mixed with restored saloons and other historic buildings dating from the town's frontier background.

Leaving Skagway, we boarded the ferry again—this time going south. Our cabin was reasonably comfortable, and the restaurant served a variety of delicious fish.

Going south we stopped at several small towns, then Juneau again and Sitka on our way to Ketchikan. At each stop we were able to explore the towns briefly and buy a few souvenirs. Ketchikan was especially interesting for me because I remembered that a college chum had come there to teach many years ago and had married a man who ran a lumber company. "Ketchikan to catch-a-man", some of us thought (perhaps jealously). I couldn't find her name in the phone book, so she must have long ago moved on—where, no one seems to know.

We continued down the Alaskan and Canadian coasts through the Inland Passage, past Vancouver Island and on to Seattle where we disembarked. Instead of flying home immediately, we explored Seattle. It was fascinating to see the merchants throwing fish back and forth at Pike's Market! Then we rented a car and drove south to Oregon to visit my sister, Austin, and her husband, Art. On the way, we stopped overnight in Portland with friends from Guatemalan days, the Reiersons; then we drove by Mt. Rainier and headed south through the Cascade mountains.

It was good to see my sister again, and while in Ashland we saw several plays. The town is well known for its Shakespeare festival, as well as offering other plays during the season. Pressed by our schedule, we drove back up the dramatic Oregon coast to Seattle for the flight home.

We continued our classes at the Institute for Learning in Retirement and kept busy with friends and family, but in May we were off again to explore the Outer Banks and Cape Hatteras National park, a region we knew little about. There we visited the site of the Wright brother's first flights, realizing again how far aviation has come since those early days. I wonder what those pioneers would think of the international space station recently launched.

Our summer trip to Europe in 1990 began in early June. After a week in London, we joined a British Airways tour to Vienna, and later, Budapest. How good it was to see the beautiful, sophisticated city of Vienna again, reminiscent of Geneva with its international ambiance. It was our first visit to Budapest, and after a boat trip up the Danube, we disembarked with anticipation of exploring the old cities of Buda and Pest. It was a perfect time to visit Eastern Europe, since the Berlin wall had been torn down and Hungary had just become independent from Soviet domination. All the statues of Lenin were being removed and many streets were being renamed to reflect their own national history. There was a definite feeling of excitement in the air. One taxi driver gleefully showed us the new name that would soon replace Leninstrasse (or whatever Lenin street is called in Hungarian). Even though we didn't speak the language, we were able to communicate and thoroughly enjoyed our visit, which included several excursions to mansions and museums as well as outings on the Danube. Our tour group was small and friendly, most of them British.

We stopped often at riverside villages on these trips, sometimes climbing steep cobblestone streets from the dock and occasionally being taken from the boat for a short bus ride. These side trips added a lot to our understanding of the country and its people. At one village we witnessed a colorful wedding group outside a lovely old church.

July was a pleasant month, with visits to Colchester and Beechamwell in Norfolk where Peggy has her cottage. Her garden there is filled with lovely flowers and shrubs, a delightful spot for relaxing. The grandchildren were growing fast and together we explored nearby ruins, wildlife refuges and other places.

An interesting side trip that summer was a visit to our friends the Neaths, in Southsea, where we saw several old reconstructed ships, among them, the Mary Rose, which had been recently raised from the waters off the coast. It had been deep in the English Channel since the days of King Henry VIII, and was a crumbling shell, but still recognizable.

We just made it back home in time for the birth of our fourth grandchild, Lucas Thompson Hua Ray on the 15th of August. Little Lucas was perfect and the next months were busy for all of us.

Christmas was another wonderful reunion with all the immediate family, including an alert four-month old charmer hanging his stocking for Santa for the first time. It was a joy seeing the grandchildren together on Christmas Eve at a candlelight service at River Road Unitarian Church that Bob and I now attended.

Early in January, to escape the winter cold in Bethesda, we drove down to Florida. We had not been there since 1976 and we were curious to see all the changes. In Jacksonville we stopped to see many of my old haunts including Landon High School and other places. We visited Mother and Dad's graves in Arlington which was now an oasis surrounded by modern development. My old homesite on the St. Johns River was changed but still brought back many memories. The people who now owned it had raised a large family there, as our parents had. The log house was gone, of course. A new wood-batten house, basically an H shape as ours had been, had replaced it, blending in well with the slope of land and surrounding live oaks. There was still an impressively broad view over the river from the bluff. I wandered around, caressing my favorite trees, including the oak with the huge grapevine still twisting around it where I had spent many hours. Surprisingly, I even discovered my "M" carved years before on the large magnolia tree in the Indian mounds.

While in Florida we also visited Bob's cousin, Bill, in Homestead. He had recently lost his wife to cancer and although very lonely, was trying to put his life back together. We went to a rodeo with him while there—a first for me. Later, we stopped to see another of Bob's cousins, Clark, in Jupiter, Florida whom we had not seen for many years.

In March, we flew to San Antonio to see my sister, Rosemary, and her husband, Bob. There we visited the extensive headquarters of the Bible Study Fellowship where Rosemary served as director. It was just being built when we were there about ten years earlier, and had now become an attractive, efficient center, due in large part to Rosemary's energy and leadership.

In the spring we flew to England where we joined our friends, the Mallers and the Neaths, to visit the island of Guernsey. We spent several days exploring, seeking out-of-the-way sights and special gardens. In the attractive port town where we stayed, we toured Victor Hugo's house, high on a hill overlooking the active harbor. He had written many of his masterpieces there including Les Miserables. Rather eccentric, he was a stickler for privacy, it seems, and even had most of his meals sent up to his studio by dumb waiter so he wouldn't have to converse with anyone. He also stood at a tall desk while writing, which seemed strange to me. The house was furnished with beautiful things from that period.

Later in the summer Bob and I set out to explore Maine and Nova Scotia. The towns along the Maine coast lived up to all we had heard of them. We visited Arcadia National Park, then stopped in Bar Harbor at a lovely hotel looking over the bay. Graceful sailboats passing by added to the idyllic setting.

Driving up through New Brunswick was less interesting, but we both relished the lobsters there before going on over to Nova Scotia.

While driving the loop around Cape Breton, we came across a sign for McEachern Road. Could other ancestors of mine have settled there? We admired Halifax and fell in love with the area south of there, where we stayed in a small fishing village. Peggy's Cove was interesting with its lighthouse set on broad flat rocks, but unfortunately so popular that it was crowded with tours.

Back home, our Peggy stopped over for awhile on her way to explore Guatemala and the Yucatán with a small group of adventurous souls. Then in early December, my sister Austin flew to Washington to attend a ceremony celebrating people active in the fight against world hunger. We were proud of Austin who had arranged many activities and raised consciences in her town of Ashland for this cause. She was amazed at some of the changes that had taken place since she left Washington.

Christmas that year was spent in North Carolina with Jeanne and Lee in their beautifully decorated mountain home. Before returning to Bethesda, we drove down to see Dan and Joanne in South Carolina, where they had retired on a lake near Anderson. The unpleasant part of this winter trip, unfortunately, was bad colds for both Bob and me, mine later turning into pneumonia, which took six weeks to get over. I realized that my immune system had not really come back to normal.

Because of my health we had to cancel a January trip to Costa Rica and a long trip to China later, which we had arranged with a class from the Institute for Learning in Retirement. It seems that China is not a good place to go if you have any respiratory problems. I had been studying the country with this group and this was a big disappointment.

As compensation for these canceled trips, with the doctor's permission, we flew over to Bermuda. We both appreciated the brilliant sunshine there after the past dreary months. We stayed in a centrally located guesthouse and took buses all over the island, pacing ourselves but not missing much, since the island is small. We took several boat trips to see the coral and colorful fish and visited the old capitol, St. Mary's. There, we were intrigued with the little church on the hill and the reconstructed boats that celebrate the early settlers. The brilliant display of colors, turquoise waters and pink-sand beaches offered photo-ops all along the coastal areas. I tried to capture this beauty of the island in an abstract painting after we returned home.

We didn't go to England until late June in 1992. After visits with the family, we flew again to Geneva and from there went up into the mountains to Zermatt, which we had not seen for some years. It was a welcome relief to leave the heat of the Rhone valley to take the narrow gauge train ride from Visp up along the rushing stream.

In Zermatt, we stayed at the chalet-style Hotel Julian, its flower boxes cascading with pink geraniums. We wandered around, trying out different places for lunch, and exploring the old cemetery with graves of the many climbers who has lost their lives on the Matterhorn. We spent several relaxing days taking hikes and funicular rides into the surrounding mountains.

In September we were off again to visit Quebec and Montreal. We flew in to the sophisticated city of Montreal, staying at the Hotel Queen Elizabeth for several days. Our first trip to this part of Canada was exciting for us and we were impressed with its beauty. We visited the site of the former Olympic games and other sights. Then, taking the comfortable train from Montreal up to Quebec City, we splurged and stayed in the world famous old Hotel Frontenac high on the hill. We loved exploring this city with its varied cultures and attractions. British reminders were on all sides, but the French influence was prevalent. In addition to the French signs, the croissants and other such things reminded us that this was very much a bit of France. We returned to Montreal by train before flying home, enjoying impressive views of Niagara Falls on the way back.

We had not often traveled on Amtrak, but in November we decided to take the train up to New York to see the special Matisse exhibition there at the Museum of Modern Art. We had booked a room in the Wyndam, a small hotel near the Plaza and only a block from 5th Ave. When we arrived we found that somehow the hotel did not have a reservation for us, even though we had made it many weeks earlier. Confusion on all sides, finally resolved when we were given the fancy bridal suite—decorated all in pink!

In addition to seeing the unforgettable Matisse Show, I enjoyed showing Bob a lot of the special places I remembered from my time living there in 1945-47. While visiting the World Trade Center towers it was satisfying to see that the Federal Building at 90 Church St. where I had worked during Navy days, was still standing nearby. We were impressed with the Lincoln Center, and attended a concert in Avery Hall there. The last night we had cocktails in the famous Oak Room of the Plaza, which I remembered visiting with various boyfriends when I was young. It was a good season to enjoy this exciting city these many years later with my permanent boyfriend!

November 1992 was a momentous time for another reason. After a long and sometimes bitter campaign, Bill Clinton was elected President of the United States, an event that was to have an impact on our whole family.

Barbara had left her demanding job on the Hill with Senator George Mitchell, in order to spend more time with the family when Lucas was born. She was asked to serve on the President's transition team leading up to the Democratic takeover in January, and was then offered a plum job in the White House in the Legislative Affairs Office. It was to prove to be a challenging, once-in-a-lifetime job, and we were all enthusiastic and happy for her, even though it meant some family adjustments for Steven and the children. Everyone was eagerly looking forward to the new year.

XVII

FOLLOWING THE DREAM

The philosophical adage to "live life fully and live it whole" appealed to me from an early age. I hope to follow this dream as long as possible, as both Bob and I look for different parts of our fascinating world to explore. At the same time we value a balanced life, so in addition to family activities, we try to create our niche in the community contributing what we can. In the nineties we continued our active participation in the life of River Road Unitarian Church, chairing various committees and serving when needed. At the church we found a supportive group of like-minded people and made good friends.

To appreciate each day is easy when life is good, to accept those not so good, a bit harder for most of us. During the last decade of the century the years seemed to pass faster and faster. Getting older really does speed up time. Wasn't Einstein quite old when he discovered the fourth dimension?

January 1993 ushered in a new administration in the White House and there was a rising sense of optimism in the air. We were all impressed with the intelligence and energy of the new President. After Barbara joined the President's staff, Bob and I occasionally enjoyed some special "perks". As well as special tours of the White House, we were thrilled to have lunch in the White House Mess. What fun seeing the workings of the administration up close! Another time we enjoyed a National Symphony concert from seats in the President's box. There, we offered Barbara a champagne toast in the private adjoining reception room.

At a later lunch at the White House Mess, we were able to meet first lady, Hillary Rodham Clinton, when we happened to be in the arcade by the Rose Garden as she came by with her entourage. She was gracious when Barbara introduced us, and I was impressed by her natural confidence and interest in people.

Bob and I soon took off again, this time on a trip to Costa Rica with our friends, the Neaths, from England. Together we explored the country, sometimes driving through neglected or unpaved roads. We managed to see many of the volcanos, archaeological ruins, the Cloud Forest and other sights. It was good to become acquainted with a part of Central America that we had not seen and more fun when joined by old friends.

After arriving in England for our summer visit, we saw the girls and grandchildren briefly, then flew to Paris. There we visited the glass pyramid addition to the Louvre and the Musee D'Orsey, both of which had opened since we left. Then, always drawn back to our favorite part of France, we took the TGV (fast train) to Avignon in Provençe.

In our rental car we revisited St. Remy, Les Baux and Gordes, seeking out special restaurants along the way. One lunch I'll never forget was in the small town of Tavel. There, guided by the owner, I had a delicious dish of *fleur de la courgette* stuffed with mushrooms in a fabulous sauce. This was accompanied by a goblet of cool rosé wine, a specialty of the region.

On the last night before returning our car we stayed in an elegant hotel in Villeneuve-les-Avignon. La Magnaneraie was built within a sprawling residence of the 15th century. It was a perfect ending to our visit before taking the train over to Toulouse.

Our friends, the Chinals, were most gracious in showing us around there, and we saw their daughter Juliette who was studying law at the University. From Toulouse we took the fast train back to Paris then flew to England, knowing we would never tire of this part of Europe.

After returning to Bethesda, we looked forward to a visit by Carol and the children in August. It was an unusual summer trip for the Lewis family and we tried to make it memorable. While they were in Washington, we did nearby sightseeing, going to Mr. Vernon and Luray Caverns. They toured the White House and together we saw the musical "Annie Get Your Gun". Carol saw "Phantom of the Opera" at the Kennedy Center with Barbara, and was thrilled to be seated in the President's box.

Later we drove with Carol and the grandchildren down to North Carolina, stopping overnight in the Blue Ridge Mountains. The children were delighted when we saw deer and a bear family along the way. While staying with Jeanne and Lee, we went to Sliding Rock, an attraction nearby that the young ones especially enjoyed. Then we visited the Youngs in Bonclarken before continuing on down to South Carolina to see Dan, Joanne, Cindy and her husband, Jerry. There we all enjoyed boating and swimming in the lake. Too soon the London family had to leave for home.

During the Christmas holidays we went to the White House again, this time to see all the fabulous Christmas decorations. Every room was beautifully transformed into a seasonal fairyland. Choirs and other musical groups performed here and there, and a complicated gingerbread house in the East room had a place of honor. We had never dreamed we would enjoy the privilege of seeing all this and were properly impressed.

Our niece, Kathy Cook, and her family had moved to the Washington area in June 1993. We were so pleased to have more family nearby. She and her doctor husband, Duane, had three delightful children and we were sad to see them move to another area a couple of years later when Duane had finished his residency at Walter Reed Hospital.

Christmas spent on a Caribbean island with loved ones was another dream come true. That was our good luck when Peggy joined us for a ten-day vacation in Puerto Rico. The spacious penthouse apartment we rented was ideally located in the Condado area, looking out over the lagoon with the ocean only a block away. In addition to Christmas presents we brought down for each other, Peggy, with her usual flair, had carried a small, decorated tree all the way from England! It was fun and a unique way to spend the holiday.

Our excursions took us to different parts of the island. Since Bob and I had vivid memories of the year we spent there when we were newly married, we drove around the Rio Piedras area visiting the university and even locating the actual apartment house we had lived in. I well remembered taking Linda up and down the four stories when she was a puppy!

Many changes had occurred, of course, and the traffic was heavy at times. One day we wandered around the picturesque streets of Old San Juan, visited Morro Castle and other sites. We sought out a seafood restaurant we had remembered, but, alas, they no longer served sea turtle steak (now on the endangered list). The Navy Building overlooking the water where I had worked was still there and also the Navy Club, which didn't look as if it had fared well, or maybe it just wasn't as attractive as I had remembered.

All of us wanted to see other parts of the island so we began by driving along the coastal road west as far as Arecibo, stopping at lovely beaches along the way. On the way home, we stopped for tall, iced drinks at one of the patios overlooking the sea at the huge Dorado Beach Resort.

Our day trip to the rain forest of El Yunque brought back pleasant memories as we revisited wandering trails and waterfalls. Clusters of huge bamboo and all kinds of tropical trees and plants—ferns and flowering shrubs seldom seen—grew in profusion on all sides.

We drove to Ponce on the south coast one day, showing Peggy the beautiful fountain in the main square and the famous firehouse with its red-checkered design. Going back we took smaller roads through the mountainous central area. In one small town we came across a festival of some kind, complete with carousing locals and roadside offerings of Puerto Rican foods, all accompanied by blaring music. It was a typical island scene and we were reminded of the high-spirited fiestas that seem to be celebrated every week or so in this part of the world.

One of our final days in Puerto Rico was spent at lovely Luquillo Beach not far from San Juan. We relaxed under the palm trees, as Peggy tested the chilly aqua-tinted water. A coconut we found there stayed in our car (never opened as planned) until we returned the car to the airport. It was a vacation to remember, a memory to cherish.

We decided we had come home too early from sunny Puerto Rico when a heavy ice storm hit the Washington area the end of January 1994. We determined to get to warmer climates the following winter, as there were several days when I couldn't venture out of the house because of the thick coating of ice on all the walks and roads. Promises of spring came along in March, however, and Barbara invited us to a surprise birthday party for Steven in the White House. There was delicious food and a large cake to share with his friends and colleagues at NIST in a special setting.

We had never taken an organized cruise, but that spring we were lured into accompanying a group to see the waterways and small towns of Holland. We flew over early to London then to Amsterdam for a short visit before joining our tour. The ship carried one hundred passengers and our cabin was small but comfortable except for the tiny cramped bathroom with shower over the toilet! The people we met were friendly and the food excellent so we couldn't complain. It was also a chance to see many places not easily accessible by car.

Spring is the perfect time to visit Holland when the tulips are in full bloom and we saw field after field of gorgeous colors. One day, the group went to the fabulous garden of Küchenhof. Flowers of all kinds are set in natural settings around small lagoons with waterfalls and tall trees adding to the beauty.

Our ship cruised down to Utrecht with a side trip to Arnhem to see one of my favorite museums from earlier visits, the Kröller-Müller, with its wonderful

outside sculptures. From there we followed the river south, meandering in and out of the islands to the Walchren peninsula to visit several small towns. Coming back north we stopped in Amsterdam and then looped north as far as Enkhuizen and Hoorn. One special side trip we took from Lelystad was to the small village of Giethoorn (Goat Horn), where canals are used instead of roads. One man was moving his cow by boat! The children even go to school by water "buses". This charming town, its canals bordered by large trees, was one of the most interesting places we saw on our trip. We picked among the other day trips offered, sometimes preferring to explore on our own or to stay on the ship as it proceeded to the next stop to meet the group going by bus. By the end of the week we were glad we had seen all we did, but the experience strengthened our preference for making our own travel arrangements.

Luckily, we had made plans to go off for our own adventure after the cruise. With our Eurail passes we left for Germany, stopping in Koblenz, and then took a day trip on the Moselle River over toward Trier, admiring the numerous castles among the vineyards.

Back on the train we continued along the Rhine, then over to Heidelburg where we had arranged to rent an apartment. It was a few miles out of town in a riverside suburb called Neckarhelle. I later learned that Brahms had written some of his music there! Bus service was convenient into Heidelburg and we had no trouble exploring the attractive town with its narrow streets, plazas and historic buildings. It's a romantic setting, complete with an imposing castle looming on the hill above.

After a day's cruise on the Neckar River one day, we took the train to Bern, which we both loved from our days living in Switzerland. There we stayed in a delightful residential type hotel looking over the river Aare. After revisiting this always fascinating city, we took the train to cross some of the high passes over the Alps to Lucarno in southern Switzerland. The scenery was dramatic with gorgeous views of mountains and waterfalls. We had to change trains and move to a narrow gauge train at one point. Many of these passes are inaccessible by car.

After exploring the lakeside resort of Lucarno, we headed back to Bern. This time we chose a different route taking a train that went north through Lucern. We both wanted to see how the city's famous covered bridge had been restored after it had been damaged by fire some years earlier. Rebuilt in its original style, the wood is still too new to be as attractive as it was. Perhaps age will help. It does mellow some things (as well as people!). We returned to Bern staying in the same hotel, high up in the large, raftered room, happily snuggled under duvets and enjoying all the special amenities that a good Swiss hotel offers.

In Geneva we picked up a car and drove along the lake to Nyon, where we stayed in one of our favorite hotels, Les Alpes, for several days. It was fun to explore our old home area, noting all the changes that had taken place in Founex (few) and elsewhere. The view of the Nyon castle from our hotel room, this time with a full moon over the lake, added to the magic. We were able to see many old friends at a party given by friends, Joan and Claude Hislaire.

We continued with our Railpass, taking the TGV to Paris, where we had chosen a charming, small hotel, Abbaye St. Germain, in the St. Suplice area. In spite of its central location in the Latin Quarter, we had a quiet room looking out over the small, shady terrace garden where a delicious *petit déjeuner* was served.

An unexpected surprise awaited us when we arrived at the hotel. The concierge said we had mail waiting for us, and we were delighted to get a note welcoming us to Paris from our daughter, Peggy. Then, imagine my astonishment when I heard, "Hi, Mom!" and turned to see her standing there! She had come over from England with a friend for the weekend and was taking a flight back later in the day. We had a delightful few hours together before she left. Bob and I arrived home by way of England in June, earlier than usual since we had gone over early.

The highlight of that summer was the purchase of my piano, as a forty-fifth anniversary present from Bob. I had missed having a piano since leaving Geneva, even though I could not play all that well. I began reviewing some of the fundamentals, and picked away happily at easy arrangements of songs I remembered.

Going to British Colombia was another trip we had postponed earlier, so as a relief from hot summer weather, we flew to Seattle, then took the ferry over to Vancouver Island. It was the season of World Cup games there and Victoria was crowded with visitors, but we found a place in a small guesthouse within walking distance of the attractive port. We saw the exciting "extras" that were going on— skulling races and other events, even though we didn't attend the games themselves. From Victoria we drove north to the famous Butchart Gardens. Numerous varieties of flowers and trees were arranged on different levels, with paths leading here and there. I'm not sure how they managed it, but everything seemed to be in full bloom—quite impressive, especially for those of us who love flowers.

Leaving the gardens, we drove as far north as Nanaimo, taking side trips to the west coast seeing Englishman River Falls and the magnificent Cathedral Grove with its huge hemlocks and fir trees towering up above. Some of them are nearly 800 years old! The island is full of fascinating places to explore, many of which we had to forego, due to our schedule.

From Nanaimo we took the ferry over to Horseshoe Bay on the mainland of British Colombia. We remembered visiting there with our small children and wondered what had become of our friends, Diana and Harvey Henderson from those days (and earlier in Peru), since we had lost track of them over the years. In the city of Vancouver we found a wonderfully convenient hotel on the north shore overlooking the port and the ferry.

The center of the city, which was a short ride across the river, had been attractively restored and was lined with trendy shops. We were able to track down the Hendersons, and found that Diana, divorced from Harvey for many years, was now living in Sidney, off Vancouver Island. Talking to her we were sorry to learn that we had been so near to her earlier without knowing it, so missed getting together. From Vancouver we drove south to Seattle, before flying home to Bethesda.

Later in September, restless again, we took our first trip to Vermont to see the autumn leaves. The White Mountains were already showing their autumn colors—a promise of later vivid hues. We stayed in Bennington and explored the nearby areas, seeing among other things, Arlington, the hometown of the popular American artist Norman Rockwell. The small museum there had originals of many of his magazine covers. An elderly woman showing us around told us she had been one of the child models for several of these.

We sought out covered bridges and were captivated by the small New England towns. Our niece, Miriam and her husband, John, met us for lunch in Lenox, Massachusetts, halfway between Bennington and their home in Amherst. Together we visited nearby Tanglewood, a summer music center I had always wanted to go to when I was a young violin student—a wishful dream! Bob and I drove home along the Hudson River, past Hyde Park, West Point and Poughkeepsie, another first for us. Having fallen in love with Vermont, we both wanted to return soon.

Autumn was marked by a special tour of Air Force One at Andrew's Air Force base, which had been arranged for Steven, Bob and me. Fun to see what the "oval office of the sky" was like, in addition to seeing the President's sleeping quarters, the press area and other things. Barbara had been on several trips with the President since she started working at the White House, so we imagined her in this setting. When the airmen showing us around learned that all of us had been pilots at one time they were especially accommodating, and I was even invited to sit in the pilot's seat—which I did!

Our grandniece, Maggie Moebius, arrived in Washington that year where she wanted to find work. We helped her get settled in an apartment and provided a few necessities, along with our moral support. We were glad that another attractive young relative had to chosen to come to "our" city to pursue her career. Later her sister, Corinna, also settled in Washington.

After Christmas Bob and I headed south again to escape the winter cold, this time stopping over briefly to see various relatives and friends on the way. Our trip to Florida was one of several we took during the next few years. We were vaguely looking for a winter vacation home, and explored areas along the Gulf coast as well as along the Atlantic.

Among the unusual things we saw in Florida was the largest living cypress tree in the world. We also visited Ebo city, a Cuban section of Tampa, that I remembered going to with my dad when I was a child. The area had been restored and revitalized and we found the actual restaurant I remembered, the Columbia. It was still charming with its colorful tiles and good food.

Genealogy had not previously drawn me to do research on my ancestors, although Bob had had become quite interested in the subject even teaching courses at ILR and at the church. In the spring of 1995 I finally visited the library of the DAR headquarters in Washington to see what they might have recorded about my family. I knew that my Uncle Jim had gone into our ancestry in some detail many years earlier.

During the next few months, my research led to some interesting findings. It seems that my great-grandfather on Mother's side, Dr. Henry Smith, had served for a time as Surgeon-General with Robert E. Lee in the Civil War. I found out that his father, George Smith, was born in London. The next time I was over there I tried to find records of his birth but could find nothing. Unfortunately, Smith is not a distinctive name and what's more, he wasn't Church of England. It seems that those records were kept in the 1600s, but Presbyterians were among those thought of as "non conformists". I guess I live up to that distinction a bit in my own life!

One of my ancestors (curiously named Instance Hall) had been a state representative in the early Congress of Virginia. Another, Lewis Hall, served in the Revolutionary War. Later when Bob and I checked records in the county courthouse in Surry, Virginia, we discovered a 1732 will of Lewis Hall's father, Isaac Hall. In it he bequeathed large land holdings to each of his four sons (with nothing mentioned about leaving anything to daughters!). It seems logical to conclude that Isaac Hall either came to the U.S. in the 1600s or was born here then. I have not been able to check farther back on that particular branch of the family. I did find records and the graves of three generations of Austins (my mother's father, grandfather and great-grandfather) at the Old Stone Presbyterian Church in Lewisburg, West Virginia. I may do more research on that branch some day. Genealogy continues to interest me, but since "the world is so full of a number of things" I am not an avid researcher.

A fun excursion Bob and I took about this time was a short visit to Philadelphia, a city Bob had never seen. I had been there a couple of times during the time I lived in New York, but didn't remember much. We took Amtrak and stayed in the city center. In addition to seeing the Liberty Bell, Quaker Meeting House and other sights, we visited the U.S. Mint, an interesting place where coins and official medals and seals are made.

June found us in Vermont again, this time in a rented house on one of the small lakes. It was a delightful setting and would have been perfect if I hadn't had a stupid accident when, perhaps thinking I was twenty years old, I leaped in the canoe for a ride on the lake. It was not the stable kind I had been used to, and I was thrown violently forward into the boat, resulting in bad bruises. This quickly put a crimp into my enjoyment of the rest of the week. Later x-rays showed I had not broken a rib as I had feared. Miriam and John came up from Amherst to stay with us a few days, which brightened our stay.

Ireland has always appealed to the imagination of artists as a place of literary history, and continues to provide inspiration to those who seek out its unique beauty and simple charms. In spite of its turbulent history of religious division and a desperate poverty in earlier times, we all know it is full of magic with leprechauns and other wee folk much in the thinking of the Irish people. Their wonderful music and the conviviality of the local pubs continues to draw people from all over the world to the Emerald Isle. What better place to go for a special vacation?

So, in August as the weather got hotter, Bob and I made plans to rent a cottage in the southwestern peninsula area. We invited the girls and grandchildren in England to join us during their vacations. Before the children arrived, we explored parts of the country we hadn't seen. We were intrigued by the old churchyards with their characteristic Celtic crosses.

During our touring we stayed in country houses that accepted a few guests. One was in a converted convent, and one night we stayed on a huge working farm. (One of the guests there arrived in his private plane!).

The house we rented was at Ballydehob, south of Bantry, which proved to be a convenient base for exploring. We took day trips south to Skull, then around the peninsula to the rocky cliffs of Mizen Head and over to Skibbereen, where we chanced on a lively street fair.

One day we visited the Bantry Bay area, and then north beyond Glengariff. The sub-tropical gardens on Garinish Island are reached by boat. There old Italian style formal gardens have been transformed with groupings of flowers, shrubs and trees set among unusual rock formations. Going home, we drove over some isolated country where herds of lonely sheep grazed on the hills above the bay.

After leaving Ballydehob, Bob and I stayed a few days in Kinsale, south of Cork. The children joined us briefly before heading back to England. Our small hotel in Kinsale had an ideal setting overlooking the harbor filled with sailboats. A special treat was watching part of the annual Fastnet sailing race from our balcony.

I was interested in learning that it was there off the coast that the Lusitania had been torpedoed and sunk in 1915 during World War I, resulting in a loss of more than 1500 lives. This tragic event had made an impression on me when I heard of it as a young student, since it had happened on a May 7, later to become my birthday, and I did not like to have such a blight on my day! But this summer there was nothing to spoil our pleasure, leaving us with only happy memories.

XVIII

THE DREAM GOES ON

Monet and Chicago—what more exciting combination? The largest Monet exhibition ever collected was showing at the Art Institute in Chicago during the fall of 1995 and we did not want to miss it. Since Bob had never been to Chicago, we decided it was the perfect time for a visit. A lot had changed since I was there at age twenty but I was pleased to find many landmarks I remembered, including the big department store, Marshall Field, where I had seen my first escalator.

We stayed in the city center at the old Blackstone Hotel where many U.S. presidents and other well-known people had stayed through the years. We selected it because of location and historic interest—certainly not for luxury, as we found out. The lobby, with statues and large paintings, is reminiscent of better times, but the amenities left much to be desired. Not recommended. Hotel aside, our trip was a great success. The Monet exhibition was fabulous—a magnificent display of this popular Impressionist's works. Among other things, there were whole rooms full of paintings of the Notre-Dame of Paris seen at different times of day, a scene we know Monet painted over and over.

We toured the city, and viewed it from the top of the Sears Tower, at that time the tallest building in the world (later to be topped by twin towers in Malaysia). In addition to visiting Marshall Field and the historic old Palmer House Hotel, believe it or not , we saw a snow-white alligator, one of the few in the world, at the Aquarium.

During the Christmas holidays, we were invited to a special party for the families of White House staff.. Again the historic mansion was beautifully decorated with glowing lights. Another special surprise we enjoyed, was a luncheon party at the White House Mess for Bob's birthday on Dec. 19th, complete with birthday cake!

The cold winter caught us before we could get away for our annual trek south in 1996. The Washington area was hit with a heavy blizzard bringing deep snow and record cold temperatures in early January. It was so dramatic—cars in the streets completely covered—that we were actually glad that we had not missed it, but nevertheless we were happy to head south later in the month.

After several winters checking out different parts of Florida rather extensively, Bob and I both decided we had really "done" the state. With a vague idea of looking for another place to rent during the cold months we stopped by Hilton Head, South Carolina on the way home. Exploring this island near Savannah we soon became interested in buying a place there instead of renting each year.

After checking several places we found just what we were looking for in the Evian development of Shipyard Plantation. Situated among tall trees, it looked out over a lagoon and lake with the ocean just a few minutes away. Besides the advantage of being near the interesting cities of Savannah, Beaufort, and Charleston, the island itself has playhouses, an Art's Center, restaurants and shops, plus beautiful beaches and sports attractions. We closed on the purchase of our villa apartment in February 1996.

A sad event of that spring was the unexpected by-pass heart surgery of my sister Jeanne. It was quite a traumatic time for all the family and everyone rallied to offer support. Jeanne was depressed, but brave as she fought to gain back her strength and independence. We all hoped for a full recovery and many more happy days together.

When we heard the large Cezanne exhibition would be showing in Philadelphia, Bob and I immediately made plans to see it. It was a magnificent show, the largest ever assembled and shown only in Philadelphia in the U.S. after runs in Paris and London. There were early paintings as well as the later portraits and glowing still lifes and landscapes for which he is so famous. Cezanne has always been one of my favorite artists, and I was vividly reminded of the visit we had made to his hillside studio outside Aix en Provençe years earlier. It is maintained exactly as he left it, complete with an arrangement of the fruit and other objects seen in his paintings. Since we had been to many of the places he painted (such as Lac d'Annecy), the exhibition brought these memories back with renewed appreciation.

Later in June, we left with a group from the World Affairs Councils of DC and Philadelphia to visit Poland and the Czech Republic, countries we had not been to. The tour featured music and politics, with all kinds of exciting activities scheduled. We took Amtrak to Philly to join the tour group, then flew to Warsaw. Thankfully, our travel companions proved to be intelligent and well traveled, and with only twelve in the group, we soon became friendly.

Warsaw, which had been almost completely destroyed during World War II, presented a rather grim picture since it had been rebuilt by the Soviets—never known for their imaginative or even interesting architecture. It was now a busy, fast developing city with many changes going on since Poland led in toppling communist control by the Soviets in eastern Europe, gaining their independence in 1989. Lech Walesa, who had led the fight through the Solidarity trade union movement and who had later been elected president of the country, was now out of power. He had not been too successful in carrying out reforms in the new democracy. With the new president elected in 1996, an era of free trade and progress toward full democracy seemed to be developing. The American

Ambassador to Poland, Mr. Nicholas Rey, gave us a thorough briefing on the present political situation during a morning coffee visit to the embassy residence. Ambassador Rey had been born in Poland, spoke the language fluently, and even though he was a political appointee, seemed well qualified for his job.

We saw the main sights of Warsaw, including the old town with Castle Square and the historic column of King Sigismund III Vasa, originally erected in 1644. After having been destroyed during World War II, the column and many houses in the old town had been restored. The Royal Castle was also restored and is now a museum. The tallest building in Warsaw is the Palace of Culture and Science, a grim reminder of Soviet domination.

In the Jewish section all of us were affected deeply by the vivid accounts of their treatment during the years leading up to the war. Even though we all knew about this bloody stain on history—a horrible example of man's inhumanity to others different from themselves—it was dramatically impressed upon our consciences as we visited the site. Where the Jewish Ghetto stood is now a peaceful section centered around a memorial park with trees planted by many of the survivors who escaped to the United States and elsewhere. A large monument with struggling stone figures captures the horror of those evil days.

A more lighthearted vision of Warsaw was gained by a visit to an attractive park in the suburbs where we saw the Ostrogski Castle, now monitored by colorful peacocks preening in the sun. In the evening we heard a Chopin concert in a beautifully decorated salon of the castle. A local pianist sensitively interpreted the music of this native son—perfect music for the setting, reminding us again how music can rise above many of history's horrors.

We next visited Kraków (or Cracow) that was recorded as an important city as early as the end of the 10th century. King Casimer made it the capital of Poland in 1040, and it developed as a center of trade, craft, fine art and science. Despite being destroyed by the Tartars in the 13th century, it was reconstructed according to its original plans and this town-planning arrangement has been preserved through the ages. The city proved to be much more interesting to visit than Warsaw. Some of the town walls still stand, and the town centers around the Main Market Square, a thriving place with shops and sidewalk cafes.

At one corner of the square stands St. Mary's Basilica, a Gothic church built in the 15th century on the site of an earlier church. Its ornate wooden altar was carved over a period of twelve years. Another attraction for the tourists to St. Mary's is the playing of a trumpet from the highest tower of the church every hour. The simple melody had been played in medieval times as a warning call. As we listened, it broke off abruptly to commemorate the Tartar invasion which destroyed the city. When the watchman on duty spotted the enemy he sounded the alarm until an arrow pierced his throat in mid-phrase. This dramatic reenactment continues to bring history to life for all the citizens and visitors.

High on Wawel Hill the cathedral and the castle dominate the other medieval buildings. The cathedral has beautiful stained glass windows illuminating its many chapels, and in the castle we saw one of the largest collections of detailed tapestries in the world, made by masters in France and Belgium.

In our tours of Kraków, again we were shown the old Jewish section of the

city. Most of the present population is Catholic, with only a few Jews living there. The ancient streets, some still cobbled, are lined with medieval buildings. Because Kraków is such an educational center, there were many lively young people—not too different in appearance from students in other countries.

Happily, during our free time, we were able to visit a museum near the city walls where we saw the beautiful portrait by Leonardo da Vinci, La Dame avec L'ermine (Lady with an Ermine). This shows the same serene, enigmatic smile that we see in the Mona Lisa in Paris, and was the most outstanding painting we saw during the whole trip.

Before we left for the Czech Republic, we visited the concentration camps, Auschwitz and Birkenau. This was such an emotional visit for me I could not manage to see it all. So much has been kept just as it was, and to see the actual places where these evil deeds took place is a horror to haunt us all. Photos, obtained after the war from the Nazis, had been enlarged and are displayed in the camp. The pictures of the innocent children on their way to the gas chambers were almost too much to bear.

As we drove from Poland into the Czech Republic the landscape became more attractive with rolling hills and forests—a mixture of evergreen and deciduous trees. The white birches reminded me of the forests I had seen near Moscow. After a long bus drive we arrived at our modest hotel in a small town near Litomysl, a cultural center where the International Opera Festival was being held.

The town is dominated by a large Renaissance castle full of Baroque furniture. Across from the castle is the Smetana Museum, former home of

Smetana's father, a local brewer and good friend and drinking companion of the castle's owner. Chess sets and areas for smoking in the castle are reminders of the times they spent together, according to legend.

In the museum I was entranced by the various displays, especially the small violin (half size) which Smetana began playing when we was three years old! His music is featured in frequent concerts in the courtyard of the castle, and we were able to enjoy his light opera "The Kiss" there one evening. Later we attended two short operas—Mascagni's "Cavaliero Rustico" and Leoncavallo's "Comedians" (Pagliacci), both well performed. This was an unusual experience since a light rain threatened to stop the performance and we listened from under umbrellas from time to time! It was amusing to see the pattern of colored domes sloping down to the stage as we music lovers huddled to hear the well-known arias.

Before leaving this area we visited an unusual Renaissance chateau in Opocno. The chateau was begun in the 15th century and added on to by various owners. It contains all kinds of Italian art and ceramics as well as a large library. One owner was an avid explorer and a whole floor is taken up with stuffed animal heads, skins and other trophies. A large room was crammed with weapons of all kinds—one of the largest private collections of guns in the world. This man was also a dedicated equestrian and I noticed many portraits of favorite horses. One was life-sized, dominating the men's smoking room. I'm sure psychologists would have fun analyzing this man—certainly a swash-buckling type!

We finally arrived in Prague—the gem of the tour, as far as I was concerned, and the main reason I had wanted to come on the trip. We were especially impressed with the architectural wonders of the city. The local guide throughout our stay, Sonya, was a treasure of information; but after a few days of hearing her rather loud explanations and dates, I turned off a bit and resorted to ear-plugs from time to time. It was good to have a guide, however, in countries where we knew nothing of the languages. One of the first things we noticed in both Poland and the Czech Republic was how unpronounceable many of the signs were—composed mostly of consonants, with no discernible connection to any of the Romance languages. We were able to catch on to some of the shorter words, but it was rather amusing to see great long strings of consonants, completely unintelligible. Luckily, the employees of the hotel spoke English. Also, since Germany was not too far away, we could occasionally dredge up a few phrases to order coffee and such. Gestures are often lifesavers, of course, and at least we were not faced with different letters of the alphabet (as in Russia, Greece and other countries).

The Czech Republic was rapidly becoming an important player among European countries. Prague was leading the other capitals of Eastern Europe in economic development at that time, aiming to become a member of NATO and later to join the European Union. Our visit came at an opportune time to witness the energy and changes taking place. I had long admired Vaclav Havel, the playwright with such an appealing philosophy, who became the political leader. I remembered hearing his moving speech to the U.S. Congress a few years previously. As President of Czechoslovakia, (then, after the split, of the Czech Republic), he was devoted to human rights and a civil society. The other Vaclav, Vaclav Klaus, head of a three-party coalition, was the most powerful figure in this post-communist country, and he did much to promote free-market policies. The people (and the world) still hold Vaclav Havel in their hearts, but most of them appreciated what Klaus was doing. The political maneuvering continues, of course.

Prague Castle and the beautiful St. Vitus cathedral stand high on a hill over the Vltava River that divides the city.

There are many other outstanding churches and the Old Town Square was especially beautiful. The Town Hall there displays a large astronomical clock, complete with the signs of the Zodiac, and each hour it draws a crowd to see the emerging figures. In Prague, we were invited to the studio of the sculptor famous for the death mask of the student protester who immolated himself to dramatize the oppression of the communists. A memorial of this horrible event now stands in Wencelas Square, a long street lined with shops—the center of the city's commercial activities.

Charles Bridge, linking the two sides of the city, is open only to pedestrians and is always crowded. The only commercial activities permitted there are artists and craftsmen with their offerings—some quite good and others dreadful, as one can imagine. From here we had good views of the river and city. There are so many architectural gems in Prague, I was entranced just looking around and up everywhere we went.

Following the musical and political themes of our tour, we attended a Dvorâk chamber music concert in the courtyard of Nelahozeves Castle outside the city. Nearby we saw the house where Dvorâk was born and the small church where he played the organ. We learned that his father had been a butcher (pronounced "bachelor" by our guide, much to our amusement!).

Another evening we went to a wonderful recital in what is now the Mozart Museum. The composer lived here for several years and harpsichords and other instruments he had played are displayed. I was surprised to see his violin was made in Vienna in 1778, which means it was made several years later than my own violin, also from Vienna.

Our tour of the Czech Republic ended with a farewell dinner and folk dancing in a country restaurant near Prague. It was the 4th of July, and with another group there, we were happily able to celebrate being American. The other group was made up of descendants and families of Czechs who had emigrated to South Dakota many years before. Except for the 83-year-old leader of the group, it was their first trip back to their ancestral homeland—a poignant celebration for descendants of all ages, including a three months old infant.

Flying home, Bob and I left the group at Zurich to fly to England for a visit with the family there. Looking back on our trip, we were both grateful to have learned something of a part of Europe that has been enmeshed in the threads of history through the ages.

In Colchester, we were pleased to see that Ryan and Anika, then 13 and 11 years old, were continuing to develop into the ideal grandchildren we expected! In addition to raising the children alone, Carol was adding to her education, working toward another degree through The Open University, as well as teaching at the Colchester Institute.

Peggy, meanwhile, had become a successful family lawyer (solicitor) in London, heading her own law firm with a large staff. We are proud of all of our children's accomplishments.

Before flying home, we got together to see the Irish dancers in "River Dance - The Show", an outstanding display of intricate footwork. We arrived back in Washington on July 17th, coincidentally just a few hours before the catastrophic plane crash off Long Island.

Before the November elections, we left the Washington hubbub to return to Hilton Head, where we were visited by Thunes, then Peggy, who had just spent three weeks driving through many of the northeastern states getting reacquainted with her native country. During her short visit she had a few days to relax before returning to England. I cherish the time I had walking with my daughter on the beach and looking for "our" alligator in the lake.

XIX

LOOKING FORWARD

Everyone gathered in Washington for Christmas in 1996. After the usual festivities (including seeing the trees and lights in the White House), we all drove up into the Blue Ridge Mountains to Wintergreen, Virginia for a few days of skiing. What fun to watch all the young ones maneuver down the slopes. It was quite warm and the slopes had been covered with man-made snow, which didn't seem to stop anyone from skiing day and night. I'll never forget six-year old Lucas zooming straight down, passing everyone. He skied without poles and seemed to balance perfectly. "I just like to go FAST and STRAIGHT", he said. No snow plows (or so-called wedges) for him! The grandchildren were well on their way to becoming excellent skiers. All our children took the slopes with ease, having learned to ski in Switzerland.

One challenge we did not expect or welcome in 1997 was a diagnosis of prostate cancer for Bob. No one is ever ready for something like this, but we were relieved when tests indicated there was little chance the cancer had spread. Since his father had died of prostate cancer, Bob decided to have surgery as soon as it could be arranged. He was operated on in early February. It proved to be a bit more complicated than anticipated and we were thankful that there was a good team of doctors and supportive staff at Sibley Memorial Hospital.

Recuperation went well and we managed to cope with all the inconveniences. Bob was patient and optimistic and I certainly learned a lot. As I had to do many new things on my own, I realized again how much I had depended on him.

After Bob's health improved we headed for Hilton Head just before Easter. We had a leisurely trip stopping over at country inns. It was a perfect time of year, with dogwood and azaleas in the full glory of spring. The Magnolia Plantation azalea gardens near Charleston were ablaze with color. Another interesting stop was in Georgetown, a rice-growing center north of Charleston founded well before the Civil War. I never thought I would see a rice museum! The whole trip was a relaxing change from the trying days that had preceded it.

We continued our exploration of the U.S. and Canada in June with a ten-day trip around Lake Ontario. Again we stayed in country inns along the way—some more memorable than others—but all different and interesting.

It had been over thirty-five years since we had visited Niagara Falls and we were again awed by its power and beauty. We chose to stay in the small Canadian town of Niagara-on-the-Lake where the Shaw Theater Festival is held every year. There we saw Lillian Hellman's "The Children's Hour", so controversial in the thirties when it was first produced. It is still pertinent today, dealing with the problems of homosexuality and bigotry.

In Toronto our modest hotel was centrally located and during our short stay we were able to see much of this thriving international city. Except for getting a ticket for illegally stopping in front of the hotel to unload baggage, all went well. High point of our stay in Toronto (literally) was going to the top of the needle-shaped 1,815 foot CN tower, the highest freestanding tower in the world! At one section you can walk over a glass floor looking down on the tiny objects below. This took a bit of nerve, but we both ventured out on it, while many would not! The Harbourfront development extending along the lake was impressive.

Driving home we explored the Finger Lakes region with its rolling hills and vineyards. We drove through Syracuse to see the Erie Canal Museum, which evoked memories of a canal boat song I had learned in Girl Scouts years ago. We returned home to Bethesda in time to witness (via TV) the turning over of Hong Kong to China by the British, surely a milestone of history.

Since our return to the U.S., I had often thought I would like to have a small dog as companion to brighten our later years. Encouraged by our good friends, the Clevelands, (fellow dog lovers), Bob and I were thrilled when we found a lively six month old Cavalier King Charles spaniel to join our family—a real beauty with champions on both side of her ancestry.

Her registered name is "Edenglen Winter Solstice", since she was born on the twenty-first of December. We named her "Linnie", since she reminded us of our little puppy, "Linda", my first anniversary gift from Bob when we were in Puerto Rico. Now our new puppy came to help us celebrate our forty-eight years together. She did bring some changes to our schedules, but her lively, affectionate personality and clever antics made each day brighter!

Another milestone around this time was the dramatic success of the NASA mission to Mars. The robotic Pathfinder landed on the surface of the planet on the fourth of July. What a celebration! The world waited in awe as pictures sent from the Pathfinder showed the rover, Sojourner, sent slowly gliding down the ramp to explore the surrounding terrain. Taking samples of the soil and sending data from different kinds of nearby rocks to be analyzed by geologists was a feat not believed possible. It was the first time a robotic machine had landed on another planet and been directed by engineers from Earth. The earlier Voyager mission to Mars had collected soil samples, but did not have specific ongoing direction by the engineers. It also had not landed on such an

interesting and varied site. The Pathfinder, in contrast, seems to have settled in what was once a flooded valley strewn with rocks, and pictures showed several good-sized mountains in the distance. It was a thrill to see the events unfold on the TV and we look forward to witnessing more NASA explorations. Is this a great time to be alive or what?

The highlight of our summer in 1997 was the arrival of Carol, Ryan and Anika for a holiday. We had a good week together in Hilton Head, exploring the island, swimming and fishing (Ryan caught a turtle as well as a fish!). Katie drove down with us to spend a few days before flying back (her first flight on her own!). We explored nearby Savannah before taking Katie to the airport for her flight back home. I'm sure it was a flight she will always remember.

After leaving Hilton Head, the family entourage drove to Flat Rock, North Carolina where we had a brief visit with Cecil, Reynolds and those of their family who were there (Jennifer and Cecile with their children). Then on to Anderson, South Carolina where the Ray-Dowling cousins had organized a reunion. Five first cousins—Bob, Dan, Bill, Jack and Clark with as much of each family as could be assembled made it a lively group of 29. I had not met most of them before—nor had Bob. It was a busy, happy day filled with swimming, boating and water skiing on the lake.

Those from England were able to meet more relatives when we stopped in Roanoke, Virginia to see Mayhoward, Terry and family (Austin, Nathanael, Silar and John). Too soon, Carol and the children had to fly home but we all looked forward to being together for Christmas.

The world was shocked in early September when Princess Diana of Great Britain was killed in a horrible accident in Paris. An astonishing reaction of grief swept over the world at this abrupt end of a young life—a beautiful and glamorous dream princess for many people. It was somehow a fairy tale gone wrong. Her public fight to get rid of land mines and her sympathetic attention to the sufferers of poverty and AIDS brought a deep response, reflected by the expressed grief of millions.

The death of the saintly Mother Teresa of Calcutta came shortly after Princess Diana's death and was somewhat overshadowed by that event. Revered by Catholics worldwide and admired by millions, she had aroused the moral consciences of thoughtful people in many nations. The elaborate state funeral given to her by India was an official acknowledgment of her service to the poorest of the poor.

Before leaving for Guatemala for a family get-together, Bob and I enjoyed the Christmas celebrations at the White House again. Barbara had changed jobs, and was now an Associate Director of OMB (Office of Management and Budget), with offices in the Old Executive Office building next door. Steven had also received a promotion, and was now a Division Chief at NIST, supervising about one hundred scientists, which made us proud of both of them.

Christmas in Guatemala! What could be more exciting than a holiday vacation in that lovely country where we had spent three happy years some thirty-five years earlier. Having two of our three children, plus two grandchildren with us made it all the more delightful. There were many changes, of course, especially in Guatemala City. I was struck by the masses of people in the streets, more than twice as many as were there before, and traffic was hectic. The others arrived in the country before we did, and Peggy and Ryan met us at the airport with a driver for our trip to Antigua, about an hour's drive away. Before leaving Guatemala City, we arranged for him to take us by the first house we had lived in. Instead of being relatively isolated, backing onto a coffee *finca*, it was now surrounded by development. Alas, our second house there had been completely swallowed up by high-rise buildings. We had expected this spreading development, of course, and had arranged to spend our Christmas in the old town of Antigua.

We were welcomed there by the other family members and Peggy's friend, John, who had also come over from England. We were enchanted with the charming colonial house, which dated from about 1567. The high-ceilinged rooms opened onto a center courtyard with tropical flowers, plants and even a grapefruit tree. A central fountain attracted unusual birds. Our family group had taken over the complete house, now run as a Bed and Breakfast. Bob and I stayed in the master suite—complete with a huge bath looking out to a private terrace draped with glowing bougainvillea vines. Each room had a fireplace and morning and evening fires made them comfortable and cozy.

The most welcome arrangement was having a private cook, and other help. They were not intrusive and Bob, especially, was able to communicate freely with them. My Spanish also came back—admittedly a bit mixed with French! Peggy, who had been taking lessons, got along quite well, as did Carol, who I am sure had much of her earlier language skills tucked away in her head. The delicious meals featured local dishes. Terri, the cook, who had previously worked seven years for the local monks, was cheerful and willing to shop as well as cook.

Before we arrived the others had taken day trips to Lake Atitlán and Chichicastenango, both places Bob and I remembered well from previous trips, but which the children had no memory of, even though they had been there years before. They evidently had exciting trips this time. Once their bus was escorted by police, as it seemed tourists had been robbed on the route only the day before (unknown to them when planning the trip).

On our first evening in Antigua the girls had planned a surprise celebration for Bob's 73rd birthday. They arranged a gala party, complete with a colorful piñata. It was tied to the large grapefruit tree and each of us took turns breaking out the candies—just as we used to do for the children's birthdays many years ago.

We had an unexpected awakening during the first night we were there. A brief, but strong earthquake shook the house about 4 a.m. The adults woke up but the children slept through it, much to their disappointment. Bob and I knew exactly what it was from the first shake, having witnessed such things years ago, but we figured if the house had stood all these years there was little danger. We did go outside to the courtyard where we saw brilliant stars in a clear sky and heard the distant barking of dogs, who sense these things much better than humans.

During the following days, we visited some of the church ruins scattered around the city, and the colorful local market. In Parque Central we admired the array of costumes worn by natives from various parts of Guatemala. The children enjoyed having their shoes shined by small boys in the parque for a few quetzales.

Christmas day was delightful with presents stacked around the unusual tree—a bare branched affair, sprayed white and decorated with small lights and attractive local ornaments. A cheerful fire broke the morning chill and the noise of firecrackers in the streets mixed with the church bells. All the servants were off with their families on Christmas day, so we had lots of fun cooking our own meal as we celebrated being together.

We had lunch one day at the old Hotel Antigua that we remembered from years ago, although it had changed a lot. Later, all of us enjoyed a typical meal at a local restaurant. There we listened to the marimba bands as a Guatemalan woman made fresh tortillas in the garden beside our table.

While in Antigua we were able to have brief visits with some friends from our days there in 1959-62. Hank DuFlon, who worked with Bob in the USAID mission in Guatemala City, and his wife, Bobbi, had retired to Antigua years earlier. We visited them for tea in their lovely home—a huge place sprawling over almost a complete block next to the attractive ruins of a church.

A Guatemalan artist friend, Maria Castillo, and I had kept up with each other through the years. We used to go to different places to paint together, including Antigua, and when she heard we were there she had her chauffeur drive her from Guatemala City for a visit. Over a family tea we caught up on recent happenings in the country. It was good to get a local perspective on changes and current developments. Maria had never married but comes from a large family and has numerous nieces and nephews. We continue to keep in touch.

It was difficult to say goodbye to the family. Our trip home to Bethesda was uneventful except for a hectic transfer in Miami, then finding our car with a dead battery in the snow at BWI airport. Carol and the children left Guatemala for the long flight home to England, but Peggy and John stayed to visit Tikal and Belize, with Peggy planning later travel. It was a most satisfying, exciting Christmas—perfect except for not having Steven and family with us. Memories of that time spent with loved ones in a delightful place stay in my heart.

XX

FACING THE NEW MILLINIUM

There are times when it seems prudent to move to the beat of a different drummer. We all do get a year older each year and as Bob and I realized the end of the century was approaching we had to face this in a practical way. We had vaguely discussed the idea of settling into some kind of a retirement community before it was really necessary to do so, recognizing that even as life is precious it is also fragile. Neither of us wanted to have to make such major decisions in an emergency, nor did we want to burden our children with that onerous task.

These thoughts were much in our minds while we were in Hilton Head during the winter months of 1998. When the Thunes were visiting us there, we explored a retirement community, TidePointe, which had opened the previous year not far from our place in Evian. Situated on Broad Creek it had many attractions, including a well-equipped spa, social activities and meals in a spacious Clubhouse. There was also a health clinic with facilities for assisted living if needed. We had not considered moving so soon, but shortly afterward when we saw an attractive veranda home for sale there, we decided to buy it.

Back home in Bethesda, we faced the difficult task of putting our townhouse on the market. This meant getting house and garden in pristine order, choosing a real estate agent and even more traumatic, making seemingly endless choices. What a hassle! An exhausting time, both emotionally and physically, a job we hoped never to have to tackle again.

The hot summer days seemed even more stressful when the sexual misconduct of President Clinton came to light. His lies to the White House staff and to the American people about this affair further complicated things. How depressing to learn that such a strong leader in other ways was personally so weak. It seems an inborn part of his character—a real tragic flaw, reminding one of a Euripides drama, with irrational emotion taking over from reason and self-control. This usually leads to a tragic downfall, which the American people, as well as those in other countries, watched with horrible fascination as events unfolded.

By contrast, we were thrilled to hear that our daughter-in-law, Barbara, was to be honored at the Women's Equality Day Celebration. At a surprise reception held in the Indian Treaty Room of the Old Executive Office building she was presented with the Lucy Stone Achievement Award for the contributions she had made through her work. She was honored especially for helping to restore Food

Stamp benefits to 250,000 legal immigrants, including 75,000 children. I joined Steven and the children to witness the presentation and to meet speakers, Erskine Bowles, the President's Chief-of-Staff, and Donna Shalala, head of the Department of Health and Human Services, among others.

The months passed quickly and our townhouse did not get sold, even when we lowered the price. Since we were committed to moving to Hilton Head in mid-November, we gathered as much cash as possible, then arranged a carry-over loan to complete the purchase of the property there.

Moving day loomed, our packing made more stressful by prospective buyers looking at the house up to the last minute. The actual days of the professional packing and loading went fairly well, and since it was out of our hands at that point, less stressful. Whatever, it is always a relief to get what has to be done finished.

Peggy flew over from England to help us move into our new home at TidePointe. It was a godsend to have her. We signed to close on the house on November 16th, and movers arrived early the next morning with everything intact. Rather hectic getting it all in place or stacked in our large garage for later sorting. We were relieved to find that things fit in quite well. Peggy was indispensable as we faced the numerous decisions. Linnie, who had spent several days in the kennel while all the hectic activity was going on, soon explored everything and found her own "special places" to relax (always where she could keep a good eye on one of us). Peggy had to leave too soon! She flew back to England by way of Washington, where she spent Thanksgiving with Steven and family.

Little by little Bob and I got things unpacked and our new place soon felt like home. Weather seemed to be sunny and balmy most of the time during the winter months. Hearing about the snow and ice farther north made us doubly glad we had moved to this benign climate.

A short time before Christmas, we had an unfortunate experience with Linnie. To celebrate her second birthday on Dec. 21st, we took her for a late afternoon walk on the beach. It was quite foggy, but she loved to run and came when we called, so we let her off the leash as we walked in front of Shipyard Plantation. All was fine until she saw some sandpipers ahead and began chasing them, soon disappearing into the fog. We called frantically, but with the roar of the surf plus the fog she became disoriented. The tide was out and she somehow missed us. We searched up and down the beach to no avail. Several frantic hours later, someone said they had seen a small dog headed north toward Palmetto Dunes Plantation. That was over a mile from where we had started walking, so we drove there to see if anyone had seen her. No luck. We alerted entry guards at both plantations, plus the concierges at hotels along the beach and continued our search for hours. People were most helpful, one nice young man even going for a large flashlight to lend us.

About ten at night, surrounded by darkness and dense fog and with the tide coming in, we went home with heavy hearts. After a sleepless night, we were back on the beach at dawn the next day. The entry guard at Palmetto Dunes reported that she had seen a small dog a short time before, but it had disappeared when she turned to let a car enter the plantation. Our hearts leapt up thinking that Linnie had at least survived the night, and we returned to the beach hoping against hope to find her. After about a half hour, in answer to Bob's call he saw a small white head lift above a nearby sand dune. In a flash, a shivering, whining little bundle jumped into our arms, madly licking our faces. She was covered with burrs and even had patches of tar in her coat, but she seemed more than beautiful to us. We can only surmise where she had hovered during the last 12 hours, but I am sure her guardian angel was watching over her. At home, after an hour getting out the burrs and giving her a bath, she collapsed with exhaustion— sleeping almost two days straight. Having her back was the best Christmas present we have ever gotten.

Christmas 1998 was spent without family, one of two times that had happened, but things were festive all over the island with carol concerts and other things going on. The Clubhouse at TidePointe was decorated with lovely flower arrangements and trees glowing with lights. New acquaintances invited us to join them at the elaborate Christmas buffet, so the first Christmas in our new home was pleasant.

People at TidePointe are from various parts of the U.S., with many of them having moved from previous homes on the island. Few arrive directly, i.e., "cold", although I am sure that is one reason for their move! We were among the minority in more ways than one. We found a few Democrats but most here are quite conservative, which is not surprising, I guess. There are many activities to choose from on the island as well as at TidePointe so it would be hard to become bored, even without private interests.

Bob's major interest, the computer, takes a lot of his time, but is most helpful in keeping all our various taxes and accounts in order. His study is perfect for that. I managed to create a small studio in the dinette area of the kitchen for my art work. My computer fits nicely in the corner of the big master bedroom and the piano is conveniently placed in the living room—satisfactory arrangements for each of us.

Having Linnie gives us a quick introduction to many people as we take her for walks. We especially look forward to our late afternoon walks by the water. The sunsets cast glowing colors over the expanse of Broad Creek and the marshes, with twisted oaks silhouetted against the sky. Birds of many species frequent the lagoons. We've seen herons of all kinds, pelicans and different kinds of ducks. According to the expert bird watchers, hundreds of different species migrate to the island during the winter months.

After almost a year of obsession with the scandal of President Clinton's dalliance with Monica Lewinsky by both the public and the media, the president was finally impeached by the House of Representatives in early December 1998, the first elected president in U.S. history to have been so judged. He was duly tried on two counts by the Senate according to the rules of the Constitution. On February 12th he was acquitted on a charge of perjury and on an obstruction of justice charge, with close votes, but with neither resulting in a two-thirds majority. Whatever one felt about the verdict, everyone seemed to want to move on to the business of running the government after this stressful event. We only hoped President Clinton could redeem himself in some way for the pain he brought to the nation. We do have renewed confidence in the due process of the law, although we, along with many others, were saddened by the personal weakness of the president, and felt somehow betrayed by his lying to the American people as well as to his friends and staff.

During the early months of that year we had visits from family and friends. Steven drove down from Charleston for a couple of nights after a conference there and he seemed to approve of our house and the community. Dan and Joanne, as well as Cindy, Jerry and children visited. Cecil and Jeanne also came over from North Carolina for a few days. How wonderful to have sisters so close by—only about a five-hour drive away. It's convenient to be on the east coast corridor to Florida, so friends and family can stop over.

In late April Bob and I flew from Savannah to Dulles, for our long anticipated trip to England. We had a few hours stopover in DC and were able to see Steven and Lucas briefly before our flight. Using accumulated frequent flyer miles, we flew Club Class—one of the most comfortable trips we've had, with minimal jet lag.

It was good to see Peggy's welcoming smile when we arrived at Heathrow next morning. It was the first time we had visited her new home—a charming cottage in the London suburb of Islington. Peggy had painted and decorated with her usual flair and we were made most welcome. We divided our time between London and Colchester, where we always feel loved and wanted. Grandchildren were growing up fast, Ryan now as tall as Bob.

Both of us had long wanted to try the Eurostar train under the channel to Paris. This time we indulged ourselves and arranged to spend three nights in that beautiful, exciting city. It was amazing to get from the center of London to the Gare du Nord in Paris in just three easy hours via the so-called "chunnel".

Our small hotel was near the Seine in the Latin Quarter, perfectly located among art galleries, sidewalk cafes and bustling street markets. It refreshed my soul to soak up the unique ambiance of that part of the city, and it brought back vivid memories of earlier days in Paris. When I was studying painting that year I had spent happy hours wandering around dreaming of all the artists who had lived and worked there. Now having a *café crème* at Café Deux Maggot while looking up at the San Germain Cathedral, these dreams were reinforced. Next to us, the distinguished man with long, flowing white hair surely was an artist of some kind! There was something psychologically satisfying about going back— almost as if I had never left, or imagining that I was returning to a place where I belonged. Speaking French added to the feeling, of course, and although consciously I know I am not Parisien it was easy to project a different dream life altogether.

The highlight of our stay in France was a day trip to Giverny, about fifty kilometers from Paris. There, Claude Monet lived and painted for many years, creating a lovely estate with extensive gardens and lakes. All, including his house and studio, has been authentically restored with delightful vistas on all sides. The famous Japanese bridge—literally dripping with wisteria blossoms— and the ponds with waterlilies shown in so many of his paintings, looked as if they were lifted straight from his canvases.

We were driven to Giverny in a mini-bus with a few others, and were given a quick tour through the center of Paris going and coming, enjoying the thrill of dashing around the Arc de Triomphe with cars zooming by on all sides in the usual frenzy. On the way back from Giverny we drove above the valley of the Seine through small historic villages. One of  these is where General Montgomery had his headquarters for awhile during World War II. We also drove through Suresnes, crossing the bridge there for the drive through the Bois de Boulogne. Much had changed since we lived there, with high buildings now rising above the river. We thought we could see a few open spaces at the top of the hill and were sure our house must still be up there!

Back in London, we took a most interesting tour of Shakespeare's Globe Theater, which had recently been reconstructed as nearly as possible to the original. Looking down from the side balcony to the hard-packed dirt floor, I could imagine the crowds of people centuries ago who would stand throughout the popular performances, joining in with loud comments.

History will mark the spring of 1999 with the horror of the "ethnic cleansing" taking place in Kosovo in southern Yugoslavia. The Serbian leader, Slobodan Milosovic, and many of the Serbs living in Yugoslavia had a long-held hatred of the Albanian Muslims, most of whom lived in Kosovo. For months, Milosovic had been ordering his army to raid, rape and kill many Albanians, gradually "cleansing" that area. NATO countries became increasingly alarmed as these atrocities became known. Diplomatic overtures and threats of dire consequences failed to stop Milosovic. In late March NATO planes began heavy bombing of military centers, selected roads, airports and bridges used by the Serbian army. This added to the horror, and though unavoidable, harmed some innocent victims. In spite of mistakes made, including the bombing of the Chinese Embassy in Belgrade, the bombing continued until June when Milosovic capitulated and ordered the retreat of the army, thus allowing the refugees to return. NATO peace keeping forces monitored the departure of the Serb military and the return of the refugees, many of whom had no homes to go back to, their towns vandalized beyond belief. Mass graves were testament to even more untold horrors. No one could watch all this unfold without compassion for all the innocent people on both sides who were affected. Milosovic, indicted as a war criminal, will go down in history as the evil "Hitler" of the 1990s. Who knows what the future will bring to this Baltic region, where centuries of conflict have occurred?

As summer arrived in South Carolina and the temperature rose, Bob and I and Linnie headed for the cooler mountains. in North Carolina We stayed several weeks at the higher altitude and were able to see lots of family. While we were there I looked up old friends from Montreat days—the Hudsons and Bunny Stroup Lake, whom I had not seen for fifty years! Montreat was especially beautiful with numerous rhododendrons in bloom.

One of the highlights of our stay in North Carolina was a visit to the Biltmore Estate, a huge chateau built in the nineteenth century by George Vanderbilt. Lavishly furnished rooms of all kinds with original family portraits by Sargent and Renoir reflect an opulence not seen in the States before or since. The mansion with its surrounding acres and broad views over the Blue Ridge Mountains, gives us a peek into a life few can imagine.

July was marked by a sad event. John Kennedy, Jr. met a tragic death when the private plane he was piloting plunged into the sea near Martha's Vineyard. Caroline, his wife of a few years, and her sister were passengers and they were also killed. People all over the world were shocked and grieved, reminded yet again of the assassination of President Kennedy in 1963 and Robert Kennedy a few years later. The family, unfortunately, seems fated to be plagued by these tragic events.

Bob and I faced a milestone in August, 1999 when we celebrated our fiftieth anniversary. Having all our loving children and grandchildren with us made it a joyful time and one to cherish.

The family stayed at our villa in Evian and at the guest villa at TidePointe, near our veranda home. We received flowers, cards and calls from all our siblings. Bob gave me an elegant, antique brooch dating from 1867 and some pearl and diamond earrings. He seemed to like the gold watch I gave him.

Our gala dinner was held in the private dining room at the TidePointe Club. We had ordered a lovely mixed flower arrangement for the long table and a large cake. The children, meanwhile, were making secret plans on their own.

As we entered the dining room we were amazed to find it transformed into a fairyland of gold. There were gold and white streamers, candles, balloons and wonderful little touches around, even tiny gold confetti "50"s sprinkled over the tablecloth. Gifts of all kinds were piled by our plates. Perhaps the most amazing gift was a series of three videos prepared by Steven from selected home movies Bob and I had made over the years (and later passed on to him). They start with our wedding and progress through the films of children growing up in various countries where we lived. Later Steven added video shots of the elegant dinner celebration creating a gift we will enjoy for years.

To top it all, imagine our surprise when the lovely cake was presented, lavishly decorated in gold and glitter with the names of all the children and grandchildren added. A small replica of our wedding picture as we came out of the chapel those fifty years ago, was placed in one corner of the cake, held by a delicate gold stand. All this was done secretly by the children, involving phone conversations to the Club staff from overseas and elsewhere. Champagne flowed and Steven offered us a memorable toast from all of them. It couldn't have been a more perfect celebration.

The following days were happy times, as the children and grandchildren enjoyed the beach and other activities on the island. We were sad to see each group leave, but in our hearts, the family will always be together.

Late August brought the season's first hurricane scare to the island. Bob and I had never been on the island during one of these threatening weather events. We were soon made aware of the dangers, plans to evacuate and other precautions. As hurricane Dennis approached nearer and nearer we, along with other residents of TidePointe, got ready to go farther inland to a safer place. The storm proved to be indecisive and hovered nearby for several days. Impatient with the uncertainty (as well as the sweltering heat!), Bob and I decided to drive to North Carolina where the Youngs graciously welcomed us. We followed the storm via TV as Dennis "tiptoed past Hilton Head", causing severe wind and waves on the North Carolina coastline and farther north. While with the Youngs, we had a chance to see our nephew Matthew and meet his wife Cindy for the first time.

A much more serious hurricane followed Dennis two weeks later. Hurricane Floyd moved fast and carried winds of up to 150 mph. This time there was a mandatory evacuation ordered and carried out for the island. Bob and I anticipated the traffic backup and left an hour or so early, driving with Linnie over to Hendersonville again. Those leaving a bit later ran into long delays—with traffic back ups to 120 miles in some places. We stayed with the Youngs until the authorities said it was safe to return.

Some trees were down in TidePointe but we were relieved to find no serious damage had been done. Evian also escaped heavy destruction since Floyd did not actually hit the coast until reaching North Carolina where severe winds, rains and record flooding caused major damage. Thousands there were made homeless and over forty were killed. No one wanted to go through a hurricane season like that again.

Our villa in Evian was put on the market in October and, luckily for us, was sold within a few weeks. In a way, we hated to say goodbye to the attractive apartment where we had spent some happy days as "snow birds", but since moving to TidePointe we no longer used it except for the rare visits by the children.

Steven and family in Washington welcomed us for a lavish Thanksgiving celebration in 1999. In addition to catching up with activities there, Barbara had arranged a special treat for us. Again we had privileged seats in the President's box at the Kennedy Center where we saw the play, "Side Man", an innovative production that had received a Tony award in New York. Just being back to enjoy the cultural life in DC was appreciated. Best of all, of course, was being a part of the active, young family there in our favorite big city.

Christmas and the welcoming of the year 2000 were celebrated in high style at TidePointe. Music, dancing and champagne added to the excitement of the new century's beginning. We could only imagine what the future would hold, but that night everyone seemed to be optimistic.

The past century had brought more changes than any in history, as technology continued to shape a global civilization. It did seem the world was becoming better for many more people. Unfortunately, natural disasters as well as violent conflicts continue, many arising from inborn hates; and there are still areas of unbelievable poverty. We can only hope and work as a nation for a more just, connected world society.

Since we had come to TidePointe I had missed having my own car. In early January I was glad to get a new Toyota Avalon, which gave me more freedom to take part in the art activities of the island. I soon enrolled in a watercolor class taught by an accomplished artist living nearby. Although I usually paint in oils it was good to broaden my art experience. Bob, aided by a new efficient mat cutter, became expert in producing mats for my amateurish efforts. The active art community of Hilton Head Island offers many opportunities to enjoy painting and be inspired by others.

Our house in Bethesda was finally sold, with the closing in March. The woman stockbroker who bought it seemed delighted with it, so I'm sure it is in good hands. Bob and I were relieved to close that chapter in our lives, even though we had thoroughly enjoyed living there after returning from Switzerland. Being near Steven and his growing family was our greatest pleasure during those years.

Of course, change seems to be a constant for us, and in the spring there was a new development. We went to North Carolina again to see Jeanne and Lee, who had sold their house in Black Mountain and moved into a retirement apartment in Hendersonville. While staying with the Youngs we began looking for a summer vacation rental in the mountains, since Hilton Head becomes so hot and humid. We arranged for a short-term rental for part of July, but it seemed impossible to rent a nice place all summer that would accept pets. We soon decided that perhaps we should look for a place to buy. As luck would have it, we discovered an attractive condo for sale in a development on the outskirts of Hendersonville. We arranged for settlement the last of June.

The summer of 2000 somehow seemed to be both a closure and the opening of the last years of my life. Perhaps getting together with all my sisters and brother for a family reunion helped define this time. Our coming together as different, independent thinking adults with various experiences and philosophies was both revealing and reassuring. Frank discussions were loving, if at times stressful. Perhaps reunions are always that way, but our love for each other emerged as the dominant feeling. As we went our separate ways we seemed to understand our differences better, and I knew we would always be there for each other.

The cooler air and beauty of the mountains refreshed our souls as well as our bodies after the oppressive summer heat of Hilton Head. As Bob and I were

getting the condo ready with basic furniture and other essentials, Steven, Katie and Lucas drove down from DC for a brief vacation. We went to see Chimney Rock, Sliding Rock and other nearby sights together. During a return trip to Hendersonville in October to witness the brilliant fall foliage Peggy flew over from England to see our new summer home. We looked forward to many more family visits.

The presidential election of 2000 was perhaps the most controversial in U.S. history, certainly in the last one hundred years. Court cases challenging ballot counts plus charges of politically motivated interference in recording voter's choices, created a real brouhaha for well over a month. Whether the sharply divided congress will be able to get anything meaningful done in the near future is problematic. We can only hope that time and concern for the country will result in some measure of cooperation as President George W. Bush takes over the new administration.

Our Christmas holiday package of the year 2000 was wrapped in love and glittering lights as we joined the family in Washington, along with Peggy from

London. We attended the year's presentation of medals to outstanding celebrities in the Arts and the Humanities, and were privileged to take a final special tour of the White House. Not only did we marvel at more than thirty decorated trees, but we actually walked through the rooms of history. Guided by Barbara we were allowed to go into the Oval Office and into the library where President Roosevelt gave his "fireside chats" in earlier days, as well as visiting such seats of power as the Cabinet room and the Roosevelt room. It was a walk through history beyond my dreams.

History will mark the twentieth century as the most phenomenal in recorded time. The changes that have come about since its beginning have changed the world in more ways than anyone would have imagined. I feel privileged to have witnessed many of these changes during the nearly four-score years of my life.

Many eminent and influential painters and musicians bridged the nineteenth and twentieth centuries, creating a renaissance in the arts. Cezanne, Monet and Picasso, and composers such as Stravinsky and Ravel join the classical artists we cherish, gaining popularity through the years.

Even more dramatic changes have come about in science and technology. The discovery of new planets, man's exploration of space and other breakthroughs continue to offer challenges. The mapping of the Human Genome is a major accomplishment that is bound to lead to new discoveries. We can only trust it will work for the good of all. Social development, shaped by war and economic changes, unfortunately, has moved at a slower pace than that of science—human nature being what it is.

To look back at one's life is like slipping into a favorite old sweater and snuggling down with a good book. We begin as a child looking out a protective door with wondering eyes. Too soon we find ourselves caught up in the swirl of human relationships and striving. Where does it all lead? Sometimes to fame or fortune, sometimes to disappointment and failure, usually a combination of both. Is happiness lurking there somewhere? Whatever—as we get to the latter chapters of our life there is a certain satisfaction along with sadness as closure takes place. Our eyes dim, but other things come more into focus. Days of sunshine become more beautiful and precious as we retreat again behind our protective doors, watching the sun set on the wonder of our world.

As we individually—and ultimately alone—are caught in the current of human frailty and face the finality of life, we often look for understanding through our dreams—realized or sought for. Close relationships and the joys of music and art can give these days a special poignancy. At this time people find solace and hope in different ways. To feel embraced by the complex mystery of the natural world can in itself be exhilarating as the circle of dreams closes. We need not analyze these feelings to appreciate their existence, for in the boundless world of nature and the unknown force behind it lies the veiled mystery beyond imagination.

About the Author

Marguerite "Candi" Ray was born and grew up in Jacksonville, Florida. After college years in North Carolina and Tennessee, she joined the U.S. Navy WAVES, serving in Miami and New York. She left the service in 1947 as a Lieutenant-Commander.

During graduate school at Vanderbilt University, she met her future husband, Robert Ray, who had served in the Navy as a pilot. They were attracted by their similar interests and backgrounds, since Candi had also gotten a private pilot's license while in the Navy. Bob was an international economist, and for the next fifty years plus they lived and worked in eight different countries on four different continents. During over thirty years overseas, they had many adventures while raising their three children. After returning to the U.S. in 1986, they continued to travel widely, and now live on Hilton Head Island in South Carolina.